Celtic Saints of Scotland, Northumbria and the Isle of Man

Celtic Saints of Scotland, Northumbria and the Isle of Man

ELIZABETH REES

FONTHILL

Front cover illustration: Lindisfarne Gospels, f.26v.
Back cover illustration: St Patrick's Chapel, Heysham.

Fonthill Media Limited
Fonthill Media LLC
www.fonthillmedia.com
office@fonthillmedia.com

First published in the United Kingdom and the United States of America 2017

British Library Cataloguing in Publication Data:
A catalogue record for this book is available from the British Library

ISBN 978-1-78155-601-6

Typeset in 10.5pt on 13pt MinionPro
Printed and bound in England

CONTENTS

Preface

The title of this book is not strictly accurate, for the nation that we call Scotland did not exist until after the time when Celtic Christians lived, worked, and prayed. Furthermore, we know little about early Christianity in north Britain, since no early texts survive from this region—apart from a few poems, hymns, and an eighth-century *Life of Columba*.

In his comprehensive volume, *The History of the Celtic Place-names of Scotland*, first published in 1926, Professor William Watson described local landmarks and settlements named after some 600 early monks and a handful of nuns, but we know almost nothing about most of them. Still, many clues have emerged from the study of place names and early inscriptions, while excavations continue to reveal fascinating details about the lives of our northern Christian forebears.

This book attempts to summarise what we know at this point, although most pieces of this very large jigsaw are irretrievably lost. The book is illustrated with photos that I have taken at early Christian sites across northern Britain and the Isle of Man. I thank my sister, Frances Jones, for her help with their reproduction. I am not primarily a scholar; as a single-vowed woman, I write from within a lived tradition, and try to identify what energised our northern Christian ancestors.

It was the late Professor E. G. Bowen, a pioneer of Celtic studies, who first inspired me as a teenager to explore the locations where the Celtic saints lived. I am grateful to Jonathan Wooding, Professor of Celtic Studies at the University of Sydney; to Dr Karen Jankulak, a specialist in Celtic hagiography; and to Tom O'Loughlin, Professor of Historical Theology at Nottingham University, all of whom have helped me over the years; any errors are my own.

Elizabeth Rees

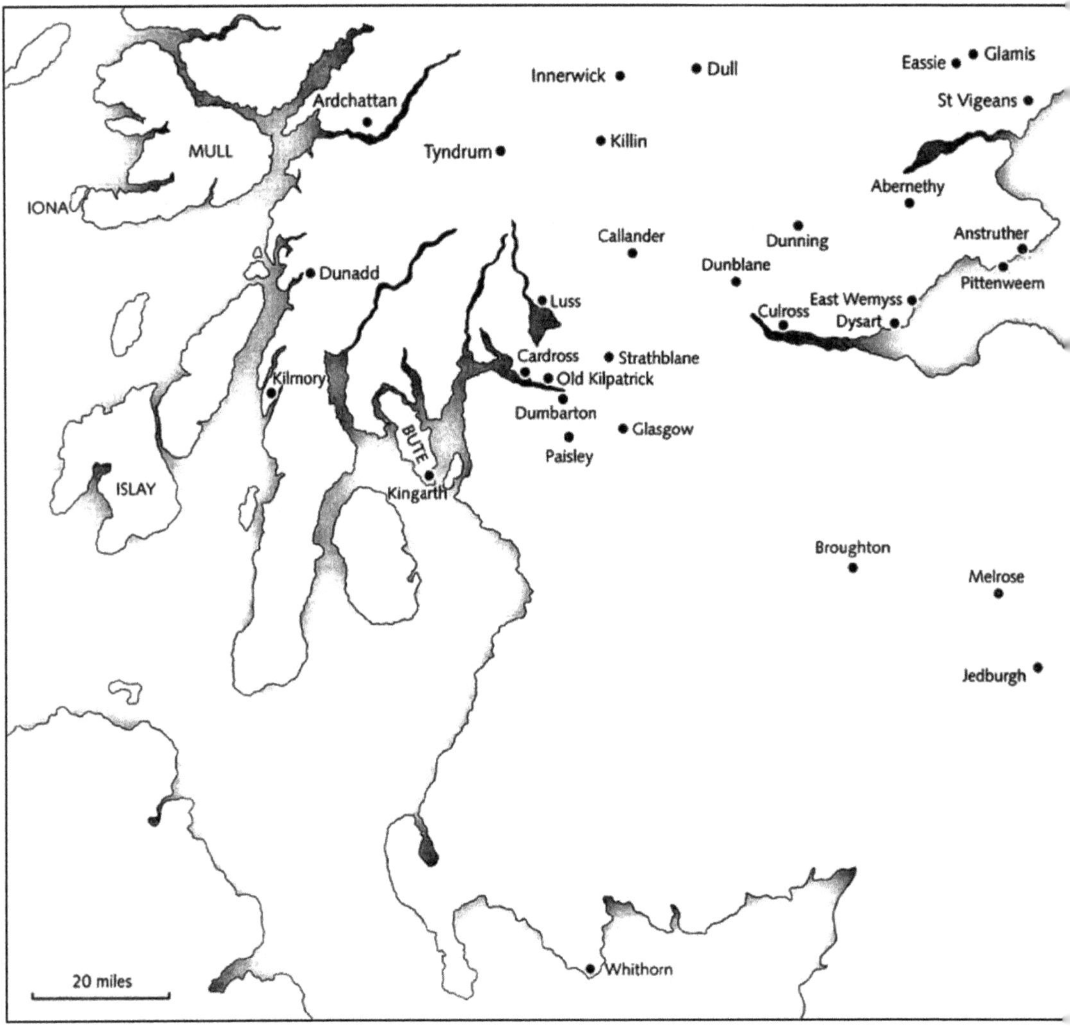

Early Christian sites of southern Scotland.

Introduction

In early Christian times, before the emergence of Scotland as we know it, north Britain was divided between the Picts (who mainly lived in eastern Scotland, north of the Firth of Forth, and the River Clyde) and the Britons (who lived to the south of this natural divide). In addition to these two groupings of peoples, there were Scots in Argyll, while the Angles of Northumbria extended their kingdom of Bernicia north to the Firth of Forth and west to the Irish Sea.

We know little about the Church in north Britain at this time. According to rather late sources available to Bede, a bishop named Ninian came to a post-Roman Christian community at Whithorn and evangelised 'the southern Picts', but we do not know exactly what area Bede implies by this term. In Chapter 3, we shall explore some of the problems arising from Bede's narrative.

Columba brought Christianity to Iona in the later sixth century, and Bede states that he evangelised 'the northern Picts', but again we do not know the full extent or permanence of his influence. Bede is more likely to be accurate when he describes times closer to his own—he relates how Northumbrian Christianity reached British areas north of the Forth by the later seventh century. Bede adds that the Northumbrians brought the Christian faith to eastern areas ruled by the Picts in about AD 710.

Early Christian sites can be identified by a combination of clues: place names, an oval enclosure, the presence of early carvings, burials or church buildings, or a well. The name elements *cill-* or *kill-* (from the Latin *cella*, suggesting a monk's cell or chapel) or *annait* (meaning 'mother church') may indicate a date between AD 500 and 900, especially when combined with the name of an early saint, but some saints were popular for a very long period, or their cult was revived in later medieval times.

Medieval Christian Texts

A number of writings survive from the monastery of Iona—hymns, poetry, an elaborate gospel book, chronicles, and a *Life of Columba* written by Adomnán, the ninth abbot of Iona. These will be considered more fully in Chapter 1. The *Book of Deer* is a small gospel book dating from *c.* AD 900, which was perhaps written at a monastery in Aberdeenshire;

it will be described in Chapter 6. Otherwise, little survives until the late medieval period, by which time sources record legends rather than historical facts.

This is partly because a saint's life was designed to be read aloud during the liturgy on his or her festival. It was therefore intended to inspire devotion, rather than convey accurate detail. This is true of the *Life of Ninian* written by Aelred, abbot of Rievaulx in Yorkshire in 1165, and it also applies to the *Life of Kentigern*, composed by Jocelin, a monk of Furness Abbey in Cumbria in about 1184. However, both authors make use of some earlier sources.

A few written texts survive from eastern Scotland. These late sources tell us how medieval Scottish Christians viewed their Celtic predecessors. The earliest of these were written in about 1400 in metrical verse in a vernacular dialect; they include the lives of St Ninian and of St Machar, a follower of Columba. Their chief source is the *Legenda Aurea* (or 'Golden Legend'), a collection of stories about the saints compiled by a Dominican friar named Jacobus de Voragine in about 1260. This collection became immensely popular—over 1,000 manuscripts of its text survive.

The *Aberdeen Breviary*

The *Martyrology of Aberdeen* contains brief statements about the lives of saints and a calendar that lists their feast days as celebrated in Scotland. The *Martyrology* was perhaps assembled shortly before the production of the *Aberdeen Breviary* (or *Breviarum Aberdonense*). This is an important source for the lives of Scottish saints, but since it was compiled 1,000 years after the death of Columba and his fellow monks and nuns, its historical accuracy is minimal.

This was Scotland's first published book, and the first national breviary, or collection of liturgical texts prayed throughout the year, to be produced in Europe. Bishop William Elphinstone, founder of Aberdeen University, oversaw the collection of material for it in 1509–10. Elphinstone employed researchers to travel around and record what was known about the lives of the saints and compile information about their shrines.

We shall begin by examining the region about which most is known: Argyll in the time of Columba. Adomnán's *Life of Columba* offers us a unique glimpse of Celtic Christian Scotland. It is our only biography from this region that dates from early times.

1

Columba and Iona

Perhaps the most outstanding of the Celtic monks, Columba (AD 521–97) was a warrior and politician, a scholar, priest, and poet who played an important role in both Scottish and Irish history. The name Columba (or *Columcille* in Irish) means 'Church dove'. According to the Old Irish *Life of Columba* (or *Betha Coluim Cille*), he was born into the royal family of the Northern Uí Néill at Gartan, near Letterkenny in Donegal. We know a considerable amount about him because in about AD 690, the abbot of Iona, Adomnán, wrote a long and informative *Life of Columba*.

A source available to Adomnán was a *Book of the Miracles of Columba* written by Cummene Find, the seventh abbot of Iona (AD 657–9), which is now lost. The earliest surviving text of Adomnán's *Life of Columba* was written on Iona by Dorbbéne, a monk who succeeded him as abbot and died in AD 713. We are fortunate to possess such an early copy, written on goatskin parchment in a heavy Irish hand.

Columba began his schooling under the care of a foster father, a priest named Cruithnecan; this suggests that he was intended for the Church at an early age. Adomnán describes 'the blessed boy's foster-father, the priest Cruithnechan, a man of exemplary life', and the training that the lad received: 'Even from his boyhood he gave himself up to the Christian apprenticeship and the pursuit of wisdom'.[1] He also studied under a Christian bard in his mother's country of Leinster.[2]

Columba and Abbot Finnian

Columba became a monk at a young age, and was ordained as a deacon in the Irish monastery of Finnian at Movilla beside Strangford Lough in County Down. Adomnán alludes to Columba's time as a monk under Abbot Finnian of Movilla, referring to the abbot as Findbarr or Finnio. He writes that Columba 'was staying as a young deacon in Ireland with the holy bishop Findbarr ... acquiring knowledge of sacred scripture while still a young man'. Theirs was a relationship of master and disciple: Columba 'went to the venerable bishop Finnio, his teacher, as a young man to an old'.[3]

Finnian was a British monk who went to Ireland as an exile for the love of God. He is likely to be the same monk as the famous Finnian, abbot of the large monastery of Clonard in central Ireland.[4] This may not, in fact, have been his real name. In minuscule handwriting, '*n*' and '*u*' are easily confused, while '*f*, '*v*', and '*u*' are fairly interchangeable; thus 'Finnian' is likely to be a later misreading of the name 'Uinniau'.[5] Following convention, however, he will here be referred to as Finnian.

Later, Columba was ordained a priest, and in about AD 546, he founded his first monastery at Derry in his family's territory, on land given to him by his tribe. He established various other communities in Ireland; Durrow in Offaly and Iona are the only Columban foundations mentioned by Bede. Irish accounts of Columba relate how on a visit to his former abbot, Columba borrowed a book from the library and secretly copied it at night. He was discovered when he had almost finished, and Finnian demanded the copy. This first recorded breach of copyright was brought to trial before the High King, who ruled in Finnian's favour.

Columba Departs for Scotland

Columba set sail for Scotland with twelve companions in AD 565 at the age of forty-one, for reasons that are not entirely clear. Adomnán explains that Columba had been wrongly excommunicated at a synod at Teltown, in Meath, just before his departure to Scotland as a pilgrim for Christ, and that the synod's verdict was later reversed.[6] Columba established a monastery on Iona, where he largely remained for the rest of his life, although he returned to Ireland for occasional important events.

While it seems that Columba sailed to Scotland as a 'pilgrim for Christ', as a successful warrior-prince, politician, and abbot, he may also have been invited by his relative Conall, the new king of Dál Riata (or Argyll), to help him repel the Picts. One tradition relates that Columba was given the island of Iona by King Conall as a site for a monastery.

Dál Riata

In early times, Argyll was known as Dál Riata; its royal centre was at Dunadd. The Dál Riata were Scots Gaels who had connections with the Antrim tribe of the Dál Riata in north-east Ireland. The name means 'Riata's portion of land', and perhaps refers to a legendary founding figure. Until recently, it was thought that this Scottish kingdom was founded from north-east Ireland, as Bede recounts.[7] However, there is no archaeological evidence of migration from Ireland to Argyll at this time.

In Ireland, people lived in stone-walled ring forts, but there are none in Argyll, although there are suitable locations for them. Instead, people in Argyll lived in forts on hilltops (or *dúns*) from at least 500 BC onwards. Some lived on crannogs, or artificial islands, a tradition that only later spread to Ireland in the sixth century AD. Personal ornaments, such as brooches and dress pins, in Argyll are different from Irish types.

There are several hundred pillars in Ireland inscribed in ogham, an alphabet invented in Ireland, but only two in Argyll, which suggests that few Irish settled in Argyll.

It now appears that early genealogies were altered by later rulers in order to strengthen their territorial claims. For a time, the Scottish and Irish Dál Riata were ruled jointly. A founding legend that described them coming to Scotland from Ireland conveniently helped the Scots to claim sovereignty over the Irish Dál Riata. Indeed, they spoke the same language, which differed from that spoken east of the Grampians.[8]

Áedán of Dunadd

For most of the seventh and eighth centuries, Argyll was ruled by sub-kings with an over-king chosen from one of two leading kinship groups. The first significant king was Áedán mac Gabráin, who reigned from about AD 574 to 608. His main fort was probably Dunadd, and he was well-known to Columba. He is recorded as mounting many successful expeditions to Orkney, Ireland, the Isle of Man, and the Scottish Borders. He fought more widely beyond his own territory than any other king of Dál Riata, and was finally defeated by the Northumbrians in AD 603 as he tried to halt their advance into southern Scotland.[9]

The kings of Dál Riata seem to have been on friendly terms with neighbouring British kings to the south, but were often in conflict with the Picts to the east. By the mid-ninth century, the kings of Dál Riata had extended their control eastwards into the land of the Picts. We do not know whether the people of Dál Riata held off the Norse as they attacked from the west, or whether the nobility moved east for safety. They moved away from their royal forts and hilltop settlements into unenclosed farmsteads. Centres of power shifted eastwards from Dunadd and Iona to Scone, St Andrews, and Dunkeld. In Argyll, artistic achievements declined as metalwork became plainer and stone crosses less elaborate, and the kingdom of Dál Riata slipped into obscurity.[10]

Royalty at Dunadd

As a highborn warrior and abbot, it is likely that on his arrival in Dál Riata, Columba would first have visited the royal fort of Dunadd, which is 5 miles north-north-west of Lochgilphead. Rising from flat, boggy land beside the River Add, Dunadd made an excellent fortress. A surprise attack was impossible as its main entrance is a natural gully through massive walls of rock, which was closed by great gates with a timber superstructure. From this vantage point, the king's warships commanded the sea route to Ireland and his army was poised to fight the Picts. The fort was occupied until AD 1000.

A small peak was used as an inner citadel, where the king was inaugurated (he apparently placed his foot in two footprints carved in the bedrock to symbolise his dominion over the land). Nearby is a rock-cut basin perhaps used for libations, and a natural formation possibly used as a throne. These features may date from pre-Christian times. Later additions of a

Above: Entrance to Dunadd fort, Argyll and Bute.

Left: View from the royal footprints across the fort of Dunadd, Argyll and Bute.

carved boar and an ogham inscription in Gaelic dating from the ninth or tenth centuries suggest that these features were still recognised in Christian times. Surrounding Dunadd are prehistoric burial monuments—a stone circle, cairns, standing stones, and rock carvings, which emphasised that the king was part of this ancient ritual landscape.

There is a similar carving of a footprint at Southend in the Mull of Kintyre, near the fort of Dunaverty, while there are pairs of footprints at the Iron Age fortified settlement of Clickhimin in Shetland and on a large boulder now in the church at Burwick in Orkney. Late medieval records describe initiation ceremonies involving stones with footprints both in western Scotland and Ireland. The Lords of the Isles were proclaimed at a ceremony that included placing a foot in a carved footprint to show that the new Lord would walk in the footsteps of his predecessors.[11]

Agriculture and Metalwork

Charred grain from seventh-century layers at Dunadd showed that oats were grown on the surrounding gravel terraces; many querns for grinding corn were also found. Cattle bones indicated cows about half the size of modern breeds of cattle. Metalwork was an important industry—hundreds of discarded fragments of crucibles with traces of gold and silver, moulds from brooches, metal droplets, tools, and unfinished items were found. Raw materials, such as tin from Cornwall, came from distant sources. There was a remarkable tiny setting of a deep-red garnet surrounded by twisted gold filigree extracted from a piece of Anglo-Saxon jewellery, perhaps to fashion into something else.[12]

A buckle mould of Anglo-Saxon type was found with silver adhering to it. Since this was not a Celtic item of dress, it appears that a Saxon craftsman worked at Dunadd. Anglian princes and their retinues from Northumbria were in exile at the court of Dál Riata throughout the seventh century. Fragments of a very large brooch were found, resembling that of Tara—it seems that this, too, was locally produced.[13]

The deposits full of debris from Dunadd's seventh-century metalworkers demonstrate a fusion of interlaced animal ornament, complex spirals, and knotwork derived from Anglo-Saxon, Irish, and Pictish art; by the eighth century, these had become integrated into a single 'Insular' style, one that was uniquely British, rather than European. Excavations at Dunadd suggest that Dál Riata was a region where this style evolved.[14]

Christians at Dunadd

There may have been a monastic site close to Dunadd. A small slate disc was found at the fort, inscribed with the letters *Inomine*. This forms the first two Latin words of a blessing, 'In the name [of the Lord]'; it shows the presence of a literate cleric at the royal site. One of the more sophisticated quern stones found at Dunadd bears an incised cross in a style used by monks on Iona.

Another indication of a monastic presence at Dunadd was the discovery of a small piece of orpiment, a yellow sulphide of arsenic that was used as a pigment in illuminated manuscripts including the *Book of Kells*. Orpiment is a rare mineral, imported perhaps from Mount Vesuvius, near Naples, or from Asia Minor.[15] Red or purple pigment was also found.[16]

Dunadd's occupants may have worshipped below the fort at Kilmichael Glassary, a mile to the east, where a monk's iron hand bell was found dating from the seventh to the ninth centuries; it was encased in a twelfth-century shrine. Its hereditary keepers (or *dewars* in Scots) were the McLachlans of Dunadd until the seventeenth century.[17] Early Christian grave slabs survive both at Kilmichael Glassary and at Kilmartin, 3 miles to the north.

Kilmartin

Near the Scottish west coast, 19 miles south of Oban, Kilmartin (or 'cell of Martin') may have been a foundation made from Iona by Columba's monks. It was probably dedicated to Martin of Tours, a fourth-century bishop who founded a monastery at Marmoutier, which became the model for many others in Western Europe. The Irish monk Óengus the Culdee described Martin as 'the mount of gold of the western world'.[18] At least five Scottish sites were named after Martin of Tours.[19]

The earliest mention of a church at Kilmartin dates from the fourteenth century, but there are four early Christian crosses here—three simple Latin crosses and a richly carved, free-standing cross probably dating from the tenth century. In a shelter in the churchyard is a fine collection of fourteenth- and fifteenth-century grave slabs carved by a group of sculptors who worked around Loch Awe. This group of tombstones was brought from nearby Poltalloch.

A Monastery at Ellary

According to local tradition, on his way to Dunadd and Iona, Columba landed at Ellary, where he stayed in a large, airy cave at the head of a small bay in Loch Caolisport, off the Knapdale peninsula. The cave has produced evidence dating from Mesolithic times onwards, and there are early carved crosses on the walls. It contains a freshwater pool caused by condensation dripping from the roof, and an altar built of flat stones. Outside is a ruined thirteenth-century chapel. There is a stream with a waterfall nearby and, in earlier times, there would have been a view from the cave across to an islet in Loch Caolisport, where seals play.

The tradition that Columba landed here cannot be verified, but an early monastery was established nearby by monks from Iona. A mile away from the cave, a small cemetery, set among trees, is named *Cladh a' Bhile* ('Burial ground of the holy tree'). It contains almost thirty early grave markers, mostly simple in design, but including a large pillar with a 'marigold-petal' cross above an ornamented equal-armed cross; it probably dates from

Right: View from Columba's cave, Ellary, Argyll and Bute.

Below: Map of Iona.
1. Columba's monastery
2. *Cladh an Dìsirt* cemetery
3 and 5. Pre-Christian forts.
4. Site of the monks' massacre by Norse invaders.
6. Flat plain where the monks grew food.
7. Curragh Bay, where Columba possibly landed in 563.
8. Arrival point for boats that ferried the dead from the mainland, for burial.
9. Augustinian convent, *c.* 1200.

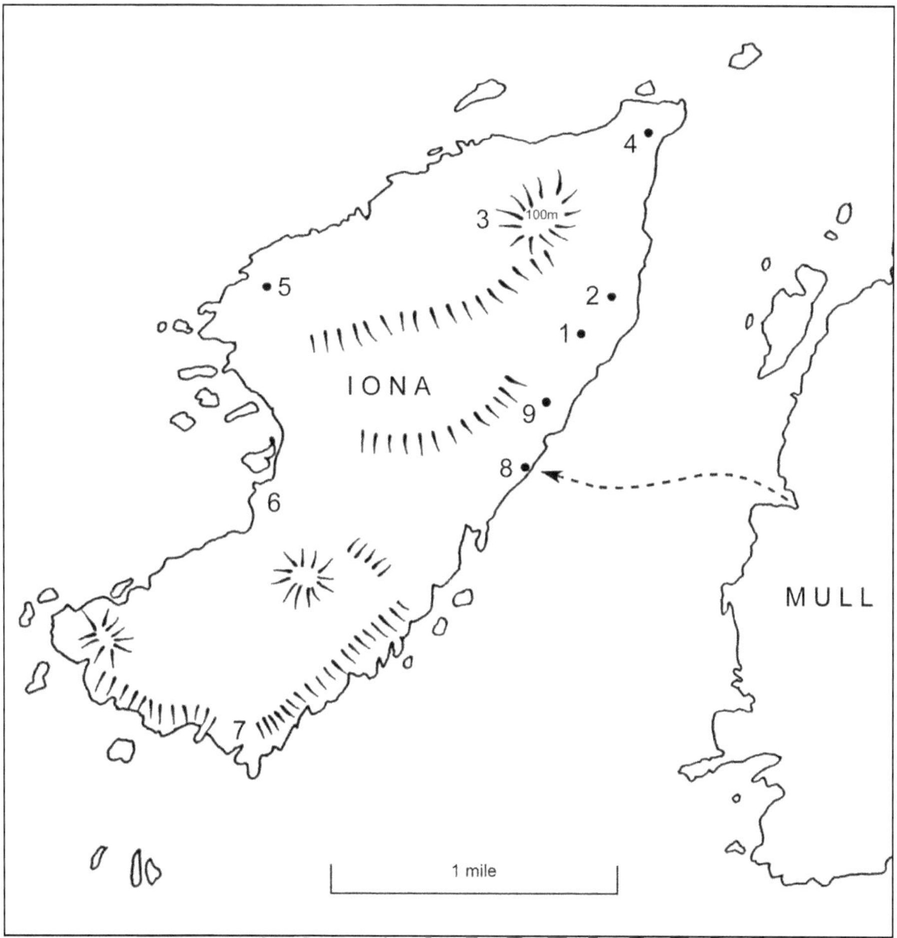

the eighth century, after which the cemetery was no longer used. Its modern wall appears to follow the line of the original enclosure. A gap in the grave markers on its west side suggests that there was once a small chapel at this point, oriented east–west.[20] Querns for grinding corn were also found here.

Ellary is a small settlement on the Knapdale peninsula, 11 miles south-west of Lochgilphead; it is reached by driving south on the A83, turning right onto the B8024, and turning right again at Achahoish. Large-scale maps indicate that one can reach Ellary from Kilmory to the west, but this is a private road, and the journey from this direction can be made only on foot. There is an annual pilgrimage to the cave.

Iona

Iona is an island 3 miles long, a mile off the western tip of the larger island of Mull (see colour plate 1). It can be reached from the Scottish mainland by taking the ferry from Oban to Mull. A coach crosses the island, and its journey ends at Fionnphort, where a small boat takes passengers across the Sound to Iona. If you take the first ferry out from Oban in the morning, and catch the last ferry back in the evening, there is time for a couple of hours on Iona. In order to visit the island at greater length, one must stay in Mull or on Iona itself.

We learn a great deal about the monastery on Iona from Adomnán's *Life of Columba*. This is not a biography, but is divided into three books, entitled *The Prophecies*, *The Miracles*, and *The Visions* of Columba. However, many of the so-called prophecies simply describe the abbot's foresight and his knowledge of the character of his monks. The *Life* offers us a fascinating glimpse of Columba's personality and his community.

In one 'prophecy', Columba gently chides Baithene, who was his first cousin and his favourite disciple, for wasting another monk's time. Baithene was copying out a manuscript of the 150 psalms. As we have seen, the letters '*m*', '*n*', '*v*', and '*i*' were written with identical strokes, and it was very likely that Baithene would have omitted a stroke. However, monks chanted the psalms by heart, so this was of little consequence. Adomnán recounts:

> One day Baithene came to the saint and said, 'I need one of the brothers to go over with me and correct the psalter that I have copied.' On hearing this, the saint spoke as follows: 'Why do you give us this trouble for no reason? For in this psalter of yours of which you speak, not one letter will be found to be added, nor any to be missing, except the vowel 'i' which alone is missing.' And just so, when the entire psalter was read through, what the saint had foretold was found to be true.[21]

In the following 'prophecy', we are given a homely glimpse of the monastery, with its hearth and its pitchers of water. Columba evidently knew which youngsters were responsible and which were careless:

> One day similarly, while [Columba] was sitting by the hearth in the monastery, he saw

> Lugbe, of the family mocu-Min, some distance away reading a book. Suddenly he said to him, 'Take care, my son, take care. I believe that the book you are reading is going to fall into a jar full of water.' And this presently happened. For after a little while that young man stood up to carry out some duty in the monastery, forgetful of the holy man's word, and the book which he carelessly put under his arm fell into a pitcher of water.[22]

Columba the Copyist

Adomnán describes how Columba spent time writing until the day of his death. He implies that in his own day, a century later, the monastery on Iona possessed books written by Columba: 'Many circling years had run by after the blessed man's passing to the Lord, when a certain young man, falling from his horse, was drowned… he had books under his arm packed in a leather satchel.' After twenty days, the dead man was hauled out of the water and the satchel was opened. The books were rotten, but 'there was found a page, written by St Columba's holy fingers, which was dry and in no way damaged, as if it had been kept in a book-chest'.[23] In a similar way, 'a book of hymns for the week, written in Saint Columba's hand, dropped from the shoulders of a boy who fell from a bridge'. This too was preserved.[24]

At the end of Columba's life, he 'sat in his hut copying a psalter. And as he reached that verse of the thirty-third psalm, where it is written, "They that seek the Lord shall want no manner of thing that is good", he said, "Here, at the end of the page, I must stop. Let Baithene write what follows."'[25] In this way, Columba indicated that Baithene should succeed him as abbot.

Books written on Iona include quotations from all the major biblical commentaries and indicate an extensive monastic library. The earliest surviving book written in Scotland is probably that known as the *Cathac* (or '*Battler*') of Columba, written in about AD 600, possibly by Columba himself. It is a copy of the psalms; after his death, it was encased in a shrine and used in Ireland as a battle-standard by the O'Donells of Donegal to secure victory in battle.[26]

Columba's Cell

Columba lived in a hut built on planks on a small rocky mound in the monastery compound. The mound can still be seen in front of the large Benedictine abbey that was later built on the site, near to the fine high cross known as St Martin's cross. The mound may also be the 'little hill overlooking the monastery' from which, according to Adomnán, Columba gave his final blessing to the monks before his death.

The *Life of Columba* refers to fifty-five sea voyages back and forth between Iona and elsewhere. Experienced monks acquired an intimate knowledge of the tides, winds, and currents, and Columba is described advising monks about the time of day at which it

St Martin's cross, Iona, in front of the mound on which Columba's cell stood.

was safest to set sail in various directions. Monks and pilgrims came to visit or to join the community. Those travelling from Scotland crossed the island of Mull and then shouted across the Sound to Iona for a brother to ferry them over. From his hut on planks, Columba could see them coming.

In the following 'prophecy' recounted by Adomnán, Columba is copying a manuscript—ink was precious and could not be wasted. Columba may well have known the visitor whom he heard calling across the Sound for a boat to fetch him:

> On another day also, there was a shout across the Sound of the island of Iona. The saint heard the shouting while sitting in his hut built on planks, and said, 'The man who is shouting across the Sound is a man of no fine perception; for today he will upset my inkhorn and spill the ink.' Hearing this, his attendant Diormit stood and waited a little while before the door for the tiresome guest to arrive, so as to protect the inkhorn. But he soon withdrew from there on other business; and after his withdrawal the troublesome guest appeared, and in his eagerness to kiss the saint upset the inkhorn with the hem of his cloak and spilled the ink.[27]

The Seal Robber

Columba acquired neighbouring islands to provide resources for the monastery—the monks grew grain on the islands of Coll and Tiree (or 'Barley Island'). Seals were a useful source of meat, oil, and shoe leather. It is likely that Columba knew the thief in the following prophecy, and waited for an appropriate opportunity to confront him:

> At another time while the saint was living on the island of Iona, he summoned to him two men from among the brothers, whose names were Lugbe and Silnan, and gave them these orders: 'Cross the Sound now to the island of Mull and look for Erc, a thief, in the plains near the sea. Last night he came alone and in secret from the island of Coll, and he is trying to hide by day under his boat, covered with hay, among the sand-hills, in order to sail across by night to the little island where the seals that belong to us breed; then, greedy robber that he is, he intends to kill some of them by stealth and fill his boat, before returning to his home.

Columba's compassion is evident as the narrative continues. Erc perhaps killed seals because he and his family were hungry, and so Columba tells the monks to give him wethers, or castrated rams, to take home instead:

> They obeyed and set out; and they found the thief hidden in the place foretold by the saint, and brought him to the saint as he had ordered them. Seeing him, the saint said to him: 'Why do you break God's command and keep stealing the property of others? When you have need, come to us and ask, and you will receive what you need.' And saying this, he ordered wethers to be killed and given in place of the seals to the wretched thief, so that he should not go back to his home empty-handed.[28]

Life on Iona

Adomnán describes the monks walking across the island with their farm implements on their backs, to reach the sandy plain on the west side of the island where they grew their crops, using seaweed as fertiliser. On the Scottish west coast, people still harvest seaweed to enrich poor soil. In the autumn, they take their scythes to the beach and cut the seaweed when the tide lifts it into the water; they then bind it into large bundles and wheel it away in barrows. They spread the seaweed on the soil, and the frost breaks it up—they can then plant vegetables in the springtime.[29]

Cattle were bred for dairy products rather than for beef, as we can tell by their sex and their age at death. In his *Life of Columba*, Adomnán emphasises the value attached to cattle, with his accounts of Columba increasing peoples' fortunes by causing their cattle to multiply. Horses were used for transport and haulage; excavation at Iona indicates that they were sometimes eaten at the end of their working lives, and their hides were used for leather.[30]

In the *Life*, we are told of a white horse that carried the milk churns from the cow pasture, and of expeditions to larger islands to fetch wood for building when there were no longer trees on Iona. Adomnán pictures the monks praying in the small church, where Columba's clear voice could be heard above the others. He could also be recognised by his white cowl, or hooded cloak, for the other monks wore unbleached cowls.

A white pony on Iona.

Loch Ness

It seems that Columba twice travelled north to Inverness, perhaps on political missions to confer with Bridei, King of the Picts. His first visit may have been to negotiate peace between King Conall and the Picts, and to ask permission to settle on Iona, which King Bridei considered to be in Pictish territory. Columba and his companions sailed up the Great Glen to Inverness, and Adomnán recounts that on the journey they encountered a creature in the River Ness that people have equated with the Loch Ness monster. A local person who died after being bitten by the monster was being buried near the bank of Loch Ness. Disregarding their experience, Columba told one of his monks to sail across the loch and retrieve a boat. The account continues:

> [The monk] obeyed without delay, and taking off his clothes except his tunic plunged into the water. But the monster, whose hunger had not been satisfied earlier, was lurking in the depths of the river, keen for more prey. Feeling the water disturbed by his swimming, it suddenly swam to the surface and, with a mighty roar from its gaping mouth, it sped towards the man as he swam in midstream.[31]

Columba ordered the monster to return to the depths, and the monk reached the safety of the boat.

Columba Returns to Ireland

Columba lived on Iona for thirty-five years. In AD 575, after an absence of twelve years, he returned to Ireland to attend an assembly of the Uí Néill clan at Druimm-Cete in Derry, as adviser to Áedán, the new king of Dál Riata. The assembly agreed to Dál Riata's independence from Ireland. The standing of the Irish bards was also discussed, and Columba argued in their favour.

It was during this visit to Ireland that Columba is likely to have established a monastery at Drumcliffe, 5 miles north of Sligo city. Drumcliffe is close to the site of the fierce battle of Cúl Dreimhne, which had taken place at the foot of Ben Bulben's almost vertical slope in AD 561, two years before Columba sailed to Argyll. The *Annals of the Four Masters* inform us that this took place in revenge for the killing of a hostage prince who was under Columba's protection.

Although he was successful, it may be that Columba was wounded in the battle. Adomnán apparently alludes to his battle scar, tactfully suggesting that it was inflicted by an angel: 'Its livid mark on his side endured for all the days of his life'.[32] Columba returned to Ireland ten years later, in AD 585, to visit his monastery at Durrow and that of Ciarán at Clonmacnoise. Columba's monastery maintained close links with his Irish homeland—six of the eight abbots who succeeded Columba over the next 107 years came from his own Cenél Conaill branch of the Northern Uí Néill.[33]

Columba's Death

Columba died on Iona. Adomnán describes the abbot's final tour of the island, when he was pulled in a cart because he could no longer walk far. He blessed the island, the monks, the barns, and the white horse. He returned to his hut and, as we have seen, tried to complete a psalm that he was copying, but was unable to do so. That night was Whitsun Eve. Columba went to church for the midnight office, but collapsed there and died. Adomnán described his last hours:

> At midnight he rose up in haste at the ringing of the bell and went to the church, and he ran ahead of the others and entered alone; and kneeling in prayer he sank down beside the altar. Diormit, his attendant … entered the church and cried in a tearful voice: 'Where are you, father, where are you?' And groping through the darkness, as the brothers' lamps had not yet been brought, he found the saint lying before the altar, and lifting him up a little and sitting beside him, put his holy head in his lap.

It is possible that Adomnán heard older monks in the community tell the story many times. He continued:

> Meanwhile, the assembled monks ran up with lights, and began to lament at the sight of their dying father. And, as we have learned from some who were present, while his soul had

> not yet departed, the saint opened and raised his eyes, and looked round on both sides with a wonderfully cheerful and joyous expression.... Diormit then raised [Columba's] right hand to bless the saint's company of monks.... And after his holy blessing, signified in this way, he at once breathed his last.[34]

His monks prayed around him for three days before burying him. They were left to grieve in peace, since storms prevented visitors from crossing the Sound.

Iona's Influence

From Columba's time onwards, Iona was considered to be the centre of Celtic learning. Irish monks came to Iona to study and pray, as did Irish-trained monks from across Europe. Meanwhile, brothers from Iona played a leading part in the spread of Christianity among the Picts of eastern Scotland and the Anglo-Saxons of Northumbria. The Columban monastery of Lindisfarne was founded by Aidan, a monk from Iona, and these two communities became focal points of the Columban family, its cultural traditions, and its manuscript art.

After Columba's death, Iona suffered a number of Norse raids. In AD 806, during their third attack, Vikings killed sixty-eight monks, and the abbot of Iona then took his monks to a safer location in Ireland. This was Kells in Meath—it was 25 miles inland, and therefore better protected from Norse raids. This may have been a new monastic site; it became the headquarters of the Columban monastic family network. From then on, the abbot of Kells was called 'the successor of Columba'.

Iona's First Cemetery

Today there are few remains of Iona's Celtic monastery; the twelfth-century chapel of St Odhráin stands within a much earlier graveyard—this was probably the first Christian cemetery on Iona, where royalty were buried, close to the monastery. The cemetery has yielded the second largest collection of early Christian funerary monuments in the British Isles; only Clonmacnoise beside the Shannon contains a larger one.[35] St Odhráin's Cemetery is named after an early monk who may have lived here before Columba's arrival. Nearby, an ancient winding path of large stones is known as the 'Street of the Dead'. When chieftains were brought to Iona from the Scottish mainland for burial, this was the track along which they were solemnly carried.

Columba's Shrine

The tiny chapel in front of the Benedictine abbey is built on early foundations and may mark the site of Columba's shrine. This was originally freestanding, but its importance

Columba's burial chapel, Iona.

was recognised by the builders of the thirteenth-century Benedictine abbey, who incorporated it into the larger building. In the nineteenth century, the original walls of the shrine still stood about 1 metre high.

On either side of its entrance, as in early Irish churches, the side walls project outwards to support the roof, a feature known as *antae*. The doorway and *antae* are faced with dressed stone, suggesting a ninth- or tenth-century date. The shrine is mentioned in the Icelandic saga *Heimskringla*, which describes the Norwegian king Magnus Barelegs visiting the 'small church of Columcille' on Iona in 1098, when it still retained its wooden door.[36]

Ramparts and a Hermitage

The great rectangular ramparts that surrounded the monastery on Iona can still be traced; they were constructed around the time of Columba's death and were enhanced by an impenetrable hedge of hawthorn and holly. Outside the great rampart, 300 metres to the north-east, is a Celtic cemetery named *Cladh an Dìsirt* in Gaelic, or 'Cemetery of the hermitage'. It was enclosed by a wall and entered through an impressive gateway framed by two large stone pillars; these supported a giant lintel, which has now fallen. The name *Dìsirt* derives from the Latin *desertum*, which means an empty place, a 'desert', where a solitary monk could find God. A later superior of a hermitage on the site is named in a twelfth-century list of monastic officials. There are the remains of a medieval stone chapel beside the entrance to the cemetery.[37]

Entrance to *Cladh an dìsirt*, an early cemetery, Iona.

Trees on Iona

The name 'Iona' is a misreading by a late medieval scribe who read '*u*' as '*n*'. Adomnán calls the island 'Ioua', which appears to be an Irish version of an older Celtic word meaning 'yew tree'. This suggests that yew trees grew here in the Iron Age, although they are lacking from the pollen record for Columba's time. Pollen studies indicate that in Columba's time, oak, ash, birch, willow, and probably hazel grew on the island.

However, the larger trees, oak and ash, were gradually eliminated as the monks cut down wood for timber and cleared the ground for pasture and cultivation.[38] After Columba's death, Adomnán describes hewn trunks of oak and pine towed to Iona from other islands to build 'the large house', 'for the repairing of our monastery', and 'for a long ship'.[39]

Monastery Buildings

Adomnán's vivid account of life on Iona is borne out by the many small-scale excavations that have been carried out on the island. He refers to a church with a side-chamber or chapel, and the later abbey appears to be on the site of the early church, as three high crosses stood nearby. Adomnán describes sleeping places (*cubicula*) for monks, which may have been either individual huts or compartments in a dormitory. He refers to two buildings used by Columba: the cell where he slept, with 'the bare rock for his mattress and for his pillow a stone', and a place where he wrote manuscripts.[40] There was also a communal building for the monks, probably with a kitchen and refectory, and a guest house.[41]

In the *Life*, Adomnán mentions threshing grain and baking bread. There may have also been a herb garden for producing medicines—Columba is said to have cured people suffering from nosebleeds, fractures, and blindness. There were barns beyond the main complex. The *Life* contains references to gathering reeds for thatching and to wooden planks and wattle, presumably covered with clay, as building materials. Columba sends the monks 'to fetch bundles of wattles ... to build a guest house'.[42]

Monastic Workshops

In 1979, excavations were carried out in the early seventh-century boundary ditch between the little hill on which Columba's cell was built and Odhráin's Cemetery. Objects were discovered that would have been in use at the end of Columba's lifetime, including leather from shoes. These were made out of several pieces of leather, with a tongue at the front and occasionally at the heel—unique material illustrating the type of shoe in use at this time. The leather came from cows and calves, goats, horses, red deer, and seal.

There were also parts of three elegant bowls, mostly made of alder, turned on a lathe and decorated with bands of horizontal lines. Clay moulds indicated that fine-quality metalwork was produced. A tiny bronze bell with a clapper was found, as well as sherds of imported E-ware pottery made in south-west Gaul in the late sixth or early seventh century. There had also been a glass furnace, in which glass beads were created and ornaments of various colours with twisted patterns.[43]

Crosses

Adomnán refers to three crosses erected to commemorate incidents associated with Columba. The last of these marked the spot where Columba rested halfway home from blessing a barn before his death: '... at that spot a cross was later set up in a mill-stone, which can be seen today, standing at the roadside'.[44] The mill-stone indicates that the early monastery had a mill. A stream named *Sruth a' Mhuillinn* (Mill Stream) runs south then east through the monastic enclosure and out to sea.[45]

Three fine high crosses survive, dating from the mid- to late eighth century; they were later named after St John, St Martin, and St Oran (or Odhráin). A fourth cross, named after St Matthew, was carved in the ninth or tenth century. It is possible that the ring-headed high cross was invented on Iona, perhaps from a wooden prototype, since St John's cross was formed from separate pieces of stone assembled together with mortise and tenon joints, as one finds in carpentry. A ring appears to have been added to support the weight of the arms, after the cross collapsed. As its arms had been too long, they broke under their own weight, forcing the masons to strengthen them with the addition of a ring.[46]

Later masons realised that it was easier to carve the entire ring-head from a single piece of stone; this style of cross spread throughout Dál Riata and Ireland. The elaborate bosses on some crosses derive from metalwork and sometimes represent rivet-heads, while their interlaced decoration and figures derive from illuminated manuscripts. Iona's magnificent stone crosses were carved out of rock from Doide beside Loch Sween. It would have required great skill to transport these huge slabs, up to 4.5 metres long, across 50 miles of open sea in a lightweight curragh.[47]

The decoration on the three eighth-century crosses recalls that in the *Book of Kells*, written at the same time. The crosses and the gospel book may have been created to celebrate the enshrining of Columba's relics in the mid-eighth century. The craftsmen who carved Iona's fine crosses also worked further afield. They were responsible for the construction and decoration of the high cross at Kidalton on Islay, 46 miles to the south. This ring cross with its very fine ornamentation is perhaps the finest in Scotland; its decoration is similar to that of St Martin's cross on Iona. The latest in this group of crosses from the Iona school of sculpture is at Keills, 40 miles to the south-east, on the Knapdale peninsula.[48] The monastic sites at Kidalton and Keills will be described in the following chapter.

Early Graves

About eighty grave markers survive on Iona. These are in three forms: 'pillow-stones' (or rounded boulders), upright cross slabs, and horizontal grave slabs. Many monks' graves were probably marked by wooden memorials. The simplicity of the grave markers suggests that burial rites were not elaborate. Adomnán relates that Columba's body lay in his cell while 'for three days and nights the funeral rituals befitting one of his honour and status were duly carried out'. He was then buried 'wrapped in pure linen, laid in the coffin assigned and made ready for it', apparently in a simple grave pit marked only by the stone that had been his pillow.[49]

The slabs that survive on Iona date from the sixth century onwards and continue into later medieval times. Some are carved with a simple cross, while others are more elaborate and a few have brief inscriptions in Old Irish, such as 'A prayer for Maíl-Phátraic' or 'A prayer for Fergus'. An eighth-century tombstone is inscribed 'A prayer for the soul of Éogan'; this Gaelic name is the equivalent of Ewen, or John in English.

The twelfth-century chapel of St Odhráin is the earliest building to survive on the island. It resembles Irish chapels of the period, with a single doorway in the west wall, decorated with chevron and beak-head ornament. It was probably rebuilt as a family burial vault by Somerled, King of the Isles, who died in 1164.[50]

Women on Iona

In about 1200, Earl Reginald, son of Somerled, Lord of the Isles, introduced a group of Benedictine monks to replace their Celtic predecessors; some of the Celtic monks were

Above: Tombstone inscribed 'A prayer for the soul of Éogan', Iona.

Below: St Odhráin's twelfth-century chapel, Iona.

Isle of the Women, between Iona and Mull.

probably absorbed into the new community. The Benedictines immediately began to build the present abbey church. South of the abbey, Reginald established a community of Augustinian canonesses and appointed his sister, Bethoc (or Beatrice in English), as its first prioress.

Reginald perhaps brought the first nucleus of nuns from Ireland, where there were many convents whose nuns followed the Rule of St Augustine. Much of Bethoc's convent survives, together with the remains of a massive turf dyke that crosses the island from coast to coast, to separate the nuns' property from that of the monks. However, this may not have been the first community of women to live close to the monks of Iona. There may have been an earlier group of nuns on a small rocky island in the Sound of Iona, just off the Ross of Mull, since it is named 'Isle of the Women', or *Eilean nam Ban* in Gaelic.

Columba's Mother, Eithne

Columba sailed to Scotland accompanied not only by brother monks, but also by members of his family. An early tradition recounts that his uncle, Ernán, became prior of a community on Hinba. This was probably Jura, a large island to the south-east of Iona, where Columba's mother, Eithne (pronounced 'Enya'), is also said to have founded a convent. Several high-born women in early times were called Eithne; the name may be a female version of 'Aidan', or it may mean 'a kernel, or grain'.

One tradition suggests that Columba's mother belonged to the Corpraige of the Fanad peninsula, the second most northerly point of Donegal. This was a lesser tribal kingdom that came to be dominated by the Cenél Conaill by the mid-seventh century.[51] Adomnán tells us little about Eithne, except that in the second preface to his *Life of Columba* he stated:

> Saint Columba, then, was born of noble parents, his father being Fedilmith, son of Fergus, and his mother Eithne, whose father's name is mac-Naue in Irish, which may be rendered 'ship's son'.[52]

The name of Kilmeny, in the northern half of Islay, south of Jura, derives from *Cill Mh'Eithne*, meaning 'my Eithne's church'. This may be an early reference to Columba's mother, although it is always possible that a site's name derives from the later popularity of that saint. Still, the more remote a settlement is, the more likely it is that the name may be an early one. There are also dedications to a St Eithne in eastern Scotland, including another Kilmeny in Fife. Forgandenny, near Perth, was known as *Forgrunethny* in 1382; it probably means 'St Eithne's place in the bog', suggesting a nun's hermitage. The family name Gille Ethueny (1246), also found in Perthshire, is likely to mean 'St Eithne's servant'.[53] However, these eastern dedications may refer to another early nun.

2

Adomnán and Iona's Daughter Houses

In this chapter, we will examine the life of Adomnán and consider life on Iona after Columba's death. We shall focus on some of Iona's daughter houses, and other early monasteries of Argyll. The ninth abbot of Iona, Adomnán (*c.* AD 624–704), lived a century after Columba and was his most gifted successor; his name means 'little Adam'. As we saw in Chapter 1, he was an accomplished author; he was also a wise abbot and a gifted statesman, intelligent and far-sighted. Like Columba, Adomnán was born in Donegal and came from the royal family of the northern Uí Néill. He trained as a monk under Columba's nephew, Ernán, and became abbot of Iona in AD 679 at the age of fifty-five.

A Guide to the Holy Places

In Adomnán's early years as abbot of Iona, a bishop from Gaul named Arculf visited Iona. He had been shipwrecked off the British coast on his way home from a nine-month pilgrimage visiting holy sites in the Near East, including the Holy Land, Damascus, Alexandria, and Constantinople. Adomnán welcomed him and used information from Arculf to write three volumes entitled *De Locis Sanctis* ('About the Holy Places'). He also consulted other works in the library at Iona, in order to produce a more complete account.

Adomnán included a sketch of the Church of the Holy Sepulchre in Jerusalem, which may be the oldest architectural drawing to survive from Scotland.[1] *De Locis Sanctis* became the chief guide to the Holy Land in early medieval Europe, although Adomnán never visited Palestine himself. He presented a copy to King Aldfrith of Northumbria, and Bede composed an abridged version of the book. Bede told the story of Arculf's shipwreck, and summarised Adomnán's work in his own *Ecclesiastical History*.[2]

Adomnán's *Life of Columba*

In AD 688, Adomnán visited the monastery of Jarrow in Northumbria, where he spent at least a year and would have met Bede. The young Bede describes the older abbot as 'a good and wise man, and remarkably learned in Holy Scripture'.[3] In the four years after his return to Iona from Northumbria, Adomnán wrote his *Life of Columba*. This is primarily a work in praise of Columba's holiness, but it also conveys a political message. Adomnán claims that Columba consecrated the King of Argyll, Aedán mac Gabráin, choosing him in preference to his brothers. Adomnán related:

> One night in a trance, [Columba] saw an angel of the Lord, who had been sent to him and held in his hand a glass book of the ordination of kings.... In the book he was charged to ordain Aedán as king, but refused, because he had more love for Iogenan, Aedán's brother....
>
> And so, after the angel of the Lord had appeared for three nights in succession... the saint, in obedience to the word of the Lord, sailed across to the island of Iou [Iona] and there, as he had been bidden, ordained Aedán as king; for Aedán had arrived there during these days. And as he spoke the words of ordination, he prophesied concerning the future of Aedán's sons, grandsons and great-grandsons; and laying his hand upon his head, he ordained and blessed him.[4]

An audience familiar with the scriptures would recall how the prophet Samuel anointed King David, choosing him above his brothers in a similar way (1 Sam. 16.1-13). When the prophet was instructed by God to anoint one of Jesse's sons as king, to Samuel's surprise, God chose Jesse's youngest son, David.

An Imaginary Coronation?

Aedán's coronation ceremony is described in no other early text. The monastery of Iona was a very recent foundation, with no tradition of involvement in tribal rituals, and so it was an unlikely venue for a coronation. Adomnán may have invented this story because Aedán's descendants were now important rulers. Like Columba, Adomnán belonged to the royal Uí Néill dynasty and was politically acute as head of the largest monastic dynasty in Britain. As we shall see, he was closely involved in both secular and church politics.

Adomnán wished to create a more peaceful society in which there was order and legitimate succession rather than bloodshed and feud. This might be achieved if the royal succession depended upon Iona and the Uí Néill, following a precedent that he could present as having been created by Columba.[5]

Pictish sculpture and that of Argyll, particularly on Iona, depicts the Old Testament shepherd-king David ruling wisely and peacefully, caring for his flock and defending them from ferocious beasts. Adomnán might have modelled the story of Aedán's consecration upon that of David, in the hope that people of his time would benefit from the wise and peaceful behaviour of strong kings who defended Christianity.[6] Adomnán's *Life of Columba* was widely copied and read in mainland Europe, and his inauguration ritual may have been adopted by the Carolingian kings of France.[7]

The Date of Easter

Adomnán became involved in a dispute between the Roman and Columban Churches, which was in part a power struggle, although it was ostensibly about the date of Easter and styles of tonsure, or clerical haircut. Celtic monks like Adomnán shaved the front half of their head and left the rest of their hair long, while Roman clerics shaved the top of their head. Bede informs us that in Northumbria these matters were resolved in favour of the Roman model at the Synod of Whitby in AD 664.[8] Adomnán accepted the Roman method of calculating the date of Easter in AD 688, but was unable to persuade his own monks on Iona to agree.

This would have created an awkward situation, in which the abbot celebrated Easter on a different day from his own community. Evidently, blind obedience was neither expected nor demanded in Columban monasteries, since the monks on Iona accepted the Roman calendar only in AD 712, twenty-four years later. Meanwhile, Adomnán, who was responsible for the oversight of all the Columban foundations, promoted the new calendar in other monasteries in eastern Scotland and Ireland. Adomnán hints that there were at least five Columban monasteries in Ireland in his day. It would have been a simple matter for him to arrange to be in a monastery other than his own during Lent and Eastertime, where he could celebrate the Easter liturgy together with his brother monks.

The Synod of Birr

In AD 692, Adomnán returned to Ireland, where he challenged his former friend, King Finnachta, over an annual payment of cattle tribute. Adomnán cursed King Finnachta, who died three years later. As the ruler of Columba's monasteries in Northern Ireland, Adomnán returned in AD 697 to take part in the Synod of Birr. This was an assembly of chieftains and clerics from Ireland and Scotland, including Dál Riata and the Pictish territories. It might have taken place to commemorate Columba who died 100 years earlier in AD 597. Birr in County Offaly was close to the boundary between northern Ireland, dominated by the Uí Néill, and southern Ireland, ruled by the kings of Leinster; Birr was therefore almost neutral ground, where rival kings and clerics could meet.

At the synod, Adomnán proposed a law to exempt women, children, and clergy from taking part in warfare; the new law was accepted, and additionally applied in Scotland. Penalties for transgressing it were to be paid to the Columban monasteries. It is known as *Cáin Adomnáin*, or Adomnán's Law of Innocents; it might be considered as one of the earliest international declarations of human rights. Concerning women, it proposed 'that women may not be killed by a man in any way, neither by slaughter nor by any other death, not by poison, nor in water, nor in fire, nor by any beast, nor in a plot, nor by dogs, but shall die in their own lawful bed...'[9]

Adomnán persuaded over fifty Irish kings to guarantee the law, together with the king of Dál Riata and the king of the Picts; over forty bishops and abbots also signed the document. It survives, combined with a later commentary, or narrative preface, in a treatise in Old Irish on the Law of Adomnán, which is found in two manuscripts derived from the lost *Book of Raphoe*, written *c.* 1000. The commentary attempts to explain the law; although it may exaggerate the horrors that it describes as taking place 300 years earlier, they are unlikely to be completely divorced from reality.

The Book of Raphoe

This book, named after Adomnán's birthplace of Raphoe in Donegal, describes the traditional role of women in battle, even if they were highborn:

> The work which the finest of women used to do was to proceed to battle and battlefield, division and encampment, killing and slaughter. On one side she carried her provision bag, on the other side her infant, her wooden pole upon her back, thirty feet in length. On one end of it [there was] an iron hook, which she would thrust into the opposite battalion at the hair of the other woman, her husband behind her, a fence-stake in his hand, flogging her on to battle.[10]

The treatise relates that Adomnán and his mother were on a battlefield and were touched by the sight of an orphaned infant:

> Though they beheld the massacre, they did not see anything which they thought more pitiful than a woman's head on one bank and her body on the opposite bank with a child asleep at the breast, a stream of milk on one cheek and a stream of blood on the other.[11]

Devotion to Mary, mother of God, may have helped to inspire Adomnán to introduce the law. A section of the commentary added in Latin by a scribe who was evidently less familiar with Old Irish than with Latin, reflects on Adomnán's attitude to motherhood. He felt inspired to make 'a law in Ireland and Britain for the sake of the mother of each one, because a mother has borne each one, and for the sake of Mary, the mother of Jesus Christ… Great is the sin when anyone kills the one who is mother and sister to Christ's mother'.[12]

It is possible that, as Columba's biographer, Adomnán was inspired by his predecessor's protectiveness towards the vulnerable in society. In his *Life of Columba*, for example, Adomnán relates how a man pursued a young woman, showing no respect to the clerics who tried to save her; instead, he killed her with a spear. Columba declares that he will go to hell as the girl ascends to heaven.[13]

Renewal of the Law of Innocents

Adomnán returned to Iona and died in AD 704, shortly after his final visit to Ireland. After his death, Adomnán's relics were taken back to his native Ireland and, as part of the celebrations, his Law was renewed in AD 727 as 'Adomnán's Law'. It was one of the first systematic attempts to lessen the savagery of warfare among Christians, and was without precedent in that it derived not from tradition or time-honoured custom, but took its force from its enactment at the Synod of Birr. The Law became effective in every territory where there were Columban monasteries.[14]

The Law was again promulgated in Ireland on its sixtieth anniversary in AD 757, by Abbot Sléibéne of Iona, alongside a king of Meath. Iona's next abbot but one, Bresal, son of Ségéne, proclaimed it once again in AD 778, a year after its eightieth anniversary, alongside another king of Meath. In the eighth century, law codes similar to those of Adomnán were promulgated by bishops of other leading churches including Armagh, where a 'Law of Patrick' was proclaimed in AD 834.[15]

The Influence of Adomnán and Iona

Adomnán travelled extensively, and his cult was widespread. He is honoured on North Uist in the Outer Hebrides, and a chapel was dedicated to him on the Isle of Bute at Kildavanan, which means 'cell of Adomnán'. He spent time among the Picts, east of the Grampian Mountains—he maintained a good relationship with the Pictish royal house. He is commemorated throughout Pictish lands, especially in Aberdeenshire, Banff, and Forfar. In his old age, Adomnán is said to have worked among the Picts in Glen Lyon, one of the Highland routes leading eastwards towards Loch Tay. Sites associated with him in Glen Lyon will be described in Chapter 6.

Iona became a centre of scholarship and artistic excellence, with monks skilled at carving high crosses, illuminating manuscripts, and writing poetry. Its sculptors carved crosses at Iona's daughter houses, including a magnificent example at Kidalton. The monastery at Kidalton was dedicated to 'the Fosterling', who may have been Columba's foster son and successor, Baithene. The Kidalton cross is the only Scottish ring cross to survive intact at its original site. It has four raised bosses, and is decorated with figures and scroll motifs. Beneath the central boss, the Virgin and Child are flanked by angels. Kidalton is 6 miles east of Port Ellen, near the south-eastern end of Islay, one of the Inner Hebrides.

A School of Sculpture at Keills

Keills is 12 miles south-west of Lochgilphead, at the southern end of the B8025.
Today, it is an isolated chapel at the end of a narrow 10-mile tongue of land in Knapdale, bordered by the rough waters of the Sound of Jura to the west, and the sheltered waters of a sea loch, Loch Sween, to the east. In summer, Keills can be swathed in mist; in winter, the Atlantic winds howl from the north-west. Thirteen miles to the north, where the Sound of Jura meets the Atlantic Ocean, there is a whirlpool in the Gulf of Corryvreckan that the Celts believed was the entrance to the underworld.

Keills was easily accessible by boat. An old landing stage survives beside the deep water on the north side of the peninsula, and the chapel is on its sheltered southern slope. Keills was originally named *Cill Mo-Charmáig*, or 'my Cormac's cell'. An islet named Eilean Mór, 4 miles to the south-west, was also dedicated to him.[16] It is uncertain which Cormac this might be—a number of saints bore this name. A parish church was established here in the twelfth century, and the present chapel dates from that time.

There was an early monastery with a school of sculptors here; among the carvings preserved in the chapel is a half-finished cross that was abandoned when the stone fractured, and another stone on which masons practised carving letters and patterns. An elaborate high cross was erected on the hillside 45 metres north-west of the chapel. It resembles those on Iona and dates from the late eighth or early ninth century. Only a large monastery would have commissioned such a fine monument.

A replica now stands on the windy hillside; the original has been brought into the chapel. At its centre is a nest-like boss surrounded by four lions, with the Archangel Michael above it and a seated saint or evangelist below. The remaining surface is covered with intertwined creatures and abstract designs. The high cross is the latest in a group carved by sculptors trained on Iona.[17] There are six other early Christian slabs in the chapel.

Right: High cross, Keills, Knapdale, Argyll and Bute.

Below: Original site of the high cross, Keills, Knapdale, Argyll and Bute.

Manuscript Art on Iona

It is now generally thought that two of the finest early illuminated manuscripts, the *Book of Durrow* and the *Book of Kells*, were among those produced on Iona in the seventh and eighth centuries. The magnificent *Book of Durrow* was created between AD 650 and 700, during Adomnán's lifetime. It was perhaps taken to the Columban monastery of Durrow in Ireland by monks fleeing from the Vikings. It pre-dates the *Book of Kells* by over a century, and it is the earliest surviving fully decorated insular Gospel book. Its artist was unused to depicting human figures, but was more familiar with animal forms. The book contains highly detailed carpet pages, filled with curvilinear designs and interlaced animals.

The *Book of Kells* is another very fine decorated gospel book that was created around AD 800. Its text is a poor version of the Latin gospels; it is interesting that its scholarship does not match the skill lavished on its illustrations. These were executed in the latest Northumbrian style by monks trained at Lindisfarne. At least 185 calves were killed to produce hide for its vellum pages; this would require a herd of some 600 cattle to sustain the breeding population.[18]

The pigments used were rare and expensive, and included yellow orpiment from the Mediterranean and blue lapis lazuli from Afghanistan. The manuscript was taken to Kells, but when the monastery was plundered in 1006, the gospel book was stolen and buried for three months. It was retrieved, but had lost its jewel-encrusted cover. Like the *Book of Durrow*, it is now in the library of Trinity College, Dublin.

Poetry

One of the finest poems composed on Iona in the seventh century is entitled *Altus Prosator*, or 'The High first-sower'. It takes the form of a Latin hymn, and is unique in its range and originality. The hymn proceeds through twenty-three stanzas of six lines each, and praises God's work from the dawn of time to the end of the world. It is typical of early Irish monastic hymns in its metre of eight syllables per line, following the style of the hymns composed by the fourth-century bishop Ambrose of Milan. It is also typical of Irish hymnody in its use of rhyme, with alliteration. Like some other Irish hymns, each verse begins with successive letters of the alphabet, a pattern used centuries earlier in Psalm 118(9) and the Lamentations of Jeremiah in the Old Testament.

'The High first-sower' was perhaps used in the liturgy, since a three-line refrain is given at the end, which may have been chanted by all the monks in response to the verses that might be sung by a solo voice. A later addition appears to be a metrical Collect, or concluding prayer. The hymn could have been sung at the Easter Vigil, with its readings from the Old Testament that recall the entire history of creation and set this cosmic drama within historical time. By the eleventh century, however, the hymn appears to have been used for private devotion.[19]

The Text of 'The High First-Sower'

Verse 1, beginning with the letter 'A', addresses the Trinity and describes the Father as creator, using a less usual term *prosator* or 'first-sower':

> *(A) The High first-sower, the Ancient of Days and unbegotten,*
> *was without any source, limit, or foundation in the beginning, and is,*
> *and will be throughout unending ages forever...*[20]

The author continues to describe the Trinity, using the language of the Athanasian Creed. The creation of the angels is described in verse 2, which begins with the letter 'B' *(Bonos creavit angelos)*, while stanzas 'C', 'D', 'G', and 'H' give an account of the demons, drawing on Cassian's *Conlationes* 8, a text that was popular with Celtic monks. John Cassian (d. 433) was a monk of Lérins who spent years studying with the Desert Fathers of Egypt.

Creation in 'The High first-sower'

Using phrases from the first chapter of the Book of Genesis, the author of the hymn describes the creation of the natural world in 'E' and 'F':

> *(E) The High One, looking forward to the system of the universe and its harmony,*
> *made the heaven and the earth;*
> *Brought forth the sea, the waters, the shoots of grass, the trees of the woods, the sun,*
> *moon, stars, fire and all things needed...*
> *(F) The stars and the great lights of the upper regions were made together,*
> *So viewing this wonderful and immense created body, the angels burst forth in praise*
> *of the Lord, the architect of the heavens...*

The author then turns to an unusual theme ('I', 'K', and 'L'), and considers the tides, the sea, winds, and rain as he describes the movement of water around the world. The sea and its tides were of great importance to seafaring monks; in his *Life of Columba*, Adomnán depicts Columba observing the effect of winds on ocean currents as he advises monks when to safely set sail.

In this section, the author of the hymn devises an original theory concerning the movement of water around the world, drawing in part upon Isidore of Seville (*c*. 560–636).[21] In beautiful poetry, he explains how the clouds draw up water from the sea, and how the winds drive this water overland and also dry out the salt marshes. God carefully controls the clouds so that they gradually let out their water to fertilise the land, thereby creating rivers:

> *(I) From out of their northern sources in the deeper parts of the ocean,*
> *from the three-quarters of earth covered in sea, the clouds carry in the rains.*
> *In blue whirlwinds the sea reaches up to the heavens,*

so that the grains, vines and grasses may all benefit,
and then these clouds are moved by the winds coming from their storehouses,
and these in turn drain out the water from the marshes...

(L) The Lord often shakes down the waters bound up in the clouds,
in case they burst their retainers in a single eruption.
On the earth, the more fruitful streams of water flow slowly in their paths, as if flowing from udders.
Freezing and flowing with the turning seasons, they flow everywhere without faltering.

Several words in stanza 'K' are borrowed from a dramatic description of the rough waters at the mouth of the Nile in the *Historiae* of Pseudo-Hegesippus, which dates from the late fourth century. Since Adomnán draws on the same passage in his *Life of Columba*, it is likely that this text was available in Iona's library in the seventh century.[22]

Chapter 38 of the Book of Job in the Old Testament contains magnificent poetry describing God at work in the natural world, from the constellations to the wonders of the deep. The author of 'The High first-sower' quotes seventeen times from a *Commentary on the Book of Job* by Philip the Presbyter, who died in the mid-fifth century and was a disciple of Jerome. Philip's writings were popular in Irish monasteries, and it is likely that Iona also possessed this text.[23]

The End of Time in 'The High First-Sower'

The hymn continues to describe hell ('N', 'O'), paradise ('P'), Sinai ('Q'), and the end of time ('R' to 'Z'):

(X) The banner of the cross, the brightest sign, will shine resplendent,
When Christ, the celestial Lord, descends from the heavens.
The two great lights [the sun and moon] will be darkened;
The stars will drop on the earth like figs from a tree...

(Y) Then the Trinity will be praised;
With the singing of hymns rung out with prayer;
With thousands of lively angels dancing;...
Along with the twenty-four happy elders,
Throwing down their crowns at the feet of the Lamb of God...

The hymn's refrain is a brief and sober reflection that only Christians who remain focussed on God can truly celebrate with the 'lively angels' and 'happy elders'. In monastic language, this can be achieved only through 'contempt for the world'. This observation again draws on Cassian's *Conlationes* 8:

Who can please God in the final time,
With the various orders of truth made plain?
Only those who have contempt for the present world.

The Iona Chronicle

Monks on Iona produced other important texts including the *Iona Chronicle*, which appears to have been a contemporary account of events in northern Britain and Ireland from at least the mid-seventh century. In the mid-740s, a copy of the *Iona Chronicle* was taken to an Irish monastery; the manuscript from Iona now survives only within the later *Irish Chronicle* which drew upon it as a primary source of information about earlier times. Since no other copies of the *Iona Chronicle* survive, this Irish text is one of very few early accounts of political and religious life in Scotland between the eighth and the twelfth centuries.[24]

Equally important is a collection of Church laws compiled under an abbot of Iona, named Cilléne Droichtech, who presided over the monastery from AD 726 until 752. A monk on Iona at this time, Cú Chuimne 'the Wise', was one of two scholars who compiled an immense legal code, the *Collectio canonum Hibernensis* (or 'Collection of Irish canons'). This comprised sixty-seven books of laws based on Irish and European law and patristic theology, also drawing upon British and Anglo-Saxon sources. Perhaps for the first time, it organised canons by subject matter, rather than by their date of origin. It formed the basis for Church law throughout much of Europe for centuries. It was universally welcomed by canon lawyers, and had a lasting impact on the Christian West.[25]

Bishops and Kings

In the eighth, ninth, and tenth centuries, there is mention of bishops on Iona.[26] At least two Irish kings, Niall Frossach, King of Tara, and Artgall, King of Connacht, retired to Iona in the second half of the eighth century. Óláfr Sihtricsson, a Norse king of Dublin who had formerly ruled from York, retired to Iona 'in penitence and pilgrimage' in AD 980, but only six years later, the abbot and fifteen monks were killed in a Viking raid.[27]

The monastery remained the burial place for the kings of Dál Riata. Although the royal dynasty moved eastwards into the land of the Picts, the king-lists state that Cináed mac Ailpín, or Kenneth son of Alpin (AD 810–58), and his successors were buried on Iona. However, the king-lists date from the twelfth century and later, so they are not entirely dependable. Nevertheless, it seems likely that Iona remained the chief burial place for Scottish kings until the eleventh century, when Dunfermline in Fife became the new royal burial ground.[28]

Norsemen on Iona

The first recorded Viking attack on Iona took place in AD 795. It was plundered and burnt in AD 802 and in 806 when, as we have seen, sixty-eight monks were murdered, and again in 825. A poem by Walafrid Strabo (d. 849), Abbot of Reichenau in southern Germany, commemorates a monk of Iona named Blathmac who, knowing that the raiders sought 'the precious metals wherein lie the holy bones of Columba', buried the shrine and sent away a number of monks to hide. When the raiders arrived, 'threatening cruel perils to the blessed men', Blathmac and the remaining monks refused to reveal where the shrine was hidden and were killed. The poem suggests the existence of Columba's reliquary by this date.[29]

By the later tenth century, there appear to have been Norse Christians among the monks on Iona. Three Norse gravestones survive from the late tenth or early eleventh century. The style of one of these suggests that it was carved on the Isle of Man, while another bears a carving of a boat carrying warriors and a smith with a hammer in his hand—it appears to depict the Norse legend of Weland the Smith. A third is carved with a double-ribbon cross and a runic inscription along its border that reads 'Kali the son of Olvir laid this stone over his brother Fugl'; these are Scandinavian names.[30]

Iona and the Norse-Gaels

A mixed population of Norse and Gaels settled along the Scottish west coast and in the Hebrides. In the twelfth century, western Argyll evolved into the Gaelic-Norse Kingdom of the Isles. Although Iona had been devastated by Vikings, it remained the head of the Columban monastic family in Ireland and in Scotland until the end of the ninth century. Some of the mac Ailpín kings were probably buried on Iona until the end of the ninth century and again from the second half of the tenth century.[31]

Iona became a centre for the Norse-Gaels, in a region where the Gaels are likely to have converted the Norse to Christianity. A fine carved cross slab at Ardchattan Priory, described towards the end of the chapter, dates from the ninth or tenth century, and indicates that monasteries continued to flourish in Argyll. The Norse-Gaels were to be found in the Western Isles, Orkney, Shetland, and the Isle of Man. As early as the ninth century, Norse colonists intermarried with native Gaels and adopted their language and customs; they dominated the region around the Irish Sea until the twelfth century.[32]

Early Monasteries in Argyll

A number of monasteries were founded in Argyll both before and after Columba's death in AD 597. One of the earliest is on the southernmost islet of the Garvellachs named *Eileach an Naoimh*, or 'the Holy Rocks'. The Garvellachs are 5 miles south of Mull, in the Firth of Lorne. A cluster of monastic cells clings to the cliffs of *Eileach an Naoimh*, with a cemetery and remains of other buildings; the cells were restored in the 1990s. The circular cells with corbelled roofs are joined together; they resemble those on Skellig Michael in south-west Ireland.

The community on *Eileach an Naoimh* may have been founded by St Brendan (d. *c.* 575). His *Life* relates how he sailed to Argyll, on the Scottish west coast: 'Brendan of Clonfert came to a certain island of Britain called Ailech, and there he founded a church, proposing to remain there to the end'.[33] Brendan's *Life* was perhaps written before AD 800, although the earliest surviving copies date from the late twelfth century.

The *Life* describes how Brendan 'prayed alone near the sea on a lofty rock'. The rocky islet of *Eileach an Naoimh* is very different from the more fertile islands chosen by Columba for his self-supporting monasteries. Writing in the seventh century, Adomnán says that Brendan visited Columba on the island of Hinba; as we have seen, this is likely to be the large island of Jura, 5 miles south of the Garvellachs.[34]

On top of the ridge to the south-west of the beehive huts on *Eileach an Naoimh*, a stones circle marks an enclosure containing one or perhaps two graves. A tradition recorded in the nineteenth century names this as the grave of Columba's mother, Eithne. There are three small upright stones within the stone circle, one with an early incised Greek cross. In 1861, T. S. Muir observed a *leacht*, or altar of stones, beside the carved cross: 'a pile of loose stones laid together like an altar and flanked by a short pillar bearing an incised cross'. It was said that the bones of a female were found in the grave. The burial site is most clearly visible from the shore where boats land.[35]

Columban Monasteries in Northumbria

Iona's international influence was unique: it played a leading role in the conversion of Northumbria and through its daughter houses it became one of the most important religious centres in Europe. In Northumbria, the most important foundation from Iona was established on Lindisfarne in AD 635. Two years earlier, Oswald, son of King Æthelfrith of Northumbria, had returned from exile in the west of Scotland. He had been converted to Christianity by monks of Iona and, after reclaiming the Northumbrian throne, he invited Aidan, a monk of Iona, to establish a monastery on Lindisfarne as a base from which to convert his kingdom. Bede described how King Oswald asked the abbot of Iona to 'send a bishop by whose instruction and ministry the English nation, which he governed, might be taught the advantages, and receive the sacraments of the Christian faith'.

Bede comments:

> From that time many of the Scots came daily into Britain, and with great devotion preached the word to those provinces of the English over which King Oswald reigned, and those among them who had received priest's orders, administered to them the grace of baptism. Churches were built in several places; the people joyfully flocked together to hear the word [of God].[36]

Oswald, Aidan, and life on Lindisfarne will be described more fully in Chapter 9. From Lindisfarne, monks travelled throughout Northumbria and returned to the regions of Scotland under Northumbrian control. Monasteries were founded at Old Melrose in the Scottish Borders, at Abercorn, 10 miles west of Edinburgh, and at Hoddom in Dumfries and Galloway; at these sites, there may have been earlier bishops' churches. Whithorn eventually became a Northumbrian monastery.[37] In the mid ninth-century, Iona also came to control the Pictish Church in eastern Scotland.

Blane's Monastery on Bute

One of Columba's contemporaries was Blane (or *Bláán* in Gaelic), whose chief monastery was on the Isle of Bute. At the mouth of the Clyde estuary, Bute was attractive to Celtic monks. It was low-lying and fertile, and at the centre of routes from north-east Ireland and south-west Scotland, with Iona to the north-west. The island is sheltered from the ocean, and since it is 5 miles by 15, it supported a considerable population. It is so close to the mainland that sheep and cattle could safely swim across.

In Celtic times, the southern end of Bute was the most populous. There was a fort there, and a monastery of some fifty monks, with a surrounding settlement. The community was founded by Catán, after whom Kilchattan Bay, 1 mile to the north, is named. Catán apparently arrived from Ireland in the late sixth century. Sources differ as to whether Catán was Blane's uncle or his tutor; as abbot, Catán could well have been both.

Blane appears to have been an Irish-trained Briton; his cult is mainly found in Galloway and central Scotland. Bute may have been British at this time; the twelfth-century *Félire* (or Martyrology) of Gorman describes 'triumphant Blane of the Britons'.[38] It is possible that he was a bishop in the monastery at Kingarth on Bute in the later sixth or seventh century, and less likely that he was bishop of Dunblane. The Annals of Ulster record the deaths of bishops at Kingarth in the later seventh century and of abbots in the eighth century, some of whom met violent deaths at the hands of Norsemen.[39]

Blane's monastery on Bute is in a lovely spot in a sheltered valley near the shore. It is surrounded by its original bean-shaped enclosure wall, within which are the remains of a circular fort, a well, and what may be the ruins of monks' cells, set against a sheltering cliff. By medieval times, the monks had created an inner cemetery for themselves and an outer one for lay people (see colour plate 2). In the cemetery, there are a few early crosses. A ruined medieval church stands at the centre of the site, and a twelfth-century arch separates the chancel from the nave. The east end of the church was rebuilt in the thirteenth century.

The monastery was a centre of culture and craftsmanship: a tiny ninth-century crucible for casting bronze brooches was found here, and there are designs engraved on slate which were preparatory sketches made by craftsmen. A stone bowl is set in the ground, perhaps for washing pilgrims' feet, a traditional ceremony of welcome. Norse Christians were buried here: there is a hogback tombstone in the churchyard, designed to represent a house for the dead. A Viking's gold ring was found, and a gold fillet for binding a lady's hair.

Inchmarnock

A monastery on the small island of Inchmarnock, 1 mile off the west coast of Bute, is likely to have been a daughter house of Blane's monastery at Kingarth. The island is just over 2 miles long. The suffix *-oc* is a term of endearment, and so the island's name, Inchmarnock, means 'Isle of my little Ernán'. There are other dedications to 'my little

Right: The lower cemetery and boundary wall, St Blane's monastery, Kingarth, Bute.

Below: Stone basin, perhaps for washing pilgrims' feet, St Blane's monastery, Kingarth, Bute.

Ernán', including those of Kilmarnock in East Ayrshire and Dalmarnock, near the River Clyde, 2 miles south-east of central Glasgow; Ernán was a common monastic name.

On Inchmarnock, there is an early monastic enclosure containing a number of workshops. The largest Scottish collection of slates inscribed with texts and sketches was found here. Some are practice pieces for more complex designs, or pattern books, found near debris from metal working. The slates, which appear to date from the eighth and ninth centuries, indicate that literacy was taught even at quite small monasteries.[40]

On one slate dating from the mid-eighth century, a novice monk inscribed a line from a Latin hymn composed at the monastery of Bangor, in north-east Ireland; on the other side, he carved the first ten letters of the ogham alphabet on either side of a stem line—when the letters are bound together by a stem line, they are easier to read. Ogham is a cryptic alphabet using the sound values of spoken Latin; it consists of incised lines, often grouped along two adjacent sides of a stone slab. Strokes were easier to carve than the rounded letters of the Latin alphabet.

Another slate appears to depict a Viking raider leading a captive youth or monk, carrying a bag, to his boat.[41] There are also remains of carved crosses dating from the eighth century onwards, and foundations of a twelfth-century chapel with pillars of Old Red Sandstone. There appears to have been a small cell of the early monastery on the promontory known as St Ninian's Point, on the mainland of Bute, opposite Inchmarnock.

St Ninian's Point

Excavations in 1952 and 1954 at St Ninian's Point revealed a pagan burial ground containing long cist (or slab-lined) graves. A circular enclosure with a wall of stones and turf was later built, enclosing most of the graves. When some of these had collapsed, a small Christian chapel was built of rubble and plaster, and its inner wall was lined with clay. It contained an altar of rough masonry faced with slabs, containing a cavity for relics. There were three kitchen middens piled against the enclosure wall—these rubbish heaps contained large quantities of shells and bones.[42]

Due to its simplicity, the chapel has been assigned a seventh- or eighth-century date. The kitchen middens hint that one or two monks perhaps lived beside St Ninian's chapel. Three pre-Christian standing stones 300 metres north of the chapel indicate that this was a holy place for a very long period. The chapel was abandoned after Viking raids, but was used again in medieval times, at which point it may have been named after St Ninian.[43]

Ardchattan Priory

There was an early monastery dedicated to Catán at Ardchattan; it may have been a daughter house of the monastery at Kingarth on Bute. The name Ardchattan means 'Catán's hill'—monasteries were generally built on higher ground, from which visitors,

View from Ardchattan Priory towards Loch Etive, Argyll and Bute.

pilgrims, and enemies could easily be seen. The monastery is 8 miles north-east of Oban, in a beautiful setting on the north shore of Loch Etive. A large Celtic cross slab survives in the ruined priory that was built here in about 1230 by the Vallisculians. These were an offshoot of the semi-eremitical Carthusian order; they also founded Pluscarden and Beauly, further to the north, in Inverness.

St Connán of Dalmally

The village of Dalmally is 15 miles east of Ardchattan, near the head of Loch Awe. Dalmally was formerly named *Clachán an Dìseirt*, or 'Place of the monk's retreat'. *Dìseirt* is an early loan word from the Latin *desertum*, meaning an empty place where a hermit sought God. The name Connán is a diminutive of Conn. The healing well of 'Little Conn' (see colour plate 3) is opposite the police station at the Glenview exit on the A85. An old account describes it as 'memorable for the lightness and salubrity of its water'.[44]

The site on which St Connán's church in Dalmally is built was once an island between the two rivers, Orchy and Orchy Beag; the church was rebuilt in 1909–11. In the graveyard are medieval slabs attributed to the Loch Awe School of carving; the slabs may once have covered the graves of early chiefs of the MacGregor clan. The sculptors were Irish craftsmen who came to Iona in the fourteenth century to work on the abbey buildings of Iona. When their task was completed, they crossed to the mainland and travelled through Cowal and mid-Argyll, working wherever they were needed.

They quarried most of their stone beside Loch Sween in the Knapdale peninsula, and since they worked from pattern books, their style can be easily recognised. A collection of their cross slabs at Poltalloch near Kilmartin was mentioned in the previous chapter. They carved freestanding crosses in twelfth-century Romanesque style, and used traditional motifs for grave slabs: men in armour, priests, mythical creatures, and interlace patterns. On simpler slabs, a sword or a pair of smithing tongs might show the occupation of the dead person.

Mo Luóc's Monastery on Lismore

Mo Luóc, or Moluag, was a contemporary of Columba who is thought to have trained at the monastery of Bangor beside Belfast Lough in north-east Ireland. He then went to Scotland, where it appears that he founded a monastery on Lismore, one of the Inner Hebrides, in the Firth of Lorne, north of Oban. Lismore may have been a daughter house of Bangor.

The name Mo Luóc derives from *Lughaidh*, which is pronounced 'Lua'. *Mo* is an honorific title and, as we have seen, the suffix *-óc* is a term of endearment, so his name means 'My dear little Lua'. Churches named after Mo Luóc were established at a number of sites in eastern Scotland, in the west on Skye, Mull, and Tiree, and at the Butt of Lewis in the far north. His crosier of blackthorn, once covered in gilded copper, survives on Lismore.[45] In the late twelfth century, the church of Lismore became Argyll's cathedral.

Lismore may have been a significant settlement in early times. A very fine bronze armlet indicative of wealth and status, dating from the first or second century, was found on Lismore. Its style suggests that it was fashioned in the north-east, perhaps in Aberdeenshire; it could have been given to a chieftain of Dál Riata as a gift. Lismore might therefore have been the home of a Celtic chieftain, who granted Mo Luóc land for a monastery. The line of the early monastic enclosure is thought to be reflected in field boundaries to the north, south and east of the present church. They suggest a roughly circular enclosure, approximately the same size as that of Columba's monastery on Iona.[46]

A legend describes how Mo Luóc raced to arrive on Lismore before Columba, cutting off his little finger and throwing it onto the island in order to claim it as his territory. In the 1940s, Ian Carmichael reported that on Lismore, some people thought that the saint's name derived from *mo ludag*, meaning 'my little finger'.[47] It is possible that the legend arose to explain the existence of a relic of Mo Luóc's finger at Lismore cathedral.[48]

In the sixteenth-century *Aberdeen Breviary*, one of Mo Luóc's miracles concerned an iron bell that he commissioned, but which the smith said he was unable to make, since he lacked coal (presumably charcoal). Mo Luóc collected a bundle of rushes or reeds for fuel to make the bell, which at the time of writing still existed in Lismore cathedral. The reference to an iron bell is significant. In Scotland, at least fourteen quadrangular hand bells survive, each made from a single sheet of iron, coated in bronze. In Ireland, iron bells are thought to date from the seventh to the tenth centuries.[49] Scottish hand bells are likely to date from a similar period; three of them will be described in Chapter 6.

3

Ninian, Galloway, and the Scottish Borders

It is likely that the Romans brought Christianity to southern Scotland. The British tribes who lived between Hadrian's Wall and the Antonine Wall appear to have been on friendly terms with the Roman authorities to the south, who also protected them from their belligerent northern neighbours. However, in AD 401 or 402, the Romans withdrew to mainland Europe to fight the invading Goths. The British tribes north of Hadrian's Wall now had to protect themselves and evolved their own political identity.

Christians at Traprain Law

There were Romano-British Christians living at the hill fort of Traprain Law, 22 miles east of Edinburgh. Excavation here in 1919 uncovered the richest hoard ever found in Scotland—over one hundred pieces of Roman silver plate, including parts of flagons, bowls, spoons, and a wine strainer. Four coins indicated that the hoard was buried during or after the reign of Honorius (AD 395–423). The silver had been cut up, as if for melting down, possibly as a transaction or a diplomatic bribe or payment for the service of warrior bands.[1]

There are Christian motifs on several items. The bowls of two of the spoons are inscribed with the *chi-rho* symbol for Christ, while the perforations on the base of the strainer are also in the form of a *chi-rho*, and around the upper part of its bowl, the perforations form the name 'Jesus Christ' in Roman letters. The spoons and strainer may have been used when celebrating the Eucharist, as may one of the flagons, which is richly decorated with biblical scenes: Adam and Eve, Moses striking water from the rock, the adoration of the magi, and the betrayal of Christ.[2] The hill fort at Traprain Law seems to have been abandoned by the mid-fifth century, perhaps as the centre of power shifted further to the west.

The 'Cat Stane'

A Bronze Age megalith named the 'Cat Stane' stands inside Edinburgh airport at Kirkliston, near the Firth of Forth. In the late sixth century, a Christian inscription was carved on the stone in rough Latin script: it may be translated as 'In this tomb lies Vetta, daughter of Victricus'. Vetta is likely to have been buried near the Cat Stane, which is surrounded by three clusters of graves arranged in rows, dating from the same period as Vetta's tomb. The monument indicates a Romano-British elite in southern Scotland who were Christian. They could speak and read Latin, and it was expected that others passing by such monuments could also understand Latin. Similar stones are found in Wales, south-west England, the Isle of Man, and Brittany.[3]

Traprain Law, Stirling, and Edinburgh appear to have been strongholds of the Votadini tribe; this became the kingdom of the Goddodin. To the south, there is a large number of early cemeteries in the Lothians, where people were buried following Christian tradition, without grave goods, in long cist (or slab-lined) graves, usually oriented east-west, with the head at the west end. Sometimes the graves are laid out in regular lines; each one perhaps had a wooden or stone grave marker. These are likely to have been burial grounds of small agricultural communities.[4] There is little evidence, though, of a post-Roman Church in Scotland, organised in dioceses with bishops.[5]

Whithorn

On the opposite side of Scotland, the town of Whithorn is near the Galloway coast, 40 miles south-west of Dumfries. An inscribed stone at Whithorn is Scotland's earliest Christian monument—it was erected in about AD 450 and commemorates a man named Latinus, aged thirty-five, and his four-year-old daughter. They lived on the edge of what had been the Roman Empire, whose troops had withdrawn only fifty years earlier. The memorial stone is carved in a style that developed in Gaul. Its inscription states that it was erected for Latinus by the descendants of Barrovadus, who could have been the local chieftain; his name may denote Irish origin. It perhaps marked the gift of this site to the Church, and would therefore be an inauguration stone, rather than a gravestone.[6]

Inscriptions on sixth-century grave slabs in Galloway refer to church officials, including a sub-deacon. This indicates an educated and liturgically well-informed Christian church. The monastery at Whithorn may not have been the first in the region. A group of grave stones dating from this time, found at the nearby monastic settlements of Kirkmadrine and Curghie, appear to commemorate a group of immigrant clerics from Gaul who may have introduced the cult of St Martin of Tours (*c.* 316–97) to Galloway. Bishop Martin had developed monastic life in Gaul, after learning how monks lived in the Near East.

Christians at Kirkmadrine

The tiny church of Kirkmadrine is 23 miles west of Whithorn, across Luce Bay. This may have been the principal church of the region, before Whithorn grew in importance in the 600s. Three tall pillar stones are preserved at Kirkmadrine, carved between AD 550 and

600; they are some of the earliest in Britain. A Latin inscription on one commemorates two 'holy and outstanding priests' named Viventius and Mavorius, who may have been monastic bishops.[7] Their title *sacerdotes* means 'chief priests' or 'bishops'.

Five cross fragments at Kirkmadrine date from about AD 700 to 1100. At some point after AD 800, Gaelic speakers with Norse ancestry, known as 'stranger Gaels' (*Gall-Ghàidheil*), ruled the region. They rebuilt the church and named the settlement Kirkmadrine. 'Kirk' derives from the Scandinavian *kirkya*, or 'church', while 'madrine' may be a personal dedication, perhaps to St Martin of Tours, or to Madrun (or *Materiana* in Latin), an early female saint who has two dedications in Cornwall and one in Wales.[8]

Who was Ninian?

As we saw at the beginning of Chapter 1, the name Ninian is now thought to be a scribal error for Uinniau; it is likely to refer to St Finnian of Movilla (d. 579), a Briton who also worked in Ireland, where Columba was his disciple. While Finnian may have been sent as a bishop to the church of Whithorn, he is unlikely to have founded it. Whithorn was a secular settlement that had developed from a late Roman trading station, where some people may already have been Christians.

On the coast road 12 miles to the west of Whithorn, in the parish of Mochrum, Chapel Finian may be dedicated to Finnian of Movilla. There are the footings of a rectangular chapel here, dating from the eleventh century, where pilgrims who had arrived by sea could pray in gratitude for their safe arrival. A drystone wall demarcates an area around the church; it contains a well, a cemetery, and probably a residence for a priest.[9]

The monastery of St Martin at Whithorn developed as a healing shrine where monks employed some of the healing methods practised at Epidaurus in ancient Greece. Bishop Ninian was the focus of the shrine's healing cult, and miracles were worked in his name. It is conceivable that, as a Briton, Ninian's, or rather Finnian's, relics may have been returned to Whithorn. As we saw in the previous chapter, the relics of the Irish abbot of Iona, Adomnán, were returned to his homeland.

Bede's Account of Whithorn

Bede recorded a tradition that Ninian introduced Christianity to the southern Picts, but the extent of such a mission, largely south of the Antonine Wall, is now questioned. Writing in about AD 731, Bede believed that Ninian established a monastery at a place called *candida casa* (Latin for 'white, or shining, house'). In Old English, this was *hwit aern*, from which the name Whithorn derives. Bede wrote:

> The southern Picts, who dwell on this side of [the Grampian] mountains, had ... embraced the truth by the preaching of Ninian, a most pious bishop and holy man of the Britons,

> who had been regularly instructed at Rome in the faith and mysteries of the truth, whose episcopal see is named after St Martin the bishop, and is famous for a stately church (where he and many other saints are laid to rest). It is still in existence. The place belongs to the province of Bernicia [in Northumbria], and is generally called the White House, because he there built a church of stone, which was not usual among the Britons.[10]

A stone church suggests one built in the Roman, or continental, style. Bede may have had a political motive for his enthusiastic account of Ninian, since Bede's friend, Pecthelm, had recently been appointed as the first Northumbrian bishop of Whithorn.[11]

Early Whithorn

In the 300s, Whithorn originated as a trading centre for the native British population; it probably came within the sphere of Roman Carlisle. The high quality of the objects found here, especially coloured imported glass, originally from drinking vessels, suggests that Whithorn was a royal settlement, where feasting took place at royal funerals; similar sites are found in Ireland. Later, as Whithorn developed as a monastic site, it became one of the most important churches in the land.[12]

Excavations conducted at Whithorn from 1984 to 1991 by Peter Hill in the area to the south-west of the present cathedral priory yielded potsherds, indicating contact with Europe over a long period—fragments from the Mediterranean dated around AD 500, Gaulish pieces from about AD 550, and Frankish and Gaulish plain ceramic ware from about AD 600. There were pieces of eight glass bowls from the eastern Mediterranean, or Spain or Rome, dating from the fifth or sixth centuries. There were also fragments of fine African red slipware made of glazed clay, imported from Carthage in the mid-sixth century.[13]

The community grew crops, as well as medicinal herbs. The soil was turned with a foot plough. In Celtic times, the plough's wooden sides were roughened by the addition of large pebbles, some of which were found at the site. A replica of such a pebble-board plough can be seen at Whithorn. Foot ploughs were used in the Highlands until the 1940s—the ploughman pushed it forward by kicking it from the right-hand end in the photograph.[14]

Healing Herbs

Whithorn's monks grew a sophisticated range of medicinal herbs for curing a wide range of diseases—human faeces in an early sixth-century latrine contained seeds, including a large quantity of coriander, together with dill, neither species being native to Britain. They are of Mediterranean origin, and were found together with a sherd of an amphora of Bi type pottery, imported from mainland Europe (Bi type amphorae are bulbous containers that are ribbed from the shoulder upwards). The coriander and dill may have

Model of a pebble-board foot plough, Whithorn, Dumfries and Galloway.

been used to flavour food, but both were also used medicinally. Seeds of other healing herbs were found in the faeces, including black mustard, chickweed, and dog rose.[15]

Another early pit contained elder seeds, woundwort, hemlock, and nettle, all valued for their healing properties. Elder was used for colds, influenza, and rheumatism; woundwort was made into ointments and compresses for wounds, and was also taken internally as an infusion for cramps, joint pains, diarrhoea, and dysentery; hemlock is a powerful sedative; while nettles have astringent, diuretic, and tonic properties, and are also prescribed for eczema and haemorrhage. The herbs in this second pit, found together with fragments of wood bark, roots, and stems, may be the remains of compresses for wounds or inflammation.[16]

A Northumbrian Bishopric

The Northumbrians conquered Galloway in about AD 730, and established an Anglo-Saxon bishopric at Whithorn. Colour plate 4 shows the site of the wooden church, dating from about AD 750. Beyond, wooden posts indicate the position of two timber halls, which would have had bowed walls and curved, ridged roofs. They were part of a large monastic complex. Whithorn's first Saxon bishop, Pecthelm, was a correspondent of both Bede and Boniface, the English-born archbishop of Mainz. Below the chancel of the twelfth-century priory at Whithorn, excavation revealed the stone coffins of Northumbrian clerics.

Several fine carved crosses date from this time, including one now named the Petrus Stone, which formerly stood on high ground south-east of the monastery. It reveals traces of three different periods. First, there is a damaged, dressed face from an earlier inscription or design that may have been removed. Next, in the seventh century, a stemmed cross-of-arcs was symmetrically carved on the stone; it was carefully executed.

Finally there is an irregularly placed inscription of three lines reading 'LOCI PETRI APUSTOLI'. It proclaims the *locus*, or place, of Peter the Apostle. This can probably be attributed to the Northumbrians, and reflects the popularity of St Peter, following the triumph of the Roman party at the Council of Whitby. They may have erected it beside the old road from Whithorn to the Isle of Whithorn, where it was perhaps associated with a chapel.[17]

Ninian's Cult

One reason why the Northumbrians popularised Ninian's cult was to legitimise their control of the Britons in Galloway. Early texts written at Whithorn comprise a Latin *Life of Ninian* in verse, *Miracula Nynie Episcopi*, probably written in the late eighth century, and an acrostic poem, *Hymnus Sancti Nynie Episcopi*. These were sent to the Northumbrian scholar Alcuin (AD 735–804) at Charlemagne's court of Aachen.

Alcuin thanked the community, and sent back a silk veil for the shrine at Whithorn. He refers to its reputation for healing, with a sideways stab at Asclepius, the ancient Greek god of healing: '... And is the blessed Martin [of Tours] himself, worshipper of the true God, to be worshipped less in the kingdom of Christ than the false Asclepius has power for the pagans?'[18] The two poems are preserved at Bamberg, in Germany. The *Miracula Nynie Episcopi* describes Ninian's rock-cut grave, which was now presumably empty, and his stone sarcophagus: this was a reliquary that rested beside the altar of the main church.[19]

Twelfth-Century Whithorn

In the twelfth century, King David I of Scotland brought the Scottish Church more fully under the control of Rome. He encouraged religious orders to take over native foundations, and in about 1170 Whithorn became a priory of Premonstratensian canons. This Order had been founded in 1120 by St Norbert, a friend of St Bernard. Since they were not monks but canons, they preached, undertook pastoral care, and ran nearby parishes.

By the twelfth century, the area to the south-west of the priory contained a number of wooden houses, laid out in a regular pattern along streets. Each house was about 5 metres long, with a central hearth. One street led to the hilltop, west of the new priory, where fragments of locally produced stone crosses were found. The people living here made jewellery and bone combs, and were of Scandinavian origin.

South porch in the nave of Whithorn priory, built around 1170, Dumfries and Galloway.

This was an Irish-Norse monastic settlement, with houses that apparently belonged to secular clergy who were allowed to marry. They may have remained here until the thirteenth century, though it is possible that the canons in the priory were not happy with these neighbours from a different religious tradition.[20]

Aelred's *Life of Ninian*

The Cistercian abbot, Aelred of Rievaulx (1110–67), who had been educated at the court of King David I, wrote a Latin prose *Life of Ninian* (or *Vita Niniani*) between 1154 and 1160. The two earlier poems preserved at Bamberg were among Aelred's sources. He also had access to a now lost British *Life*, but he admits that he despised its 'barbarous language'.

Aelred describes Ninian carrying out centralising policies of which King David would approve: 'Then [Ninian] began to ordain priests, consecrate bishops, distribute other clerical honours and divide the whole land into parishes'.[21] These are twelfth-century concepts; however, Aelred also travelled to Whithorn and collected stories about Ninian from the Galloway region, which then belonged to Aelred's own diocese of York.

Cures at the Shrine

Both the eighth-century *Miracula Nynie Episcopi* and Aelred's later *Life* describe cures at Ninian's shrine. Promotion of the monastery's healing cult is a primary aim of the *Miracula*. In Chapter 4, the author writes with enthusiasm:

> This is the house of the Lord, which many are eager to visit, for many who have been afflicted with a longstanding disease hurry there. They eagerly accept the ready gift of health-bringing healing, and they grow strong in all their limbs by the power of the saint.[22]

The *Miracula* focuses on Ninian's tomb, and gives clear descriptions of the symptoms of infantile paralysis, elephantiasic leprosy and blindness; this suggests that the stories are based on case histories prepared by a trained observer, perhaps a doctor. They appear to be factual accounts of a healing centre.

The cure of a boy named Pethgils involved a night vigil—the boy was brought to the church by his parents after a long illness and carried to the 'sacred tomb in the chapel'. His parents prayed for a cure and then, as night fell, left the boy lying at the tomb. Bishop Nynia entered at midnight and touched the boy's head, releasing a stream of healing energy that corrected his misaligned feet and removed the numbness from his body.[23]

A blind woman named Desuit was cured in a similar way. She was brought to the church by her parents after prolonged suffering:

> ... weighed down by her long sleep at the place where the saint's body is held prisoner by the hollowed out interior of the rock, she prostrated herself ... and prayed that the long night should be brightened, and then ... with her whole body flung down, she pressed against the earth with her forehead and lay in the hollowed-out cave. She jumped up and dazzling light filled her eyes as darkness fled away ... [and she began] to cross on foot the famous shrine.[24]

Divine intervention was probably supported by appropriate medical care. By the time the *Miracula* came to be written, the monastery buildings may have included an infirmary for the sick and accommodation for their families and servants. In one Northumbrian deposit, a possible surgeon's knife was found. The presence of more than sixty eighth- and ninth-century coins suggests offerings for healing from visitors used to cash transactions, who had the means to pay.[25]

Sleeping at Ninian's Tomb

The miraculous cures are focussed on Ninian's tomb, particularly when visited at night, unlike most cures at saints' shrines during this period, which were effected through contact with a saint's bones, through touching his or her clothes, dust from the grave, or water in which the bones had been washed. The miracles at Whithorn reflect a different therapeutic tradition, rooted in classical medicine, and especially in the cult of Asclepius, which was adapted by the early Church and used in the Mediterranean world. This appears to have been introduced to Whithorn as early as the sixth century and to have continued for some 300 years.

The custom of sleeping at a holy place in order to receive a divine revelation was practised widely in the ancient world. In the Old Testament, the child Samuel slept in the temple and was woken three times by the voice of God, who then gave him his prophetic call (1 Samuel 3. 1-9). In Christian Britain, Whithorn was not alone in its encouragement of the sick to spend the night at a saint's shrine in order to receive healing. At hundreds of holy wells across Ireland and mainland Britain, the sick came to wash in the healing water and sleep beside the well or within its adjacent chapel to be cured. This pre-Christian practice continued into the late medieval period and well beyond. The tradition was rooted in a widespread and very ancient layer of belief.

Ninian's Cave

A partially collapsed cave on the seashore at Glasserton, 5 miles south-west of Whithorn, near the end of Physgill Glen, is believed to have been Ninian's desert retreat. Excavations in the nineteenth century cleared debris and revealed seven Celtic and Northumbrian carved crosses; they date from between the eighth and the eleventh centuries. It is possible that in the seventh or eighth century, hermits may have lived in the cave. The eighth-century *Miracula* describes the cave, observing how 'Ninian studied heavenly wisdom, with a devoted mind, in a cave of horrible blackness'.[26] To find the cave, take the A747 west from Whithorn, following signs to St Ninian's cave, Physgill.

Just 3 miles south-east of the town is the Isle of Whithorn, which is now joined to the mainland. It was probably associated with the monastery throughout its history. There are traces of a Celtic fort on the island, around the ruins of a fourteenth-century chapel, which replaces an earlier structure. This was the principle port for pilgrims arriving by sea; in the chapel, they could give thanks for their safe arrival.

The Anglians in Scotland

The Angles were a Germanic people who first migrated to eastern Britain in the early fifth century. They established the kingdom of Bernicia in Northumbria in the mid-sixth century, with their stronghold at Bamburgh. In the seventh century, the Anglians advanced into Lothian in the south-east (Edinburgh fell in AD 638 and Stirling in AD 642).

They occupied Lothian until AD 973, and for a short while acquired territory north of the Firth of Forth. The Angles also conquered the lowlands of south-west Scotland that had been under British control, and gained control of the British kingdom of Rheged, an area around Carlisle, by marriage into their royal house.

Left: St Ninian's cave, Glasserton, near Whithorn, Dumfries and Galloway.

Below: St Ninian's chapel, Isle of Whithorn, Dumfries and Galloway.

The Anglians brought a new style of monumental Northumbrian sculpture, evident in the south-east at Jedburgh Abbey and in the south-west through carvings on the Ruthwell cross and on cross fragments at Hoddom. In eighth-century Northumbria, Celtic culture became fused with that of both the ruling Angles and Viking invaders. Perhaps the most outstanding example of this new style is the Ruthwell cross.

The Ruthwell Cross

It is thought that the cross could have been set up on the seashore in the first half of the eighth century as a boundary marker between the Anglians of Northumbria to the east and the Britons of Galloway and Strathclyde to the west. Alternatively, it may have marked the entrance to a monastic church. It now stands in Ruthwell church, 10 miles south-east of Dumfries. Its arms may have been a later addition; they appear to be carved from different stone.

The monument may originally have been a column. It stands 5 metres high, and its carvings express the rich faith of its unknown sculptor. On the north face, starting from the top, John the Baptist is depicted holding the Lamb of God. Beneath is the central figure of Christ in glory, portrayed as a triumphant warrior, with a moustache in Germanic style, not a beard. He wears a cloak and sash and clasps his hands, at peace.

Below Christ in glory appears a traditional Celtic theme: St Anthony and Paul the Hermit, breaking bread in the desert. The loaf they share symbolises the breaking of bread both at meals and in worship; this lies at the heart of monastic life. The lowest panel on the north face depicts the Flight of the Holy Family into Egypt.

Women feature on the south face: at the top, Mary visits Elizabeth and beneath them, Magdalen tenderly washes the feet of her Lord. Next, Jesus heals the man born blind, below which the Angel Gabriel greets Mary at the Annunciation. At the foot of this panel is a carving of the crucifixion which, because of its style, may have been added later. A Latin commentary surrounds and explains the panels; this forms the longest extant series of carved Latin inscriptions.

Runes on the Side Panels

Along the side-panels, birds and beasts play among vine tendrils. The vine represents Christ, whom John the Evangelist describes as saying 'I am the vine; you are the branches' (John 15. 5). Surrounding each of the two side panels is an Anglo-Saxon runic inscription similar to the central portion (lines 39-65) of *The Dream of the Rood*. This poem first appears in written form in the Vercelli manuscript, dating from the mid-tenth century. The outer sections of the poem may not have been known to the carvers of the text on the cross. The runic inscription on the Ruthwell cross predates manuscripts of Old English poetry.

The theme of the Dream of the Rood is one dear to warrior peoples—Christ, the young hero, fights a great battle, wounded and bloodstained, yet victorious. The story is told by the rood, or tree of the cross. The layout of the runes, which are carved on both sides and around the top of each side panel, suggests that the stone was perhaps already standing when the runic poem was added, possibly as late as the tenth century. Perhaps *The Dream of the Rood* had only recently been composed, or was, indeed, a composite poem.[27] On the west panel, the runes which enclose the vine describe the crucifixion; the words are spoken by the cross itself:

God almighty stripped himself
when he wished to climb the cross,
bold before all men.
To bow I dared not.
I held high the great King,
heaven's Lord. I dared not bend.
Men mocked us both together.
I was moist with blood
sprung from the Man's side.[28]

Anglo-Saxon runes from the *Dream of the Rood* surround birds and vine tendrils on the central portion of the west face of the Ruthwell cross, Dumfries and Galloway.

In the runes around the east panel, the cross recounts how Christ is taken down from its wood and laid in a tomb:

Christ was on the cross,
but then quick ones came from afar,
nobles, all together. I beheld it all.
I bowed to warrior hands.
Wounded with spears,
they laid me down, limb-weary.
At his body's head they stood,
they that looked to heaven's Lord.[29]

A fine cross at Bewcastle in Cumbria is similar in style to the Ruthwell cross. It contains shorter memorial inscriptions in runes, and dates from the late seventh or early eighth century.[30] Bewcastle is a hamlet close to the Scottish border, 16 miles north-east of Carlisle.

Hoddom

Hoddom is the site of a fort that has been associated with an early chieftain named Rydderch Hael (or 'Roderick the Generous'), 12 miles east-south-east of Dumfries. The *Life of Kentigern*, composed by Jocelin of Furness in the late twelfth century, associates the sixth-century bishop Kentigern with Hoddom. This is recorded in no early source; however, there was a monastery here after Kentigern's lifetime, close to the present bridge over the River Annan, where a late medieval cemetery survives. It is reached by a short footpath from the main road.

In 1991, when part of the site at Hoddom was threatened by quarrying, Christopher Lowe directed excavations that indicated the existence of an important monastic settlement in the eighth and ninth centuries. There was an earlier earthwork enclosure dating from about AD 650, and buildings dating from that time until 1250, utilising stone from a nearby Roman fort at Birrens. The site is on a bend in the river, like St Martin's monastery of Marmoutier, which was built on a meander of the River Loire, and like Old Melrose, in a similar location beside the River Tweed; in each case, the river formed part of its boundary. The monastery at Hoddom was surrounded by an outer group of buildings for non-monastic craftsmen, as at Whithorn.

Hoddom's Anglian Community

In the eighth century, the first church on the site was replaced by Anglian monks from Northumbria with a monastery of their own. Excavation provided evidence of workshops built with sandstone dating from the seventh and eighth centuries for baking, meat curing and metal working—these indicate the presence of a large community. Wheat, oats, barley, and rye were grown, and there were kilns to dry corn.[31] There were hearths for smithing, debris from metal working, and objects of wrought iron. Two bowls were found, made of willow and alder.[32]

Two fine eighth-century crosses similar in style to that at Ruthwell and part of a shrine encasing an abbot's crosier had been found previously; in addition, eight more cross slabs and a cross shaft were now uncovered.[33] It appears that the eighth-century Anglo-Saxon scholar Alcuin wrote a letter to an abbot of Hoddom named Wulfhard, whom Alcuin addressed as 'abbot of Hodda Helm'.[34]

The Northumbrian monastery became the nucleus of a large, thriving high-status settlement that dominated the daily life of the inhabitants of southern Annandale and perhaps beyond. It might have been associated with early churches at Ecclefechan, 6 miles to the north-east and at Ruthwell, 3 miles to the west. However, little has been discovered at Ecclefechan—its name, an early one, is Brythonic for 'small church'; alternatively, it could mean 'church of Féichín', alluding to an Irish monk from Sligo. The medieval church at Ecclefechan was demolished before 1737; its site is indicated by an area of raised ground roughly at the centre of the present burial ground.[35]

Christians in the Scottish Borders

We shall now examine the unfolding of Christianity in the Scottish Borders, the region of south-eastern Scotland. Rivers were important routes in early times, and a number of Christian sites are close to the banks of the Tweed. There is a cluster of inscribed Christian monuments in Upper Tweeddale, dating from the late sixth century. In Manor Valley, alongside Manor Water, near Peebles, a memorial stone to a Christian woman was found; it is inscribed 'CONINIE [ME]RTIRIE', or 'memorial to Coninia'. She is the earliest named individual from this region; the stone is now in Peebles Museum.

At nearby Lyne church, 3 miles west of Peebles, excavations in 1998 revealed three small late sixth-century graves, probably for two children and a baby. These are long slab-lined (or 'cist') graves, aligned east-west, built with small side slabs and capstones. There were probably more graves at the site, but they were later quarried away.[36] There are other small groups of early Christian graves in Upper Tweeddale, and larger cemeteries, especially in the Lothians, further to the north.

Old Melrose

The town of Melrose is 30 miles south-east of Edinburgh. The early monastery of *Mailros* (or Old Melrose) was on a bend of the River Tweed, 2½ miles east of the town. The name *Mailros* means 'bare headland', and suggests its remote setting, which would have appealed to its founding monks. Like many insular monasteries, *Mailros* was built within an abandoned hill fort. There are traces of an embankment cutting off the promontory in the meanderings of the Tweed.

Melrose Cistercian abbey viewed from the south, Scottish Borders.

The monastery bore a British name, giving rise to the suggestion that it may have been a north British foundation, before the establishment of Lindisfarne in AD 635.[37] What is more certain is that monks from Lindisfarne established a community at Old Melrose. Eata, one of Aidan's Anglo-Saxon converts, was abbot of Melrose in Cuthbert's time. In the mid-ninth century, the monastery was destroyed by order of King Cináed mac Ailpín. It appears to have been rebuilt, however, since, in AD 875, the monks of Lindisfarne, fleeing from the Vikings, brought the relics of Cuthbert to Melrose for safety.

In about 1080, a chapel dedicated to St Cuthbert was built at Old Melrose as a dependency of Durham Cathedral; it became a place of pilgrimage. In the twelfth century, King David I of Scotland invited the Cistercians of Rievaulx Abbey in Yorkshire to rebuild the monastery, but they preferred a new location in the town of Melrose.[38] The site of Old Melrose is on private land and contains no visible remains; the ruined Cistercian abbey is open to the public.

Cuthbert and Boisil

Cuthbert trained as a monk at Old Melrose, as we learn from Bede. An old monk, Sigfrid, from Bede's own monastery of Jarrow, could remember the day in AD 651 when an eighteen-year-old named Cuthbert rode up to the enclosure gate at Melrose and leapt down from his horse. Bede relates:

> [Cuthbert] knew that the Church of Lindisfarne contained many holy men, by whose teaching and merit he might be instructed, but he was moved by the great reputation of Boisil, a monk and priest of surpassing merit, to choose for himself an abode in the abbey of Melrose. And it happened by chance, that when he was arrived there, and had leaped from his horse, that he might enter the church to pray, he gave his horse and travelling spear to a servant, for he had not yet resigned the dress and habits of a layman. Boisil was standing before the doors of the monastery, and saw him first.[39]

Boisil was prior of the monastery; he was an Irish monk who later became its abbot. He welcomed Cuthbert, as did Abbot Eata, on his return a few days later:

> [Boisil] kindly received Cuthbert as he approached; and when he had heard the cause of his coming, namely that he preferred the monastery to the world, he kept him near himself, for he was prior of that same monastery. After a few days, when Eata ... was come, Boisil told him about Cuthbert, how that he was a young man of a promising disposition, and obtained permission that he should receive the tonsure [or monastic haircut], and be enrolled among the brethren.[40]

Ten years later, in AD 661, the community was struck by plague. Cuthbert became ill but recovered, although his digestion was permanently affected. The elderly Boisil became terminally ill. Bede gives a touching account of their last week together. Cuthbert asked the old man what he would like to have read to him, and Boisil chose St John's Gospel:

> [Cuthbert] asked him what he would advise him to begin to read, so as to be able to finish it in seven days. 'John the Evangelist,' said Boisil. 'I have a copy containing seven quarto sheets: we can, with God's help, read one every day, and meditate thereon, as far as we are able.' They did so accordingly, ... for they sought therein only that simple faith which operates by love, and did not trouble themselves with minute and subtle questions. After their seven days' study was completed, Boisil died.[41]

Cuthbert was soon appointed prior of Melrose; Boisil's body was eventually taken from Melrose and enshrined in the abbey of Jedburgh.

Boisil's Shrine at Jedburgh

The abbey of Jedburgh is 42 miles south-east of Edinburgh; it is set on a hilltop above the fast-flowing Jedd Water. When the Northumbrians ruled this area of Scotland, an Anglian monastery was established at Jedburgh by Abbot Aidan of Lindisfarne. The monastery included a flourishing school of sculpture: a group of monastic masons worked here from the eighth to the tenth centuries.

Some of their carvings survive, including five free-standing crosses and the end panel of a magnificent house-shaped stone shrine, dating from the late eighth or early ninth

Above left: Jedburgh Abbey, *c.* 1138, above Jedd Water, Scottish Borders.

Above right: End panel of St Boisil's shrine, Jedburgh Abbey, Scottish Borders. It depicts a tree of life, with birds and animals among vine tendrils.

century; the shrine probably enclosed Boisil's relics. The panel depicts a tree of life, with birds and animals among swirling, symmetrical vine tendrils. Similar ornamentation is found on the Ruthwell cross.

The Norman Abbey

The Anglian monastery was superseded by a Norman abbey; it was established by King David I and given to the Augustinian canons. Its construction began in about 1138, disturbing an earlier cemetery and other structures. The Anglo-Saxon monastery may have stood to the north of the present abbey church, and perhaps continued in use while the abbey was being built.

The site was chosen because it was close to the royal castle and the monastery, but it was on a steep slope, and so the abbey was difficult to build. The Normans used a combination of hillside terraces and land reclamation in order to construct the abbey. Excavation revealed substantial timber buildings beside the river, at the foot of the south-west corner of the cloister. It is possible that David I caused these to be built in preparation for the canons' arrival.[42]

Modan of Dryburgh

Just 4 miles south-east of Melrose, Dryburgh Abbey is tucked inside a bend in the River Tweed, to the north of the town of St Boswells. The medieval abbey (see colour plate 5) is built on the site of a chapel dedicated to Modan, an early monk whose cult survives in Stirling and Falkirk. The name Modan derives from 'my Aidan'. He may be the monk named Modan who was said to have ended his days as a hermit in the mountains near Dumbarton, where the church at Rosneath is dedicated to him.[43]

The vaulted chapel of St Modan that now exists at Dryburgh Abbey was originally the library and vestry of the medieval abbey. This was founded in 1150 for Premonstratensian canons brought here from Alnwick in Northumberland by the Constable of Scotland, Hugh de Moreville. The twelfth-century chapter house survives, decorated with patterns painted on the wall plaster between its stone arcading. The ruined refectory contains a fine rose window.

Stobo and Kentigern

Five miles south-west of Peebles, Stobo is a village in the Upper Tweed valley, just north of the river. Eleven dedications in the Lothians to the sixth-century bishop Kentigern of Strathclyde and his followers have given rise to the suggestion that Kentigern may have worked in this area, but it is more likely that these dedications occurred when Strathclyde was expanding southwards during the tenth century.[44]

The dedication of Stobo church to Kentigern could have occurred even later: Glasgow may not have become a bishopric until the twelfth century. Its bishop would have been keen to promote the cult of Kentigern, its patron saint. The church at Stobo, on a hillside above the village, dates largely from the twelfth century. Stobo became the mother church of Upper Tweeddale; until the Reformation, it was linked with Glasgow cathedral.

The 'Altar Stone' at Drumelzier

The hamlet of Drumelzier is 8 miles south-west of Peebles, in the Upper Tweed valley. According to local legend, a large boulder at the roadside opposite Altarstone Farm is said to be the place where Kentigern baptised a bard named Merlin Sylvestris (or 'Merlin of the woods'), who lived there in exile after the warlord Rhydderch Hael defeated Merlin's chieftain. A standing stone in a nearby field is said to mark the bard's grave.[45]

There is no authentication for this story, but the baptism of a bard may not have been unusual. To find 'Merlin's altar stone', take the A72 west from Peebles and turn left on B712. Pass Stobo and just before crossing the River Tweed, turn right into a minor road which leads to Broughton. The first farm on the left is Altarstone Farm; the square boulder is in the hedge to the right of the road, opposite the farm entrance.

Above: St Kentigern's church, Stobo, near Peebles, Scottish Borders.

Below: The 'altar stone', Drumelzier, near Peebles, Scottish Borders.

St Llôlan's Chapel, Broughton

Llôlan is said to have been one of the many Welsh monks who fled from Powys after the Battle of Chester. In the course of the battle, which took place in about AD 613, Æthelfrith, the pagan king of the Angles, massacred many Christians. Llôlan is described as travelling north-eastwards, and a tiny chapel at Broughton, 8 miles south-west of Peebles, is named after him. It was excavated and roofed in the 1920s. The footings of its walls can be seen, with an arch set low in the present wall since the original floor level was lower. This is one of the few chapels to survive from early times.

Broughton is on the A701 between Biggar and Peebles. To find the chapel, drive north on the A701, enter the village, and pass B7016 on your left. Stop at the village store on your left, and ask for the key to St Llôlan's cell in the cemetery. Continue to the next exit left. As you turn into it, you will see the old church and its cemetery up a lane, through a gate, on the right. The chapel, with its turfed roof, is near the church.

Llôlan's feast day, 22 September according to the Old Calendar, was kept as Broughton Fair until 1864. The church at Kinkardine, overlooking the Firth of Forth, is also dedicated to Llôlan. The Earls of Perth at Kinkardine preserved his staff and hand bell until the seventeenth century; the latter may be the hand bell in the Glasgow Museums collection.

A legend concerning Llôlan, related in the sixteenth-century *Aberdeen Breviary*, alludes to an early custom whereby Celtic monks returned from Rome with soil from the Roman Christian cemeteries, which they scattered in the graveyard of their own monastery. Those buried there were then considered to be buried in Rome. The Old Irish word *ruam*, meaning 'cemetery', derives from the Latin name, *Roma*.[46]

The custom was based on a tradition found in the Old Testament. When the prophet Elisha healed Naaman, a Syrian army commander, Naaman asked for two mule-loads of earth to take home, on which he could stand to worship the true God (2 Kings 5. 17). In the *Aberdeen Breviary*, Llôlan asked for four mule-loads of soil from St Peter's cemetery in Rome to be brought to Scotland, to consecrate a cemetery for himself and others. He prayed that whoever was buried there would attain heaven.[47]

Æbbe's Monastery at Coldingham

In the years after Aidan's arrival on Lindisfarne at the request of King Oswald of Northumbria, Aidan established other communities, as we have seen. Another daughter house of Lindisfarne was the monastery of Coldingham at St Abb's Head, on the south-east coast of Scotland. Its founder was Æbbe (*c*. 615–83), a daughter of King Æthelfrith of Bernicia. She had fled with her brothers to Dál Riata, when their uncle Edwin seized the throne; when her brother Oswald regained control of Northumbria, Æbbe returned home.

After the arrival of Columban monks on Lindisfarne, Æbbe founded a monastery 20 miles to the north, on the headland at St Abbs. This was a double monastery of monks

St Llôlan's chapel, Broughton, near Peebles, Scottish Borders.

and nuns that remained in existence for about forty years. The early enclosure was marked out by a double palisade; this was replaced with a bank and trench, which still survive on the headland. St Cuthbert visited Coldingham in AD 661. Royal women from Bernicia entered the community in the second half of the seventh century; in AD 671, Princess Æthelthryth (or Etheldreda) of Northumbria became a nun at Coldingham, encouraged by Bishop Wilfrid of York.

Etheldreda

Etheldreda was the daughter of a Saxon king of East Anglia, and was related to Hilda of Whitby through her mother. She married twice before becoming a nun; Abbess Æbbe was a kinswoman of her second husband. Etheldreda later returned south and founded the abbey of Ely on land granted to her by her first husband. She was abbess of Ely for several years, until she died of the plague. Bede praised Etheldreda's virtues, describing her austerity in language taken from earlier accounts of the Desert Mothers and Fathers:

> It is reported of her, that from the time of her entering into the monastery, she never wore any linen but only woollen garments, and would rarely wash in a hot bath, unless just before any of the great festivals, such as Easter, Whitsuntide and the Epiphany, and then she did it last of all, after having, with the assistance of those about her, first washed the other servants of God there present; besides, she seldom did eat above once a day, excepting on the great solemnities.[48]

By his exaggerated praise of her struggles in marriage and in the monastery, Bede unintentionally highlights how difficult it was for high-born women in the seventh century to enter monastic life.[49]

Bede describes the laxity of the community at Coldingham, and relates that a monk was sent to warn Abbess Æbbe of their inappropriate behaviour,[50] but Bede disapproved of double monasteries and was perhaps keen for this religious lifestyle to come to an end.[51] In these communities, monks and nuns lived separately, but came together in church to chant the Office and to celebrate the Eucharist. The monastery of Coldingham burnt down in about AD 683, soon after Æbbe's death. The community appears to have been re-established in the eighth or ninth century; a Benedictine priory was founded here in 1100.

4

Kentigern and Strathclyde

The Britons

To the south of the rivers Forth and Clyde, the Romans encountered a number of British tribes. By the sixth century, these had evolved into the British kingdoms of Strathclyde, based on Dumbarton Rock, and of Goddodin in the Lothian area. The name Goddodin derives from the Votadini, whose principle stronghold was *Din Eidyn*, probably Castle Rock, Edinburgh. There were other British tribes in south-west Scotland and north-west England.[1]

The Antonine Wall marked the northern boundary of Roman Britain, 70 miles north of Hadrian's Wall. Dumbarton Rock was the site of a Roman military station, perhaps at the western end of the Antonine Wall. In AD 367, the Romans declared the land between Hadrian's Wall and the Antonine Wall to be a province named Valentia, with Dumbarton as its capital. When the Romans withdrew from Scotland in AD 401 or 402, the Britons formed their own kingdom based on Valentia, but excluding eastern Scotland. It came to be known as Strathclyde, and at first Dumbarton remained its capital.

Dumbarton Rock

The Britons named their fortress *Alt Clut*, meaning 'Height, or Rock, of Clyde': it is a twin-peaked lava plug that towers above the Clyde estuary (see colour plate 6). The Irish referred to the stronghold as Dumbarton, meaning '*dún*, or fort, of the Britons'. In 1974–75, Leslie and Elizabeth Alcock excavated on Dumbarton Rock, hoping to find traces of the early fort. They selected the lower and flatter of the twin peaks, known as the Beak, but found little evidence of the hill fort; later structures had destroyed all traces of earlier buildings.

In one small area, however, they found fragments of imported sixth-century Roman glazed Samian ware and seventh-century glass, which confirmed the high status of the fort's occupants.[2] On the steep eastern slope of the Beak were the remains of a stone and timber rampart that had burnt down. This could have been constructed as early as the sixth century, but might equally have been built for protection against later Viking raids. There were ceramic and metal objects dating from the fifth to the eighth centuries, and also a few items from the Norse period, including part of a Viking sword.[3]

Early Chieftains

Dumbarton was possibly the headquarters of a British chieftain named Coroticus, a leader of British warriors who lived by slave-trading. In the fifth century, St Patrick wrote two letters to the soldiers of Coroticus. The second letter survives: its aim was to obtain the release of Christians who had been sold into slavery to the Picts by Irish pagans. However, it is not known where Coroticus lived; he might have been a slave trader in north-east Ireland, or perhaps he lived in Ceredigion in south-west Wales.

A famous British chieftain who is more likely to have resided at Dumbarton Rock was Rhydderch Hael, a sixth-century contemporary of Columba. The *Historia Brittonum* (*c.* 829), attributed to Nennius, lists Rhydderch as one of four British kings who almost drove the Saxons of Northumbria into the sea at Lindisfarne in about 590. In his *Life of Columba*, Adomnán describes Rhydderch's long reign, referring to him as 'Roderc, son of Tothal, who reigned on the Rock of Clota [or Clyde]'. He relates that when consulted over the outcome of an important battle, Columba said of Rhydderch: 'He will never be delivered into the hands of his enemies, but will die in his own home on his own feather pillow'.[4] Rhydderch's death occurred around 601.

Writing in about 731, Bede described Dumbarton Rock as 'a town of the Britons, strongly defended to the present day'.[5] The two fortified peaks of Dumbarton Rock were separated by a level area, which perhaps contained dwellings, halls, a church, and a well. The Vikings attacked *Alt Clut* in AD 870, and its inhabitants are said to have surrendered after a four-month siege, when their well ran dry. Carved cross slabs dating from the tenth century found on the Rock indicate that it was used for Christian burial after the Viking conquest. There was a medieval chapel dedicated to St Patrick on *Alt Clut*; it was destroyed in the sixteenth century. A castle inventory of 1510 records that the chapel contained 'an old parchment Mass book', a pewter chalice, and liturgical cloths.[6]

Where was St Patrick Born?

It is sometimes claimed that St Patrick was born near Dumbarton, perhaps at Old Kilpatrick, 3 miles east-south-east of Dumbarton. Here, a Roman garrison controlled the River Clyde. The fort, on a site now occupied by the bus station, commanded a view of shipping for miles, both upriver and out towards the sea.

Patrick was indeed born into a Romano-British family, but we do not know where. We are told in his autobiographical *Confessio*, or 'Acknowledgement [of God's work]', that Patrick's family had taken leadership in their local church for two generations. His father was a Roman *decurion*, or minor civic official; he was a deacon, and the son of a priest. Patrick also tells us where he was born:

> My family own a small estate near the village of Bannavem Taburniae. My father was Calpornius, a deacon, and my grandfather was Potitus, a priest. It was near there I was taken captive when I was about sixteen.[7]

However, we do not know where Bannavem Taburniae might have been. One possibility is near Dumbarton, another is Birdoswald on Hadrian's Wall, while a third is somewhere in the south-west, perhaps in Cornwall or Wales.

Mirin of Paisley

The ancient settlement of Paisley, close to present-day Glasgow airport, is 9 miles west of Glasgow city centre, at a major fording point on the White Cart River. Its name is *Paislig* in Gaelic; this derives from the early Latin word 'basilica', meaning a church, so Paisley may have been a Roman-Christian settlement.[8] A pre-Christian cemetery was discovered at Paisley Abbey, overlaid by the graves of Christians buried facing east.

An Irish monk named Mirin, a contemporary of Columba, is said to have founded a monastery here. Excavation has provided evidence of a stone chapel and an enclosure wall dating from the seventh or eighth century. The oldest surviving object in the abbey is the Barochan cross, a tenth-century ring-headed cross brought here from a hilltop near Houston; it was carved by monastic sculptors working at Govan.

According to late sources, Mirin was a disciple of Abbot Comgall at the monastery of Bangor, County Down, in north-east Ireland. Mirin his said to have succeeded Comgall, before sailing to Scotland. His shrine at Paisley became a focus for pilgrims, and in the twelfth century, Benedictine monks from a daughter house of Cluny were brought to Paisley from Much Wenlock in Shropshire. By the thirteenth century, the monastery had income from lands, fisheries, and mills in six counties, and the priory had become an abbey.[9]

In the abbey, portions of a fifteenth-century stone frieze in St Mirin's chapel illustrate scenes from his life: a panel portrays him as prior of the monastery of Bangor, and another depicts Mirin praying in his cell at night, illumined by a ray of heavenly light. A third section shows him reviving a monk who had died of heat stroke while working in the fields. The frieze may once have formed a retable, or decorative stone panel on the wall behind an altar at Mirin's shrine. The scenes depicted are described in the sixteenth-century *Aberdeen Breviary*.[10]

The abbey was founded in 1163 by the High Steward of Scotland. The English set fire to the complex in 1307 because the fifth High Steward supported Scottish independence. The seventh High Steward became the first royal Stewart, from whom Queen Elizabeth II is descended. There are extensive remains of the Cluniac monastery, including a vaulted chamber containing its main drain, constructed in about 1350. The abbey was largely rebuilt in the fifteenth century. A slate survives from its choir school, with the earliest surviving Scottish polyphonic music scratched on it, dating from around 1450. Many other objects were found during excavation of the great medieval drain in 1990.

The name of Inchmurrin, the largest island in Loch Lomond, means 'Mirin's island'. The ruins of a chapel dedicated to Mirin were formerly visible on the island, near the fourteenth-century castle. The chapel is likely to have been built much earlier than the

Part of a frieze depicting scenes from St Mirin's life, Paisley Abbey, Renfrewshire. A panel portrays Mirin as prior of Bangor (left); Mirin praying in his cell, illumined by a ray of light (centre), and reviving a monk who had died of heat stroke (right).

castle. A small enclosure nearby is known as the 'burial ground'. Its north and south walls are built of large stones; the east and west walls are constructed of turf.[11] This might be an early Christian cemetery.

St Constantine's Church, Govan

Now engulfed by the city of Glasgow, Govan lies on the south bank of the River Clyde, 3 miles west of Glasgow city centre. During excavations in the graveyard of St Constantine's church, conducted by Stephen Driscoll in 1994 and 1996, two graves were found, radiocarbon-dated to the fifth or sixth century. These were buried beneath rough walls that seem to have supported a timber church.

Grave markers with simple scratched crosses and grave stones with crosses carved in low relief were found at Govan; these were similar to those of Iona and the Northumbrian monasteries at Whitby and Hartlepool. They were carved from about AD 600 onwards.[12] A circular wall and ditch dating from the eighth century surrounded the church; it is likely to have contained a royal burial ground. Near the church, Doomster Hill was also surrounded by a large ditch. This was a 'moot', or meeting place, where justice was administered; it survived until the nineteenth century.[13]

When Dumbarton Rock was sacked by the Vikings in AD 870, Govan became the Britons' new centre of power; it retained this position until the early 1100s, when

Glasgow replaced Govan as the royal ecclesiastical centre. Govan's church is dedicated to Constantine, who may have been the legendary founding saint of the Scottish royal house. The magnificent Dupplin cross, described in the following chapter, was carved to honour an eighth-century King Constantine, and Govan's church might be dedicated to him.[14]

A School of Sculpture

The monastery at Govan had a fine school of sculptors who worked from the ninth to the twelfth centuries. In the church are four cross shafts, the arms of which are missing, and an impressive ninth-century stone sarcophagus, carved from a single block of sandstone. It is decorated with interlace panels, pairs of animals, and a scene depicting a stag hunt. It was designed to be viewed from all sides, and so it must have stood above ground on a plinth, as were royal sarcophagi on mainland Europe in Roman times.

Two other sarcophagi found at Govan in 1762, but subsequently destroyed, suggest that Govan housed royal tombs until it was superseded by Glasgow cathedral.[15] The church at Govan also contains five of the largest and heaviest Viking hogback tombs, dating from the tenth century. Each has a curved roof, wooden shingles, and mythical beasts clasping the gable ends. Other gravestones are in the form of carved horizontal slabs, decorated with crosses and interlace patterns, in a style dating from the late ninth to the eleventh centuries.

A tenth-century Viking cross shaft portrays a cross surmounted by a sun in splendour: from a central boss, four swirling rays emerge, each ending in an animal's head. Beneath the sun, a piper on horseback skirls the bagpipes as he perhaps leads troops into battle. The sculptures indicate the presence of Christianised Scandinavians, who were sufficiently influential to be buried in Govan's prestigious cemetery.[16]

Sculptures from the Govan school of carving can be found elsewhere; they mostly date from the tenth and eleventh centuries. One is the Barochan cross at Paisley, mentioned earlier. A cross shaft that still stands in the open, close to its original position, can be seen in Springhill Road, in the Arthurlie district of Barrhead, 6 miles south-west of Govan. This pale sandstone pillar was once a ring-headed cross. There are two carved stones in the grounds of the Normandy Hotel at Inchinnan, 5 miles north-west of Govan, and a third in the church porch; these three may have formed part of the shrine of an early monk named Conval.[17]

Kentigern of Glasgow

Some time between 1113 and 1124, under Earl David, later King David I of Scotland, Glasgow became the seat of a new diocese. Since Govan had been the royal centre of the previous ruling dynasty, it was therefore no longer acceptable as a royal ecclesiastical

Above: Tenth-century hogback tomb, Govan, Glasgow.

Left: Replica of the 'sun stone', with sun in splendour (above) and skirling bagpipe player (below), Govan, Glasgow.

centre. King David promoted the cult of a new saint, Kentigern, whose shrine would serve as a focus for the new cathedral church of Glasgow.[18]

Kentigern was a Briton who apparently became bishop of Glasgow in the early seventh century; his name means 'Chief Prince'. We know little about him, but we do know that he existed because his name appears in early texts. A note of his death in the Welsh chronicles, the *Annales Cambriae*, gives a date of around the year 612. However, the earliest surviving text of this collection of chronicles is a twelfth-century copy of an original, dating from the mid-tenth century, so its accuracy is questionable.

A *Life of Kentigern* was written by Jocelin (fl. 1175–1214), a Cistercian monk of Furness Abbey in Cumbria.[19] The *Life* was commissioned by his namesake and fellow Cistercian, Jocelin, Bishop of Glasgow; it was intended to replace a *Life of Kentigern* written a century earlier at the request of Herbert, Bishop of Glasgow (d. 1164), of which only a fragment survives. The Cistercian bishop of Glasgow had previously been the fourth abbot of Melrose, where he had successfully promoted the cult of the abbey's second abbot, Waltheof. He was therefore familiar with all that was required to develop a new saint's shrine in Glasgow.[20]

Jocelin's *Life of Kentigern*

The chief aim of the new *Life of Kentigern* was to edify its hearers; it was not primarily intended to be historically accurate. Jocelin's account of Kentigern's boyhood conveys that he was, indeed, a 'chief prince', and that he learnt holiness because he trained under another saint, Serf of Culross, whose cult was celebrated in the twelfth century. In reality, Serf lived at least a century after Kentigern.

Jocelin demonstrates Kentigern's nobility and his holiness through the following story: he relates that Kentigern was the illegitimate son of a British princess. Her angry father set her adrift in a coracle, and she floated across the Firth of Forth, landing on a beach at Culross, on the Fife coast. Here, she lit a fire and gave birth to her son, who subsequently became a monk in St Serf's monastery.

Kentigern Travels to Wales

Jocelin relates that when an anti-Christian chieftain came to power, Kentigern fled south, first to Cumbria and then to Wales. Jocelin describes Kentigern arriving at Carlisle and proceeding to Crosthwaite. This and a number of other churches in Cumbria are dedicated to Kentigern; they may reflect the recovery of this region by the kingdom of Strathclyde in the tenth century. The Cumbrian dedications to Kentigern will be described in more detail in Chapter 9.

Jocelin recounts that Kentigern established a monastery at St Asaph, travelling by a circuitous route. Kentigern arrives in south-west Wales and first visits St David's; this affords an opportunity for David, the chief saint of Wales, to acclaim the holiness and authority of Kentigern, whom Jocelin describes as the founding saint of St Asaph's cathedral, for reasons which are unclear.

The tradition may have been devised in about 1125, when the diocese of York was trying to acquire St Asaph and was also attempting to establish its authority over Scottish territory, although both ventures were unsuccessful. Perhaps it was considered that Jocelin, a skilful biographer from a Yorkshire monastery, could create a noble *Life of Kentigern* that would link the diocese of Glasgow with that of St Asaph. The story could plausibly be situated within the migration of political exiles from Strathclyde to north Wales.

A White Boar

A wild white boar shows Kentigern where to build his church; this is a feature found in Anglo-Norman lives of other Celtic saints. The pig acts as an instrument of God's will, showing the saint where to build a monastery. The pig foundation tales belong to pseudo-history. Typically, a saint who has been granted a tract of land looks for the best site on which to build a church; an angel appears in a vision and explains that a pig will show him the site. Next day, the saint sees the pig, which indicates the spot.

When a monk searched for the place where he would live and die, which would become the place of his resurrection, the appearance of a wild boar came to symbolise God's approval of the site. Readers familiar with the classics would remember that in Virgil's *Aeneid*, a huge white sow showed Ascanius where to found the great city of Alba Longa, the precursor of Rome.[21] Topographical features are still named after the boar, including Boars Hill, a hamlet 3 miles south-west of Oxford, which was already so-named in the twelfth century, and part of the North Downs in Surrey named the Hog's Back.

For early peoples, pigs grazing the woodland were a main source of food. The fierce wild boar was also an ancient Celtic symbol of power and authority; it was portrayed on regalia, cauldrons, and rock carvings at locations such as the royal fort of Dunadd, as we saw in Chapter 1. In Celtic saints' *Lives*, the boar came to symbolise both God's power and the authority of a saint. Jocelin related that Kentigern and his followers searched for a suitable site on which to build a monastery:

> And while they went together over abrupt mountains, hollow valleys, caves of the earth, thickset briars, dark woods, and open glades in the forest, lo and behold, a wild boar from the wood, entirely white, met them, and sometimes advancing a little, and then returning and looking backwards, motioned to the saint and to his companions, with such gesture as he could, to follow him.[22]

Jocelin's imagination roams freely as he continues:

> When they came to the place which the Lord had predestined for them, the boar halted, and frequently striking the ground with his foot, and making the gesture of tearing up the soil of the little hill that was there with his long tusk, shaking his head repeatedly and grunting, he clearly showed to all that that was the place designed and prepared by God. Now the place is situated on the bank of a river called Elgu [Elwy], from which to this day, as it is said, the town takes its name.[23]

This refers to Llanelwy, the Welsh name for St Asaph, where Kentigern was supposed to have founded a monastery.

Kentigern's Disciple, Asaf

Jocelin describes Asaf as Kentigern's finest disciple; he appears to have been a local Welsh monk, whose cult originated at Llanasa, 6 miles north-east of St Asaph.[24] Jocelin relates that Asaf, too, was of noble birth, a grandson of King Pabo Post Prydain (meaning 'Pabo, Pillar of Britain'). Pabo was supposedly a fifth-century king who was driven out of north Britain and settled in Anglesey. Asaf was virtuous as well as high-born, and therefore suitable for the monastery to be entrusted to his care:

> There was one among [the monks], Asaf by name and famous by descent and appearance, who shone in virtues and wonders from the flower of his earliest puberty. He was diligent to follow the life and teaching of his master [Kentigern], as it is possible to know completely from reading his life that was transcribed into a little book.[25]

The 'little book' (*libellum* in Latin), was a *Life of Asaf*, now lost. Jocelin relates that after the lad miraculously carried live coals in his cloak, to warm abbot Kentigern, he ordained Asaf as a priest and later appointed him bishop and abbot of the monastery:

> St Kentigern who up till then had held dear and beloved the venerable boy Asaf, from that day forward prized him as the most dear and most special of all. And as soon as he was duly able, he advanced him to holy orders. And in due time he entrusted the care of the monastery to him, and made him his successor in the bishopric.[26]

Kentigern Returns to Strathclyde

According to Jocelin, Kentigern left Asaf in charge of his Welsh community and travelled northwards with a large group of monks at the request of Rhydderch Hael, the ruler of Strathclyde. If this were so, it would give us an early seventh-century date for Kentigern, since Rhydderch is described as a contemporary of Columba (d. 597) in Adomnán's *Life of Columba*, as we have seen. Kentigern is described as spending time at Hoddom in Dumfriesshire, before continuing north to Glasgow:

> The holy bishop Kentigern, building churches in Hodelm, ordaining priests and clerics, placed his see there for a time; afterwards, warned by divine revelation, he transferred [his see] to his own city of Glasgow.[27]

Kentigern's Miracles

Jocelin relates that God worked miracles through his servant Kentigern. We are told that Rhydderch Hael's consort rashly gave away a ring to a lover. It ended up in the River Clyde and the queen was imprisoned. Kentigern was informed of this by a messenger:

> The saintly bishop, knowing the whole story before the arrival of the messenger, ordered him to go with a hook to the bank of the River Clud, to cast the hook into the stream, and to bring back to him straightaway the first fish that was caught upon it and taken out of the water.... He found in it the ring in question, which he straightaway sent by the same messenger to the queen. And when she saw it and received it, her heart was filled with joy, her mouth with praise and thanksgiving.[28]

This is an elegant reworking of a miracle of Jesus. When Peter was asked by officials if his master paid the temple tax, Jesus told Peter: 'Go to the lake and cast a hook; take the first fish that bites, open its mouth and there you will find a shekel; take it and give it to them for me and for you' (Matthew 18. 27). Jocelin conveys that Kentigern is a holy man by portraying him working a miracle similar to that of Jesus.

Papal Approval

Kentigern is depicted as travelling to Rome seven times, since seven was considered the perfect number, so seven pilgrimages indicate the fullness of Kentigern's fidelity to Rome. He returned to Glasgow with the pope's blessing:

> Holy Bishop Kentigern, having received the [Pope's] apostolic absolution and benediction, returned home, bearing with him the codes of canons, many other books of Holy Scriptures, as well as privileges, and relics of the saints and ornaments of the church, and whatever lends grace to the house of the Lord [Glasgow cathedral].[29]

Papal approval was important if a national shrine was to flourish. Bishop Jocelin of Glasgow asked the pope to designate Glasgow as a special daughter church of Rome; he thereby placed the city under the pope's direct authority. This status was extended to the whole Scottish Church in 1176, confirming its independence from that of England. In contrast, the important monastery of Whithorn had by now become part of the diocese of York.[30]

However, a problem had arisen. In 1170, Pope Alexander III decreed that no saint could be venerated unless officially canonised by Rome; this required posthumous miracles. Pilgrims flocked to Whithorn, where Bishop Ninian had healed the sick for centuries. A similar pedigree had to be created for Kentigern. Towards the end of his *Life of Ninian*, Aelred had proclaimed:

> Here the power which had shone in the living saint ceases not to make itself manifest.... For at his most sacred tomb the sick are cured, the lepers are cleansed, the wicked are terrified, the blind receive their sight, by all of which the faith of believers is confirmed.[31]

Writing twenty years later, Jocelin used similar language to describe an even greater variety of posthumous miracles that God worked through Kentigern:

> The spirit of St Kentigern being taken up to the starry realms,... the power of miracles which had existed in him when alive now burst forth. At his tomb, sight is restored to the blind, hearing to the deaf, the power of walking to the lame, strength of limb to the paralytic, a sound mind to the insane, speech to the dumb, cleanness of skin to the lepers.[32]

Jocelin was also mindful that these were the very miracles that Christ wrought when on earth, according to the gospel: 'The blind see again, and the lame walk, lepers are cleansed, and the deaf hear, and the dead are raised to life' (Matthew 11. 5).

Kentigern's Death

The description of Kentigern's last days offers the strongest evidence that Jocelin based some of his narrative on an early source, which he quotes without understanding its meaning. Jocelin relates that the elderly bishop Kentigern died after taking a warm bath during the Epiphany celebrations. In the seventh century, Celtic Christians were baptised on this feast, as they still are in Orthodox Churches, although this custom died out in Britain soon after Kentigern's lifetime.[33]

Jocelin records a tradition that Kentigern's death occurred on 13 January, at the end of the octave, or week, of celebration following the feast of the Epiphany. In Jocelin's original source, Kentigern collapsed while, in his role as bishop, he was baptising candidates at the cathedral. After preaching, he was assisted to the large baptismal font. The water was warmed and Kentigern began to immerse the candidates, but the effort was too great; he collapsed and died. Jocelin relates:

> And when the eighth day dawned from the Sunday of Epiphany, in which day the kind bishop was accustomed to wash a multitude of people in the sacred waters of baptism, it was a day surely desired by Kentigern and by the spirits of his adopted sons. Being carried by their hands, the saint entered into a small bath filled with hot water after having first

> sanctified it by the sign of salvation, and a crown of brothers surrounded him and waited the end of the affair. And when the saint had embraced a little rest in [the bath], he raised his hands and his eyes to heaven, bowed his head, and surrendered his spirit.... The disciples, seeing what had happened, raised his holy body up from that bath.[34]

In Jocelin's narrative, Kentigern died peacefully in the bath, was taken out and dressed in his bishop's clothes, and buried in the cathedral 'on the right side of the altar, beneath a stone.' However, Jocelin apparently failed to understand that the 'bath' was in fact a baptismal tank, in which candidates were immersed in order to symbolically die to sin and rise to heavenly life. This must have been conveyed in the text that served as Jocelin's source because he then, curiously, described Kentigern's followers drowning in the bath, in order to die with their aged bishop:

> The disciples lifted [Kentigern's] holy body out of the bath, and eagerly strove with each other to enter the water; and so, one by one, before the water cooled they slept in the Lord in great peace, and having tasted death along with their holy bishop, they entered with him into the mansions of heaven.[35]

Glasgow Cathedral

Kentigern is thought to have been bishop of an area roughly corresponding to the British kingdom of Strathclyde, but there is no real evidence of a church on the site of Glasgow cathedral before the twelfth century. By this time, the cathedral had become a place of pilgrimage to the shrine and relics of Kentigern, who was honoured under his pet name, Mungo, which means 'My dear one'. In medieval times, the cathedral was one of the richest in Scotland, owning extensive estates; its bishops were leading political figures.

Much of the present cathedral was begun in about 1240 and completed by the end of the century. The church stands on a steep hillside, with a crypt at the east end that allowed natural light to focus on Mungo's shrine. Excavations in the nave conducted by Stephen Driscoll in 1992–93 revealed the west fronts of two twelfth-century cathedrals, the first smaller one being consecrated in 1136 in the presence of King David I.[36] A painted stone fragment from the first cathedral can be seen in colour plate 7.

Bishop Jocelin of Glasgow began to build the second structure in about 1181; it was not completed. These two churches each had a crypt in the same location; however, excavation around St Mungo's tomb in the crypt demonstrated that the tomb was created for the second church. Arcading from its plinth, or perhaps from some related structure, still survives.[37]

Built into the wall of the lower church is a well that was probably fed from a spring associated with Kentigern. Pilgrims could fill their bottles with holy water from the well to take home with them. The excavators re-examined seventy-seven burials beneath the nave and the lower church; some of those in the nave were earlier than the two twelfth-century cathedrals.[38]

Above: Possible arcading from the plinth of St Kentigern's thirteenth-century shrine, Glasgow cathedral crypt.

Right: Well in the crypt, Glasgow cathedral.

In a trench just to the east of the shrine, an iron pestle and two large bronze mortars were found—they had been secretly buried at the time of the Reformation. They were cast in bronze, each 27 cm in diameter. One was inscribed with the name of William Wishart, bishop from 1270–72; this mortar had a convex base, and may have been held in a stand. They were probably for mixing incense: for St Mungo's feast day on 13 January, the dean had to prepare 900 g (2 lb) of incense.[39] Since it was probably celebrated from early times, the date of Kentigern's death, his birthday into heaven, is more likely to be accurate than anything else we are told about this monk bishop.

Brendan's Medieval Cult

Throughout medieval times, the Irish monk Brendan the Navigator (d. *c*. 575) was a patron of sailors, and churches in many coastal settlements are named after him. In Chapter 2, we examined an early settlement on an islet named *Eileach an Naoimh* in the Garvellachs that may date back to Brendan's time. Writing 100 years later, in his *Life of Columba*, Adomnán describes four Irish abbots, Comgall, Cainnech, Cormac, and Brendan, celebrating Sunday Eucharist with Columba in his monastery on Jura, but this may simply be a way of highlighting Columba's importance.[40]

There are many dedications to Brendan in Scotland, particularly on the west coast, but most of these date from late medieval times. St Brendan features in an early thirteenth-century psalter from Paris, which appears to have been created for a wealthy individual interested in saints who were honoured in Glasgow diocese.[41] Brendan was a patron of the Isle of Bute: Butemen were called 'Brandans', because sea travel was a way of life for them.

Kilbirnie

The name-element *kil* denotes a monk's chapel or cell, and such a settlement is often an early one. Twelve miles south-west of Paisley, Kilbirnie Old Kirk replaced an earlier church dedicated to Brendan. Its medieval tower dates from about 1490. Writing in 1872, Bishop Forbes associated Kilbirnie with saints Brendan and Birinus. St Brennan's or Brinnan's fair was held here on 28 May, which is twelve days after Brendan's feast day; this suggests a possible connection with Brendan.[42]

There were seventeen St Brendans, but the monk honoured at Kilbirnie appears to have been the most famous of them. Other Scottish dedications to Brendan include a number on the west coast: among these are Kilbrannan on Islay, with three sites each named Kilbrandon in Lorn, on Mull, and on Islay. On the north-east coast, Kilbirnie near Beauly (Inverness), Birnie (Moray), and Boyndie (near Banff) are also named after him.[43]

Kilbirnie Old Kirk tower, North Ayrshire.

Laisrén's Cave

Laisrén was perhaps a seventh-century monk from the family of Áedán mac Gabráin, King of Dál Riata, or Argyll. Laisrén is said to have lived in a cave on Holy Isle, a small island off the east coast of Arran, in the Firth of Clyde. It is named *Eilean MoLaise* in Gaelic, or 'Molaise's isle'. *MoLaise* means 'my Laisrén'; the name of the coastal village of Lamlash on Arran, opposite Holy Isle, also derives from his name.[44] On Holy Isle there is a holy well that used to be visited for healing, and evidence of a thirteenth-century friary that was in ruins by the sixteenth century.

Laisrén's cave is on the shore, about 10 metres above the sea at high tide. It was created by waves eroding a cliff that consists of bands of red and yellow sandstone. A rough flight of steps leads down into the D-shaped cave. A large number of simple crosses were carved on its walls in early times. Some of them may have been incised by Vikings, who also carved inscriptions in runes.

A Viking fleet led by King Haakon of Norway sheltered between Arran and Holy Isle before the Battle of Largs in 1263. One of the king's marshals, or officers, appears to have carved a graffito in Norse runes on the wall of the cave. Translated, it reads 'Vigleikr the marshal carved [these]'. Another reads 'Onundr carved [these] runes', while a third states 'Nikolas from Haen carved'. There are several farms in Norway named Haen.[45]

Kessóg of Luss

Luss is a town on the western shore of Loch Lomond, 11 miles north-north-west of Dumbarton; its church was the site of Kessóg's shrine in medieval times. According to the sixteenth-century *Aberdeen Breviary*, Kessóg was an Irish prince-monk from Cashel, but this is confirmed in no early source. The small town of Luss grew beside the mouth of Luss Water, at the point where it flows into Loch Lomond. In the churchyard, a four-holed cross and two grave markers, each carved with a Latin cross, indicate the presence of Christians at Luss; they date from about the seventh century.

It seems likely that Kessóg founded a monastery on the 'Isle of the Monks' (*Inchtavannach* in Gaelic) in Loch Lomond, a mile south-east of Luss (see colour plate 9). Older people still call it 'Isle of the Two Bells', referring to the bells with which the monks summoned one another to prayer in the chapel. The wooded island is 1 mile long; it was an ideal location for a monastery, being sufficiently isolated to afford an opportunity for prayer, but close to the lakeshore, providing easy access to centres of population. A cave on the island, known as St Kessóg's cave, was destroyed by quarrying in about 1860; it was a deep hollow in the rock face, and was held to be Kessóg's retreat.[46]

Kessóg was believed to have been murdered at Bandry, 1 mile south of Luss (see colour plate 8). Local Christians built a cairn of stones over the place where he fell. This was a pre-Christian custom, and Christians continued to honour their dead in the same way. In his *Life of Columba*, Adomnán describes people building a cairn on the spot where

Viking hogback tomb, Luss, beside Loch Lomond, Argyll and Bute.

a Christian had just died as a visible memorial: 'his companions buried him there, constructing a cairn of stones. This can be seen on the sea coast even today'.[47]

The cairn at Bandry was destroyed when the shore road was constructed in 1761. A carved stone head, perhaps representing Kessóg, was found beneath it; the small sculpture now rests on a window ledge in the church at Luss, which continued to be the centre of Kessóg's cult. There are two sixteenth-century references to Kessóg's hand bell, and the Colquhoun family were the hereditary keepers of his *bachuil*, or monk's staff until the seventeenth century, when it was lost or destroyed.[48]

A Viking Hogback Tomb

An impressive Viking hogback tomb can be seen in Luss churchyard, embellished with neat rows of imitation roof tiles; round its sides, arcading rises from a row of columns. Some centuries later, a Norse invasion was led by King Haakon of Norway, and Luss suffered from one of his most daring raids. As we have seen, in 1263, Haakon's longships sailed into the Firth of Clyde and cast anchor off Arran; they continued northwards through Loch Long. The boats were then hauled overland to Loch Lomond, across the *tarbert*, which is a Gaelic word meaning a narrow strip of land at the head of an isthmus, a useful short-cut between two stretches of water. The village on the isthmus is still named Tarbet.

Loch Lomond lies only 1½ miles to the east of Loch Long, and from their new vantage point, the Norsemen proceeded to ravage Luss and much of the surrounding countryside. King Haakon then travelled 20 miles round the coast to fight the inconclusive Battle of Largs. This was part of an attempt to reassert Norwegian sovereignty over the Scottish western coast. The dispute was settled three years later, when Haakon ceded the territory to Alexander III of Scotland.

In 1315, King Robert Bruce declared Luss church and its surrounding area a place of sanctuary, an offering 'to God and the blessed St Kessóg for ever of 3 miles round the church as by land and water'.[49] Here criminals could take refuge from the law, and presumably go into hiding on the islands and in the glens. Kessóg's shrine was still visited after the Reformation. The remains of a medieval chapel can be seen in Luss churchyard.

Kessóg's Mound at Callander

Callander is at the foot of the Trossach Hills, 14 miles north-west of Stirling. The River Teith winds to the south of the Trossachs, and the town of Callander grew beside a shallow crossing point in the river. A church dedicated to Kessóg once stood here: its walled graveyard can be seen close to the river, beside the road leading into the town. Between the churchyard and a large car park is *Tom mo Cheasaig*, or 'my Kessóg's Mound'—a grassy hillock where the monk is said to have gathered the people and preached to them.[50] The Mound is best approached by entering Callander from the south on the A81.The ancient cemetery is just over the bridge and the Mound is beyond it, further to the left.

Kessóg's Mound, Callander, Stirling.

St Mahew's Chapel, Cardross

Cardross is close to the north bank of the Firth of Clyde, 6 miles west-north-west of Dumbarton. After driving north through the town on the A814, Kirkton of Kilmahew is soon reached by following a road to the right. Its chapel is dedicated to Mahew or Mochta, a British monk who lived in the sixth century. There were several early monks named Mochta; this may be the saint described in Adomnán's *Life of Columba* as 'a stranger of British race, a holy man and a disciple of the holy bishop Patrick'. Adomnán relates that Mochta foresaw the future importance of Columba.[51]

Mochta was said to have first settled in Meath, but because of local opposition he moved northwards and established a monastery in Louth, where a small twelfth-century church survives, known as *Teach Naomh Mochta*, or Mochta's House. Louth became a bishopric and gave its name to County Louth. An attendant of Mochta named Angus MacRith (*Aonghus Mac Cridhe*) is named in the Irish Martyrologies (or calendars of saints) of Gorman and Donegal.[52] An abbot's servant or attendant could be his favourite disciple, and might succeed him in office, as Asaf was said to have succeeded Kentigern. Angus was the patron saint of Balquhidder, 30 miles north of Cardross and 10 miles north of Callander.

Mochta's charming fifteenth-century chapel at Kilmahew is built within a raised, oval burial ground, beside a swift stream. It fell into ruin in the seventeenth century and was excavated and restored in 1955. Outside the north wall of the nave, a standing stone was discovered on which a plain cross was carved, perhaps in the seventh century. Three later sandstone slabs were also uncovered—they appear to have formed the walls of a tomb. Another fragment with interlace patterns was dated to the ninth or tenth century.[53]

The church still contains its original 'Sacrament house' in a cavity on the inner wall of the sanctuary. The tomb of the benefactor who restored the church in 1467, Duncan Napier, is contained within an alcove that also served as an Easter sepulchre; this was a feature of medieval churches, and is found on the north side of the chancel. On Good Friday, the Eucharistic wafer was placed here, together with the crucifix from the high altar. They remained in the tomb-like structure until Easter morning. Members of the congregation were often paid to watch and pray continuously at the sepulchre until Easter Day. The tomb was lit by a blaze of tapers and candles, and the watchers sometimes became firemen when church fittings caught fire.[54]

Fifteenth-century chapel at Kilmahew near Cardross.

5

Serf and the Southern Picts

The Picts were simply Celtic Britons living in eastern Scotland. From about AD 500, the Pictish kingdoms included all of Scotland north of the rivers Forth and Clyde, except for the kingdom of Dál Riata, or Argyll, in the west. We know little about Pictish rulers; two versions of a Pictish king list exist, but one is heavily Gaelicised and neither is found in a manuscript older than the fourteenth century.[1]

The Picts occupied the most territory during the eighth century, before the Vikings attacked its fringes. At this time, Pictish culture was highly sophisticated, with its chief church at St Andrews, established between AD 729 and 747. This was a wealthy foundation, and its craftsmen produced magnificent works of art. The Pictish kings may then have been based in Forteviot, with its rich agricultural land; they are likely to have exercised control beyond their own territory, in parts of Argyll and Strathclyde.[2]

The Picts and Christianity

It is uncertain when the Pictish élite were converted to Christianity, but this must have happened quite early because, writing in the fifth century, St Patrick refers to 'apostate Picts', which suggests that these were lapsed Christians.[3] It appears that in some cases, their understanding of Christianity was not particularly deep. As one who had been enslaved himself, Patrick condemns those who were nominally Christian but were also engaged in raiding and taking captives. Even worse, they were attacking and enslaving Christians, whom they should have regarded as brothers and sisters in Christ through their common baptism.[4]

There were significant monasteries among the eastern Picts at Portmahomack and Rosemarkie in the north, and at Dunkeld, Abernethy, and the future St Andrews further south. These were probably associated with Pictish kings who were Christian. The Pictish Saint Drostan seems to have been widely honoured in the north, while further south, St Serf is associated with a number of sites.

Excavation at Portmahomack indicates that a monastery was founded there in the late sixth century, during the lifetime of Columba and the Pictish king Bridei mac Maelchon. The Pictish church was influenced by Iona, Ireland, and, later, by Northumbria.

In AD 697, one of the guarantors of *Cáin Adomnáin* (Adomnán's Law) was Bridei, son of Derilei (696–706), King of the Picts, but his brother, King Nechtán, son of Derilei (706–24), is said to have expelled monks and priests who came from Iona.

Pictish sculpture is very sophisticated. Christian crosses and carved stones depict scriptural scenes and chiefs hunting, with elaborate scroll decoration and Pictish symbols. Little is known of the Pictish language, but monks were literate and are depicted on carved stones carrying leather book satchels. There is evidence of vellum manufacture at Portmahomack, which suggests the existence of scriptoria in Pictish monasteries. A cross slab at Portmahomack is inscribed in Latin in the finest insular script of the late eighth or early ninth century.[5]

Serf of Culross

Serf appears to have been a Pictish monk who worked in central Scotland, where there are dedications to him in Fife and Perthshire. He is referred to in Irish sources as the saint of Culross, which seems to have been the centre of his cult and perhaps of his activities. His dates are unknown; a charter of Inchaffray Abbey, dating from 1219, names Serf as the patron saint of Dunin (Dunning) under the Latin form of his name, Servanus, and his name is linked with other churches in this region in the thirteenth century.[6] His cult evidently grew in popularity at this time. Although little is known about Serf, he is associated with some interesting early sites.

Serf (or *Seruan*) is an unusual name, but an uncle of King Rhydderch Hael of Dumbarton called Seruan, who may have lived in the sixth century, is named in later genealogies.[7] A legendary *Life of St Serf* (or *Vita Sancti Servani*) survives in a manuscript probably written at Glasgow cathedral in the thirteenth century.[8] The author of the story demonstrates a new interest in the exotic lands of the near East; he relates that Serf was the son of a king of Canaan and a princess of Arabia. This was a time of heightened involvement in the East during the Crusades, when Francis of Assisi attempted to meet the sultan and convert the Saracens.

The *Life of St Serf* describes him founding a church at Culross; it relates that he died and was buried there. A Pictish king and an abbot of Iona are recorded as making donations to St Serf in this region in about AD 700.[9] As we have seen, the twelfth-century monk, Jocelin of Furness, relates that the young Kentigern trained at the monastery in Culross, under its abbot, Serf, although this is unlikely; it is probably an attempt to give Kentigern a noble spiritual pedigree.[10]

Culross is a picturesque town with its cobbled streets and sixteenth-century merchants' houses with their gabled roofs. It is 6 miles west of Dunfermline, on the northern shore of the Firth of Forth. Beside the road leading into Culross are the ruins of a chapel built by Archbishop Blackadder of Glasgow in 1503, in honour of Kentigern's birth. This commemorates Jocelin's story of how Kentigern's disgraced mother floated ashore here and gave birth to her son. Only the chapel's walls and its altar survive.

A Cistercian abbey dedicated to St Mary and St Serf was founded in 1217 by Malcolm, Earl of Fife, on the hill above the town. Under its ruins are traces of an earlier church, with its altar beneath the present one. Carved stones dating from the eighth or ninth centuries can be seen in the church. A niche in the ruined south wall of the nave may have been for a reliquary containing Serf's bones.

A few streets below, a deep well in Erskine Brae was the monastery's source of water; it was covered over in the nineteenth century. Coal is plentiful on both sides of the Firth of Forth, and the monks of Culross became the region's first coal miners. Culross owes its prosperity to this discovery: the coal lay near the surface, and was easily transported by sea.

St Serf's Church, Dunning

Dunning is on the old road from Perth to Stirling, 8 miles south-west of Perth. There was an early settlement at Dunning, where six roads meet. Serf is said to have slain a dragon here with his staff; part of the village is named Dray-gon. The story may have been intended to describe how Serf released the people from the grip of paganism, through the authority of his pastoral staff. The earliest church on the site was built around 1200; it belonged to Inchaffray Priory.

The Dupplin Cross

The church at Dunning houses a magnificent cross nearly 3 metres tall, carved from local sandstone in about AD 800. It once stood on a hillside 3 miles away, overlooking the royal palace of Forteviot, which is known from written sources. This was the residence of the Pictish kings of Fortriu, from which Forteviot derives its name. Much of the palace may have been swept into the Water of May. A carved arch, probably dating from the ninth century, was found in the Water of May: this was perhaps the chancel arch of a monastery church near to the royal stronghold.[11]

A worn inscription on the Dupplin cross may commemorate King Constantine Mac Fergusa, who was king of the Picts from about 789 to 820; for the last ten years of his reign, he also ruled over the Dál Riata in Argyll. The cross might, however, commemorate a later king Constantine: from about 750, a number of Pictish, Scottish, and Celtic kings were named after Constantine, the first Roman emperor to bring Christianity to his subjects. This indicates a developing relationship between the church and the state in the eighth century.[12]

On the cross at Dunning, Constantine's authority is conveyed in military terms: he is depicted on its east face as an army general on horseback. His prominent head and moustache emphasise his authority, while beneath him and on the south face of the cross, his subjects are depicted as foot soldiers. The biblical king David, another model of courageous and holy rule, is carved on the west face of the cross, fighting a lion, while on the north face, David chants the psalms that he composed as he accompanies himself on the harp.

Above: View from Culross Abbey, Fife, over the Firth of Forth.

Below left: St Serf's church, Dunning, built around 1200, Perth and Kinross.

Below right: East face of the Dupplin Cross, depicting Constantine as an army general on horseback, Dunning, Perth and Kinross.

Forteviot Palace

A similar cross once stood on the other side of the valley at Invermay, overlooking Forteviot from the opposite side. Their dramatic impact would have been considerable because free-standing crosses are more frequently found in Ireland, Northumbria, and western Scotland; the Dupplin cross is the only complete example to survive from the early Pictish kingdoms. The two crosses may have been boundary markers of the monastery, standing beside routes into the valley. According to the tenth-century Pictish chronicle, King Cináed mac Ailpín (Kenneth son of Alpin, who became Kenneth I of Scotland) died here in 858–59.[13]

The Pictish kings may have chosen to live here because they were surrounded by impressive reminders of an earlier ritual landscape. At a time when Stonehenge was in use, around 3000 BC, Scotland's largest prehistoric religious complex was constructed here. Three very large earthwork enclosures were dug, one encircled by 200 wooden pillars, with a processional way leading to its entrance, where in 2009, a royal tomb from the early Bronze Age was discovered. A chieftain had been buried on a bed of white quartz pebbles and birch bark with at least a dozen of his possessions, including a bronze and gold dagger, a bronze knife, a wooden bowl, and a leather bag.[14]

St Serf's Isle, Loch Leven

There was an early monastery on the picturesque Isle of Loch Leven, 7 miles west of Glenrothes in Fife. The *Life of St Serf* relates that a certain King Bridei (we do not know which) 'gave the Isle of Loch Leven to God and St Serf and to the Culdee hermits who lived there'; the Culdees will be described below. A geophysical survey has shown that the chapel on St Serf's Isle was surrounded by a series of wide oval enclosures, the outer one being an earth bank with a possible ditch beyond it.[15] In the eighth century, it had links with Iona.

The monastery was revived in the mid-tenth century as a Culdee community, a dependency of St Andrews. A late Pictish cross slab from Portmoak on the adjacent shore may be related to the monastery.[16] A Latin summary of its Gaelic cartulary, or foundation charter, survives. It was issued in the time of the Scottish king, Macbeth, who was active around 1030 and died in 1057; he was a warlord from the Moray region to the north-east. In 1050, Macbeth made a pilgrimage to Rome, where he distributed money, perhaps to win papal approval. He and his wife endowed the monastery on St Serf's Isle.

The community continued until the twelfth century. Its priests were well-accepted, and some of them held office at St Peter's in York until AD 936. Canons at St Peter's were referred to as Culdees until the reign of King Henry II in the mid-twelfth century.[17] King David I granted St Serf's Isle to the Augustinians in 1150, on condition that a foundation was built there and that those Culdees who refused to join it were to be expelled from the island.[18] The shell of a Romanesque chapel survives, and there are foundations of the later Augustinian priory.

The Culdees

The Culdees originated in Ireland, where they were known as *Céli Dé*, meaning 'Clients (or servants) of God'. By the eighth century, communities varied widely in their worship and practice, and there was a desire to return to the ascetic ideals of early monastic life. A leading figure in this movement was Máelrúain (d. 792), who founded a monastery at Tallaght, now a southern suburb of Dublin. The movement spread from Munster to other parts of Ireland, and as far as Iona. Gerald of Wales (*c.* 1146–*c.* 1223) tells us of three Culdee monasteries in north-west Wales, at Beddgelert, Penmon and on Bardsey Island.

The Culdees reached Scotland in the ninth century; their churches remained independent from secular authorities, and their monks often remained aloof from the 'unreformed' monks with whom they might live. An abbot of Iona named Diarmait, who was active from 814 until after 831, appears to have promoted this lifestyle in Pictish churches such as St Andrews. Dunkeld may also have been an early ninth-century Culdee community, while Brechin Cathedral became a Culdee monastery in the tenth century.[19]

From the twelfth century until the fourteenth, Scottish records still refer to the presence of Culdees (or *keledei*) at St Andrews, Dunkeld, and in other locations, chiefly in Angus and Fife; they appear to have survived later in Scotland than elsewhere.[20] Some Culdee individuals and groups like that on St Serf's Isle were absorbed into communities of Augustinian canons.

Serf's Cave, Dysart

As the Firth of Forth broadens, east of Edinburgh, Serf is honoured on the northern shore at Dysart, now a north-eastern suburb of Kirkaldy. As we have seen, the name Dysart comes from the Latin word *desertum*, which means an empty place, where a hermit could seek God. Serf is said to have lived in a cave beside the shore, across the road from the fortified tower of Serf's medieval church. The cave is in the grounds of what is now a monastery of Carmelite nuns; its roof is visible over the enclosure wall. While it is appropriate that Serf's cave is now part of a monastery, this means that access to it is restricted.

There are a number of chambers in the cave, which was used for worship in medieval times. Seats have been carved out of the rock in the natural hollows of the cave's chambers. The main cell in the cave, known as the Rud Chapel, or Chapel of the Holy Rood (or Cross), is referred to in a Latin deed of 1540 that records the induction of a new chaplain in the cave. There was a church at Dysart in 1220; it was constructed while the cave was still used for worship. A mansion was built on the property by the St Clair family, possibly around 1560; by the nineteenth century, the cave was used as a wine cellar for the house. The Carmelites acquired the mansion in 1931.[21]

Hermits' Caves at East Wemyss

The Christian tradition of living in caves dates back to the time of the Desert Mothers and Fathers of the Near East. They took literally the words of the New Testament Letter to the Hebrews, which describes God's holy ones living in the same manner: 'They were too good for the world and they went out to live in deserts and mountains and in caves and ravines' (Hebrews 11. 38). The sea has eroded the soft sandstone around the Fife coast to create caves in a number of locations, which early Christians used as chapels and as living quarters.

There are caves used by early Christians at East Wemyss on the north shore of the Firth of Forth, 5 miles north-east of Kirkaldy. The name Wemyss derives from *weem* (or *uaimh*), which is the Gaelic word for 'cave'. These Old Red Sandstone caves have been inhabited for 6,000 years. There were nine caves here, of which five survive. Three of them contain the largest collection of Bronze Age, Iron Age, and early Christian rock carvings in Britain. Unfortunately, vandalism, coalmining, and erosion of the soft sandstone have blocked access to many of the carvings and destroyed others.

Caves with early rock carvings at East Wemyss, Fife.

St Adrian's shrine on the May

The Isle of May is 5 miles out to sea in the Firth of Forth, and 6 miles from Anstruther. Adrian is the Latin version of the Gaelic name Ethernan; he was a monk, who may have lived and died on the May. A seventh-century Iona chronicle appears to describe his death among the Picts in AD 669.[22] In about 875, Vikings slaughtered the Christians on the island; their bodies were buried in an enormous cairn, possibly of pre-Christian origin, made of fist-sized stones from the beach, north of the medieval church on the site.

The cairn was excavated in 1996; later monks were buried at this unique Christian monument, and medieval pilgrims would add a stone to the cairn as a symbol of their prayers. The burial cairn was built on a raised beach, and occupied a very large area. It had been used as a Christian cemetery from the fifth or sixth century; it was frequently restructured and enlarged.[23]

Excavation beneath the west end of the twelfth-century Benedictine priory revealed the earliest chapel on the site, which was roughly 6 metres square, with drystone foundations. This perhaps housed the bones of St Ethernan and other early monks. The chapel may date from the ninth century; it was extended, and in the late eleventh century, a square-ended apse was added—this was dated by a silver penny of William the Conqueror, a rare object in Scotland.[24]

The priory's cloister was built into the ancient cairn, bringing numerous bones to the surface. These were left to litter the area; at this time, it seems, little reverence was accorded to the bones of unimportant people. Ethernan's grave has not been found, but from the twelfth century, his relics drew thousands of pilgrims. In the priory, an unusual ten-seater communal lavatory was found at the rear of the monastic dormitory, probably designed for the use of pilgrims.[25]

The Cluniac Priory on the May

It was partly the existence of St Adrian's shrine that prompted David I (1124–53) to endow a small Cluniac priory of Benedictine monks on the May in the 1140s, as a daughter house of Reading Abbey. Its chief purpose was to celebrate the Eucharist for the repose of David's soul and those of the royal dynasty. Other reasons were more practical—the presence of a water supply, building stone, and proximity to good agricultural land. The monks used the existing church until about 1250, when they replaced it with a larger one.[26]

There were perhaps ten monks here, and a few servants. Crops could not be grown on the May, although it could support about fifty sheep and a few cattle. Excavation showed that in the twelfth century, sea birds and seals were eaten, as well as large quantities of fish. A tenth of every catch was paid to the monks by men fishing near the shore of the island; the fishermen used the monks' harbour.[27]

During the Wars of Scottish Independence from England in the late thirteenth and early fourteenth centuries, St Andrews took possession of the priory and its extensive lands. Documents record raids on the May at this time by Scandinavians who had settled on Orkney; the church and other buildings are likely to have been seriously damaged. The monks abandoned the site and built a new monastery on the mainland a few miles away at Pittenweem.

The May remained a centre for pilgrimage. The monks kept a single member of their community on the May to tend the shrine; the hermit gave hospitality to pilgrims and collected their donations.[28] The May was in an advantageous location at the mouth of the Firth of Forth, with a useful harbour for pilgrims travelling to St Andrews. By the time of James IV in the early sixteenth century, the May had become one of the chief pilgrimage centres of Scotland.[29] Today, from Easter to September, a boat sails daily to the May from Anstruther harbour, 6 miles away. The departure time depends on the tide.

Caves at Caiplie, Anstruther

St Ethernan is also associated with three caves at Caiplie (see colour plates 10 and 11), near Pittenweem on the Fife coast, 6 miles north-west of the May. One can reach the caves by turning off the A917 just west of Anstruther, to the tiny settlement of Barnsmuir, beside the shore. The caves are half an hour's walk along the shore to the south-east, in the direction of Anstruther.

One of the larger caves, 'Chapel Cave', contains Pictish symbols: a Z-rod and another symbol that is now illegible, beneath many crosses carved by pilgrims, including a Greek cross (with equal arms) and many Latin ones (with an elongated lower limb). They appear to date from between AD 800 and 1000. Excavations in the cave in about 1831 yielded remains of deer, boars' tusks, cattle bones, and a human skeleton.[30]

The view from the caves across the open sea would have encouraged prayer, and the caves were used by monks and hermits from early Christian times until the sixteenth century. Ethernan is commemorated elsewhere in the locality: 2 miles north-east of the caves at Caiplie, Kilrenny is an early name that probably means 'church of Ethernan', and at nearby Scoonie, a cross slab with Pictish symbols has an ogham inscription referring to 'Ethernanus'.[31]

St Bride's Church, Abernethy

Abernethy is near the southern shore of the Firth of Tay, 6 miles south-east of Perth. It is an early settlement dedicated to the Irish nun Brigit (or Bride). A note in the Pictish chronicle claims that it was founded in the mid-fifth century. The note relates that when King Nechtán was driven from his land by his brother Drust, he visited Brigit in Ireland and asked her to pray for him. Nechtán was restored to his kingdom, and three years later, Darlugdach, Abbess of Kildare, came to Britain as an exile for Christ.

After a further two years, Nechtán offered Abernethy to God and St Brigit. During the Mass of consecration, Darlugdach 'sang Alleluia over the offering'.[32] A number of Celtic monks and nuns like Darlugdach left their homeland as exiles, or pilgrims, for the love of God. These *peregrini* (the Latin word for 'wanderers') followed in the footsteps of the Old Testament patriarch Abraham, who heard God say: 'Leave your country and your kindred and your father's house for a land that I will show you' (Genesis 12. 1).

One of Scotland's two round towers is found at Abernethy, the other being at Brechin Cathedral. The Irish-style round tower is at the entrance to Abernethy's churchyard and stands 22 metres high. It was perhaps built in the eleventh century as a defence against the Vikings. The doorway of the round tower and the window in its belfry are each decorated with a Romanesque arch.

Abernethy became one of the principal churches of the southern Picts, with a Celtic bishop.[33] Later sources relate that in about AD 590, some of Columba's monks rebuilt Abernethy's wooden church in stone, with the blessing of Gartnaith, King of the northern and southern Picts. The scene changed, however, when another Nechtán became King of the Picts in AD 706. He declared his allegiance to Rome and expelled the Columban monks from Abernethy because they followed the Celtic tradition. After his death, Abernethy once more became the Pictish capital.

The sixteenth-century *Aberdeen Breviary* recounts the legend that St Donald's nine daughters entered St Bride's monastery; there is no other source concerning St Donald,

Above left: Round tower, St Bride's church, Abernethy, Perth and Kinross.

Above right: Pictish symbol stone depicting a hammer, tongs and an anvil, St Bride's church, Abernethy.

whose popularity might be connected with the spread of the MacDonald clan. According to the Anglo-Saxon chronicle, King Malcom III of Scotland, later nicknamed Malcolm Canmore (or 'great chief'), and William the Conqueror met at Abernethy in 1072, possibly at the church. There was a community of Culdees and other clergy here in about 1100. Abernethy remained a Celtic bishopric until about 1273, when an Augustinian priory was established here and government from Rome was introduced.[34]

Pictish Symbols

The earliest feature at Abernethy is a Pictish symbol stone near the round tower: it depicts a hammer, tongs, and an anvil, set above flowing geometric designs. It might be a tombstone for a blacksmith, but this symbolic language has not yet been deciphered. In early times, smiths were held in high regard. At Brigit's own monastery in Kildare, Conleth was a hermit and metalworker whom Brigit invited to make church vessels for the monastery and to be pastor for the surrounding people. According to a monk named Cogitosus, who wrote a biography of Brigit in about AD 650, the wooden church at Kildare contained shrines of Brigit and Conleth on either side of the altar.

Although the Pictish language has been lost, from the sixth century onwards, Pictish stonemasons frequently carved symbols on large boulders using the untreated surface of the rock. The symbols are also found on cave walls, on metalwork, and other objects. The stones frequently include two of a range of incised symbols, plus a very common one. The symbols include such geometric forms as crescents, double discs, V-rods, and Z-rods; others that are frequently found are a mirror and comb, a sword, beasts, serpents, and fish. The mirror and comb often appear at the base of other paired designs, where they appear to 'qualify' the other symbols; they perhaps indicate that the stone commemorates a woman.

Most of the animals, red deer, salmon, and wild boar, are easy to recognise and are expertly executed with single incised lines; there are also composite, imaginary beasts. The animals are often found alone or in pairs, and could possibly represent traits such as 'courage' or 'peace'. The geometric symbols, used in various combinations, may form words, probably names.[35] This theory is supported by elaborate statistical analysis.[36]

The stones may have been memorials to the dead; some are beside rivers and other features of the landscape that became boundaries, and some may have stood on burial mounds. The symbols frequently appear on Christian monuments, mainly in the fertile lowlands of the east. They resemble other post-Roman inscribed sculptures in Britain and Scandinavia, on which inscriptions consist largely of personal names.[37]

Thus the symbols on the stones might commemorate deceased nobility, who may have been Christian. Pictish symbols continued in use until the eighth century, when they were combined with Christian images such as biblical scenes and decorated crosses. They were now carved on shaped rectangular slabs, ranging from smaller grave-markers to huge monuments 3 metres high, where they feature together with elaborate ornamentation and pictorial scenes depicting warriors and other subjects.[38]

St Andrews, 'Church of the King's Mound'

The Celtic name for St Andrews, on the Fife coast, was Kilrimont, or 'church of the king's mound', so this may have been a royal Pictish administrative centre. However, medieval pilgrims were told a foundation legend whereby a monk named Rule brought relics of St Andrew to the site from Greece. According to local tradition, Rule lived as a hermit in a cave by the shore at St Andrews; it is now known as Lady Buchan's Cave.

The monastery is first recorded in AD 747, when Irish annals note the death of one of its abbots, Túathalán. Fifteen years earlier, in AD 732, Bishop Acca of Hexham was driven from his diocese and came to live at Kilrimont. He may have brought with him relics of St Andrew that his predecessor, Wilfrid, perhaps obtained from Rome. The relics of the apostle enhanced the prestige of Kilrimont, which was later renamed St Andrews.[39]

Fine Pictish crosses were carved at this time by the monastic stonemasons, and an elaborate house-shaped shrine was created in about AD 800. This richly decorated royal sarcophagus is one of the finest examples of Pictish art. As we have seen, Pictish sculpture sometimes depicts the Old Testament shepherd king, David, ruling wisely and peacefully, caring for his flock and defending them from wild beasts, since David was considered a model to be imitated by Pictish rulers.

Two high crosses, late ninth century, St Andrews Cathedral, Fife.

At the centre of the main panel of the sarcophagus at St Andrews, a mounted king attacks a lion in a woodland hunting scene, while, to the right of the king, a large figure of the biblical King David also defends his flock from a lion, breaking its jaw with his bare hands.[40] A woolly sheep above King David's right shoulder perhaps represents his faithful flock.

From the start of the tenth century, there appears to have been a succession of bishops at Kilrimont who were regarded as the most important in the kingdom. In AD 943, King Constantine II retired at the age of about seventy to the Culdee monastery of St Andrews, where he lived until his death a few years later. In the late tenth century, when Norsemen began to raid Iona and the Scottish west coast, leadership of the united kingdoms of the Scots and Picts was transferred to Kilrimont, which was in a safer location on the east coast.[41]

St Rule's church at St Andrews is perhaps the first surviving church that was built as a cathedral. Its high, square tower is attached to a tall rectangular building, which may have been the nave, to the east of the tower. It is likely that there was a chancel beyond the tower. The church is constructed of large blocks of finely squared masonry known as ashlar; it probably dates from the first half of the twelfth century.[42]

St Rule's church, St Andrews Cathedral, Fife.

Attempts to Reform the Culdees

King Alexander I, who reigned from 1107 to 1124, attempted to convert the Celtic monks of Kilrimont to Roman ways. He tried to appoint a bishop who would help him to reform the church, but the first two bishops he chose were unwilling to do so. The King achieved a measure of success with his third candidate, Robert, Prior of the Augustinian abbey of Scone. Bishop Robert determined to establish a community of Augustinian canons at Kilrimont, who would transform it into a model Roman cathedral chapter.

The Celtic monks opposed their new bishop so fiercely, however, that Robert was unable to carry out his plans until 1144, over twenty years later. The Celtic clergy, consisting of about thirteen monks and some priests, all of them married, were invited to join the new community, but they declined. They were given a permanent home in the church of St Mary on the Rock, whose foundations can be seen outside the cathedral walls, close to the shore (see colour plate 12). The church was on the edge of the promontory, overlooking the harbour. Many of the carved cross slabs now in the visitor centre were found here. In 1248, the community at St Mary on the Rock was recognised as an independent college of diocesan priests.[43]

The very large site of St Andrews contains a number of buildings enclosed within a great precinct wall. The cathedral was begun by Bishop Arnold in about 1160, and became the longest and greatest church in Scotland; only its shell remains (see colour plate 13). Beside it is a thirteenth-century priory built for the Augustinian canons who served the cathedral. North-west of the cathedral is the medieval bishops' castle, on an easily defended clifftop site.

Dunblane Cathedral

Situated 5 miles north of Stirling, Dunblane means '*dún*, or fort, of Blane'. This hill fort in the land of the southern Picts, high above the fast-flowing Allan Water, was built to defend the main route to the north. It is doubtful that St Blane lived here, but his relics were taken to Dunblane, perhaps after Vikings raided his monastery on Bute (see Chapter 2). Blane's hand bell is preserved in the cathedral, together with a large ninth-century Pictish cross slab; this suggests the presence of a community by that time.

The belfry was originally separate from the church, and was built for defence as well as for housing bells. It was erected during the reign of King David I, who endowed the bishopric. The first record of a bishop here is of Bishop Laurence in 1155. By the early thirteenth century, the cathedral had become neglected; it was rebuilt by Clement, a Dominican friar who was elected bishop in 1233.

The earliest portion of Dunblane cathedral that survives today is the bell tower. This may have been constructed by English masons in the twelfth century, though it is now incorporated into the nave of the thirteenth-century cathedral. The earlier church may have been to the north of the tower as the tower has only one doorway, to the north.

Dunblane Cathedral, Stirling, in the snow.

The ground floor of the tower seems to have contained a chapel, with an altar in a semi-circular recess in the east wall. The plain tower had only four floors; two more were added later, built of paler stone.[44]

St Findsech

The ruins of Inchaffray Abbey are 17 miles north-east of Dunblane. In 1275, Inchaffray's charters name Findsech as its patroness. Findsech (or Findoca in Latin) was a nun of uncertain date; the sixteenth-century *Martyrology of Aberdeen* describes her as 'a virgin who has a church in the diocese of Dunblane'. The Irish martyrologies of Gorman and of Donegal relate that she came from Meath; her name means 'fair lady', as does Fiona today. Like her fellow Irishwoman, Darlugdach of Abernethy, Findsech is one of very few early nuns honoured in this region.

It is not known how soon Findsech was associated with Inchaffray. This was a Culdee site, upon which an Augustinian priory was founded from Scone in 1198. Findsech has several other dedications; a church was named after her in Perthshire in the east, while in the west, she is commemorated on the islands of Coll and Mull and on the wooded islet of Inishail near the head of Loch Awe.[45] Here there are the remains of a medieval church, a burial ground, and a large early Christian cross slab, with a ringed cross carved on each side.[46]

St Bean of Fowlis Wester

The village of Fowlis Wester is 12 miles west of Perth; its name means 'western stream'. This was an ancient religious site, with a Neolithic burial cairn, dating from 3,000 BC, a mile south of the village, and standing stones nearby. Fowlis Wester lies on the old road to Perth—highlanders drove their cattle through the village to the markets, and also sold them here. The church beside the 'western stream' is dedicated to St Bean, a monk who is mentioned in an Irish chronicle dating from AD 800; his name means 'lively person'.

Beside the road, at the centre of the village, is a replica of a fine Pictish cross; the original is one of two now brought inside the church. Like many other Pictish cross slabs and other monuments, it is carved from Old Red Sandstone, a soft rock upon which intricate designs can be easily chiselled. The cross slab is unique in that its arms project 5 cm beyond the sides of the slab, to convey the impression that it is a free-standing cross; no others are known on mainland Britain, although examples are found in Ireland.

The slab is decorated with a fine carved cross on the front, while on the reverse there are Pictish symbols and carvings of animals and people. A unique group depicts a cow with a bell around its neck, led by a cowherd and followed by a procession of six men. This might depict a local legend concerning a saint, or it could refer to the Israelites worshipping the golden calf in the desert (Exodus 32. 1-6).

Pictish high cross (replica), at the centre of Fowlis Wester, near Crieff, Perth and Kinross.

Cambuskenneth

Situated 4 miles south-east of Dunblane, on the outskirts of Stirling, Cambuskenneth means 'Kenneth's creek'. There were four St Kenneths, including the Irish monk mentioned several times by Adomnán in his *Life of Columba*, after whom a chapel was named in St Andrews Cathedral.[47] However, Cambuskenneth is named after King Kenneth I, or Cináed mac Ailpín (AD 810–58), under whom the Scots of Dál Riata were gradually united with the Picts. He was buried on Iona.

Cambuskenneth Abbey was established by the Augustinians in about 1140, under King David I, beside Stirling's medieval harbour, close to the royal castle. In 2015, excavations in the abbey grounds uncovered the harbour's stone steps that allowed boats to be unloaded at both high and low tide.[48] All that remains of the abbey is its magnificent bell tower, built in about 1200.

Fergus of Glamis

In the early eighth century, a monk named Fergus is said to have lived and died at Glamis, 10 miles north of Dundee. He appears to have been a native Pict who studied in Ireland and returned to Angus. He may have been 'Fergus the Pict, a Bishop of Scotia' (meaning Ireland), who signed documents together with twenty-one other European bishops at a Church Council in Rome in AD 721; this council met under Pope Gregory II and condemned irregular marriages. However, Fergus was a common Pictish name, so this could have been a different bishop. The *Martyrology of Tallaght*, a ninth-century calendar of saints partly based on a calendar from Iona compiled a century earlier, commemorates 'Fergus the Pict' (*Fergus cruthnech*), who may be Fergus of Glamis.[49]

The *Aberdeen Breviary* names him Fergustian and relates that he was a bishop in Ireland for many years, who travelled to the west of Scotland with a group of clerics and established churches in Perth, Caithness, and Glamis, where he was said to have lived in a cave beside a holy well that flows into Glamis Burn. The cave collapsed in the nineteenth century. During the reign of James IV (1488–1513), the abbot of Scone removed his head to Scone and built a magnificent shrine for it, which no longer exists.

The church at Glamis is close to a pre-Christian standing stone; the cup-marks at its base indicate its ancient origin. The great stone was subsequently Christianised: on one side is an interlaced cross carved in low relief, flanked by warriors fighting with hand-axes, and Pictish symbols; on the other side are more symbols—a snake, a salmon, and a mirror. Inside the church are fragments of three more Pictish cross slabs; a fourth can be seen north of the track leading south from the A94, just east of Glamis.

Above left: Bell tower, *c.* 1200, Cambuskenneth Abbey, Stirling.

Above right: Holy well beside the cave of St Fergus, Glamis, Angus.

St Fergus's Church, Eassie

Eassie is a village 3 miles south-west of Glamis and 10 miles north of Dundee; its church was established in 1246. Beside it stands another fine cross slab dating from the eighth or ninth century; it was found in the stream that flows past the churchyard. The cross is decorated with interlacing; above its arms stand two angels. A warrior is depicted beneath the left arm of the cross, while animals, including a red deer stag, are carved beneath its right arm. The warrior strides forward carrying a spear and a small shield, with his cloak billowing out behind him (see photo overleaf).

A Pictish Monastery at Meigle

One of the last Pictish kings was Ferat (variously spelt Pherath, Wrad or Uurad), who reigned from AD 839 to 842. He had a royal estate at Meigle, 12 miles north-west of Dundee, and there was a Pictish monastery on the estate. An early reference to Meigle

A striding warrior carrying a spear and shield (left) and animals (right) on a cross slab at Eassie, Angus.

records the work of a scribe named Thana in the 'villa' at Migdele (or Meigle) in the time of King Ferat; Thana is likely to have been a monk who worked for the king as a scribe.[50]

Like Glamis, this was a pre-Christian holy site, and cup and ring marks dating from 3,000 to 2,000 BC decorate two giant boulders here. By the late eighth century, the two great slabs flanked the east gate of the churchyard. Like the other twenty cross slabs found at Meigle, they are carved from Old Red Sandstone; one of the two large boulders stands 2.5 metres high. One side is perhaps modelled on a much smaller, jewelled metal cross; its circular stone 'jewels' are carved in high relief, and its cross-shaft is decorated with lively animals, including sea-horses.[51]

The reverse side of the boulder features the Old Testament story of Daniel in the lions' den (Daniel 6. 1-25). This subject appealed to Celtic Christians: Daniel's struggle to tame ravenous lions reminded them of Christ who conquered the forces of death. Daniel's heroic feat also symbolised the battles in which Celtic warriors were often engaged. Daniel also appears, flanked by two lions, on the eighth-century cross of St Martin at Iona.

On the stone at Meigle, Daniel wears a long, pleated skirt or kilt. His arms are outstretched as he tames the lions; his gesture also reminds us of Christ on the cross. Two lions paw at his kilt, while another pair lick his face. Above Daniel are an angel and huntsmen with their hounds. Below him, a centaur chops down a tree and a wild beast eats an ox whose uneaten, horned head is still visible. The mighty slab may once have stood inside the church, for it has side tenons that were designed to slot into cavities in the wall.[52]

A smaller slab formed a headstone for a grave. It is carved in high relief, to give the impression of a free-standing cross. Beneath its arms to the left stands a catlike animal

Above left: Lively animals, including sea horses, surround an ornamented cross on a giant boulder, Meigle, Angus.

Above right: Cross with a cat-like animal (left) and a large bird (right) beneath its arms, Meigle, Angus.

with bulbous eyes, and to the right, a large bird perches with a serpent in its mouth. At its base, a pair of animal heads face one another; below them, out of sight, the stone tapers in order to stand firm in the ground.

The church was magnificently decorated. Part of a sculptured frieze survives, in which clawed beasts appear on either side of a mermaid with a twisty tail. The frieze perhaps adorned the outside wall. On a stone panel that was fortunately copied before it was lost, a driver holds the reigns of two horses pulling a carriage. Two passengers sit comfortably behind him under an awning, above the twelve-spoked chariot wheels.

The stone panel formed part of a low screen that perhaps separated the chancel, where the priest presided at the Eucharist, from the nave, where the congregation stood. Twenty-seven carved stones dating from the eighth to the tenth centuries can be seen in Meigle museum, which occupies the old school house near the centre of the small town.

A Monastery at St Vigeans

It appears that the saint commemorated at St Vigeans in Angus is Féichín, Abbot of Fore in Westmeath, who died of the plague in 664/65. Vigeanus is the Latin form of Féichín. The hamlet of St Vigeans is 1 mile north of Arbroath, close to the Angus coast. The church stands on a hillock, and an important Pictish monastery grew around it, where a school of sculptors carved a large number of fine monuments between the eighth and the tenth centuries. This was possibly to mark the arrival from Ireland of some relics of St Féichín, since a house-shaped shrine survives. The church was heavily restored in the nineteenth century.

Some of the monuments stood outside what appears to have been a stone church with ornate furnishings and possible internal divisions. The finial, or ornamental top stone, survives from what may have been a seat for the president at the Eucharist, and there is a pillar cross that perhaps supported a stone altar. There are also twenty cross slabs, four free-standing crosses, four recumbent grave-covers, a disc-headed cross, and a cross-marked boulder; they are now housed in the museum at the site.[53]

One cross slab depicts two monks carrying leather book satchels on straps around their necks, and each holds a staff. On another cross slab, a ninth-century mason carved 'Drostan, in the time of Ferat and Fergus'. King Ferat is mentioned on a stone at Meigle, as we have seen. The so-called Drostan Stone will be described in more detail in the following chapter, when we consider St Drostan.

Aberlemno Church and Hill Fort

Halfway between Forfar and Brechin is Aberlemno, which perhaps means 'river confluence at the elm tree'. It lies to the south-east of the Pictish stronghold of Finavon. Three impressive carved Pictish symbol stones stand by the roadside; they may date from the mid-ninth century. The largest and finest has an interlaced cross with angels on one side and Pictish symbols on the other. From the top, these are a serpent, a double disc with a Z-rod, and a mirror and comb. These stones and some early graves suggest that there was a royal burial ground here.[54]

In the churchyard half a mile away, a magnificent cross slab depicts a battle scene. Most soldiers probably fought on foot, like those depicted on the Dupplin Cross, described at the beginning of the chapter, while kings and nobles fought on horseback. The slab at Aberlemno portrays two noble warriors: near the top of the slab, one pursues the other; at the bottom of the slab, they meet and fight until, in the bottom right-hand corner, one falls to the ground, his shield rolls away, and a raven pecks at his skull. The other side of the slab is decorated in the latest Northumbrian style with a fine knotwork cross flanked by intertwined beasts and sea-horses.

At this time, the Pictish church came under the influence of Northumbria. Nechtán, King of the Picts from AD 706 to 729, wanted his Christian subjects to abandon their Celtic customs and follow those of Rome. Therefore, in AD 710, he wrote to Abbot

Above: Church on the hilltop site of St Vigeans, near Arbroath, Angus.

Below left: Pictish symbol stone with a serpent, a double disc with a Z-rod, and a mirror and comb, Aberlemno, Angus.

Below right: Knotwork cross flanked by sea-horses (bottom, right) and intertwined beasts, Aberlemno, Angus.

Ceolfrith of Jarrow in Northumbria to seek his help. Bede was a monk in Jarrow at the time, and met the Pictish delegation. He relates that Nechtán's emissaries asked 'to have architects sent him to build a church in his nation after the Roman manner, promising to dedicate the same in honour of St Peter, the prince of the apostles, and that he and all his people would always follow the custom of the holy Roman apostolic Church as far as their remoteness from the Roman language and nation would allow'.[55]

It has been suggested that a section of the tower at Restenneth Priory, 4 miles south-west of Aberlemno, may have been constructed by the eighth-century Northumbrian masons whom Bede describes. Its design incorporates a porch with a processional entrance archway, through which the monks could walk with dignity down the length of the building, like that of Monkwearmouth, where Bede was a monk. It is possible that Aberlemno church is that named 'Egglespethir', or church of St Peter, recorded in 1161 as belonging to Restenneth Priory. The churches of Meigle and Tealing were also rededicated to the apostle Peter.[56]

Brechin Monastery

Brechin is 24 miles north-east of Dundee, and 8 miles from the North Sea. Under King Kenneth II, it became a Culdee monastery, with an Irish-style round tower. This is the earliest surviving building on the site; it is now embodied within the south-west corner of the cathedral. It is one of two free-standing cylindrical towers known to have been built in Scotland, the other being at Abernethy, as we have seen. That at Brechin is more ambitious: a carved doorway with crouching beasts flanks its threshold, saints are carved on the jambs, or sides of the doorway, and there is a crucifixion at the apex of the arch. Its style suggests an early twelfth-century date.[57]

Inside the cathedral there is a fine cross with the Virgin and Child at its centre; it was carved in the eleventh century in the Northumbrian style. The first reference to a bishop at Brechin dates from about 1150, when it became a cathedral under King David I of Scotland. Three magnificent stone fonts at Brechin, Aberlemno, and Restenneth Priory are evidence of his royal patronage. The first clergy to serve Brechin Cathedral were probably Culdees; Bishop Gregory (1218–42) re-established them as secular canons. The diocese was small and consisted of scattered churches within the larger diocese of St Andrews.[58]

The *Chronicle of the Kings of Alba* was perhaps compiled at the monastery of Brechin. It contains annals and a list of kings for 150 years following the accession of Cináed mac Ailpín in 842/43. It is likely to be based on many written sources and was perhaps composed in the late tenth century; it is preserved in a fourteenth-century manuscript.[59]

Opposite: Doorway in the round tower, with saints carved on each side and a crucifixion at its apex, Brechin Cathedral, Angus.

6

Fillan and the Northern Picts

The Picts were evangelised by monks from local Pictish monasteries and also by Irish monks. A swathe of land named Strathearn extends eastwards across the southern territory of the Picts: its name derives from two words, *strath*, meaning 'a broad, fertile valley', and *earn*, which denotes Ireland, like the name Erin. The earldom of Strathearn extended eastwards to the Firth of Forth and included Culross; it encompassed the region formerly known by the Pictish name Fortriu. Within Strathearn, Loch Earn (or *Loch Éireann*) meant 'Ireland's loch'.[1] This suggests Irish settlement in this region, and in a tribal culture, monks would have accompanied their people.

The 'Early' Fillan

The name Fillan (or *Fáelán* in Old Irish) means 'little wolf'. The Irish *Martyrology of Gorman* names sixteen saints called Fillan; it indicates that two of them worked in Scotland. The earlier of these is described in Irish sources as having lived in the sixth century. A note in the *Leabhar Breac* refers to 'Fáelán of Rath Érenn in Alba (Scotland) and of Laois in Ireland'.[2] Rath Érenn means 'fort of Ireland': it is in Strathearn. Fillan was nicknamed *amlabar*, meaning 'the dumb' (perhaps he was a silent character); he is one of the earliest Irish monks with dedications in Scotland.[3] According to the Annals of Ulster, this 'early' Fillan was trained by Ailbe of Emly, a sixth-century abbot of Munster.

A bone from the arm of one of the two Scottish saints named Fillan was preserved in a reliquary; later, King Robert Bruce asked if he might borrow it from the Abbot of Inchaffray to have it carried before him into the Battle of Bannockburn in 1314, to invoke Fillan's blessing on the enterprise. The cautious abbot agreed, but removed the arm bone before handing over the empty container. In spite of this, Robert Bruce won the battle. Since the 'early' Fillan's feast day was 20 June and the Battle of Bannockburn was fought on Midsummer Day, it appears that Robert Bruce asked for a relic of the 'early' Fillan.

The 'Later' Fillan

Another monk named Fillan came to Scotland in about 717; he also has dedications in Strathearn. This suggests that he worked among the Irish in Scotland. The sixteenth-century *Aberdeen Breviary* states that Fillan came to Loch Alsh together with his uncle, Comgan, and his mother, Kentigerna. However, this could simply be an attempt to explain the proximity of three saints' cults. The Annals of Ulster record Kentigerna's death in AD 734; Irish sources give no details of Comgan's life, but there are a number of dedications to him in the Scottish Highlands.[4]

Kentigerna is honoured near Loch Alsh, on the south side of Loch Duich, where Kilchintorn (meaning 'cell of Kentigerna') is named after her. She is said to have ended her days as a hermit, 70 miles south on an island near Balmaha on the eastern shore of Loch Lomond (see colour plate 14). The island's name, *Inchcailloch*, or 'isle of the cowled women', may recall Kentigerna and other nuns. The foundations of a thirteenth-century chapel and burial ground can be seen on the island.[5] Inchcailloch can be viewed by climbing the steps up the hill in the forest park on the mainland in Balmaha; in summer, boats sail to the island.

Fillan's Cave, Pittenweem

The small town of Pittenweem is on the north shore of the Firth of Forth, 17 miles east of Glenrothes. A cave in Pittenweem is named after Fillan (see colour plate 15). It has given its name to the town: as we have seen, '*weem*' is a transliteration of *uaimh*, which is the Gaelic word for 'cave'. In the previous chapter, we examined a number of caves where hermits lived on the south coast of Fife: those of Dysart, East Weymss, and Caiplie, 1 mile east of Pittenweem. A cave was warm in winter and cool in summer, and if it looked out to sea, it encouraged contemplation.

While 'weem' is a Gaelic name-element, 'Pit' is a Pictish prefix. It appears to derive from the Pictish word *pett*, meaning 'a share, land-holding or estate'. There are 300 such names in eastern Scotland, north of the Forth and south of Easter Ross, with a few outliers. Most of these have Gaelic second name-elements, as does Pittenweem, which means 'place of the cave'. Place-names such as this are thought to date from the ninth and tenth centuries, when Gaelic-speaking Scots settled among the Picts.[6]

Fillan's cave at Pittenweem is a large one, with two outer chambers, the second of which branches into two more. An altar has been erected in the chamber to the right, while in the left-hand chamber, there is a pool created by condensation from the cave walls: this provided drinking water. The rock plug containing the cave stands among fishermen's cottages in Cove Wynd, a steep road leading down to the old harbour; the cave was restored in 1935.

St Fillan's Mill, Killin

The town of Killin is at the south-western end of Loch Tay, 28 miles north-north-west of Stirling. Fillan is said to have settled here beside the rushing water of the Dochart Falls. According to his legend, recorded in the *Aberdeen Breviary*, he built a mill at Killin. Monks who trained in Ireland knew how to construct mills and grind flour; they developed a horizontal mill wheel that could be used where there was little water, and they brought their technology to the British mainland.

A mill often became the focal point of a settlement. In a small community, the miller might supervise the sowing of seed and the cutting of peat to fuel the mill's oven, which could also serve as the village bakery. Fillan's feast day, 9 January, is still a holiday for the mill-workers at Killin. The parish church was built in 1744; it houses an early seven-sided font, carved from a huge boulder. In the grounds of the hotel next door are the ruins of Killin's medieval church and cemetery.

Fillan had a reputation for curing the sick. His eight healing stones are kept at Fillan's Mill, which now houses the Breadalbane Folklore Centre. These large black and grey stones, smoothed by the river, were considered to heal different parts of the body. A large skull-shaped stone with two 'eye sockets', for example, was invoked for diseases of the head. Two of the eight healing stones appear to have been pivot stones on which the grinding machinery of the mill revolved. People still come to hold Fillan's stones and pray for healing.

St Fillan's Pool, Tyndrum

Tyndrum is a small Highland settlement beside the River Dochart, 16 miles east of Oban. This stretch of land beside the river is known as Strathfillan, or 'Fillan's valley'. Two miles south-east of Tyndrum, where the A82 passes Auchtertyre farm, a shallow place in the river is named Fillan's Pool (see colour plate 16). It was believed to cure insanity: patients were bathed in the river, wrapped in straw, and then taken to the Augustinian priory, half a mile to the south-east. Here they spent the night with their head in the stone font, with Fillan's bell of cast bronze placed above them. The bell survives: it stands 29 cm high, and dates from the twelfth century, 400 years after Fillan's death. It was cast when Fillan's cult had grown in importance. Cures were sought as late as the nineteenth century.

The ruined Augustinian priory with its walled cemetery can be seen on Kirkton Farm. To find it, take the A82 heading north-west from Crianlarich. Turn right up a signed track to Kirkton Farm, over a slender bridge. Park facing the ancient cemetery, which is on a mound. The remains of the priory can be seen beneath trees to the left.

The magnificent silver-gilt shrine of Fillan's crosier survives, dating from the thirteenth century; it is shaped like the curved head of a staff and lavishly decorated with filigree patterns. A crystal and a carved saint's head were later added to the shrine. It encloses a less elaborate bronze crosier head dating from the late eleventh or early twelfth century.

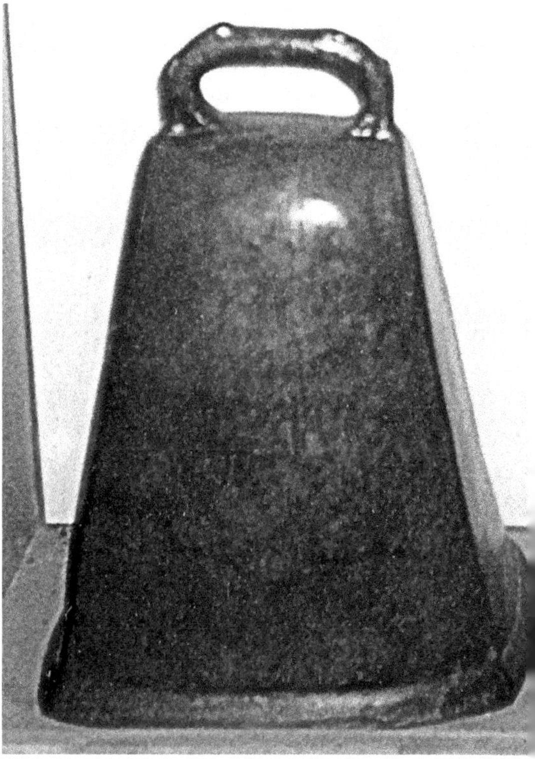

Above left: The Dochart Falls, Killin, Stirling.

Above right: Replica of St Fillan's bronze bell, Killin, Stirling.

Fillan's original wooden staff contained within it has not survived. The shrine can be seen in the National Museum, Edinburgh.

Columba and the Picts

It appears that Columba's immediate followers established monasteries in the same region, among 'the tribes of the Tay'. A poem said to have been composed on Columba's death in AD 597 describes him preaching the gospel around the River Tay, although this may be a more general term, referring to the Picts. The poem is entitled *Amra Choluimb Chille*, or 'Elegy of Colum Cille'. Its author, probably Dallán Forgaill (*c.* 530–98), laments:

> *For he has died to us, the leader of the nations who guarded the living,*
> *He has died to us, who was our chief of the needy,*
> *He has died to us, who was our messenger of the Lord,*
> *For we do not have the seer who used to keep fears from us,*

For he does not return to us, he who would explain the true Word,
For we do not have the teacher who would teach the tribes of the Tay.[7]

Later in the poem, Dallán implies that the Pictish king authorised Columba to convert his people: '[Columba's] blessing turned them, the mouths of the fierce ones who lived on the Tay, to the will of the king'. Dallán, a pet name meaning 'little blind one', was an Irish monk poet who was killed by pirates at the island monastery of Inniskeel, off the coast of Donegal. Copies of his elegy survive from the eleventh century.

North-east and north-west Scotland are separated by the long Grampian mountain range, which the Celts named *Druim Alban*, or 'the Spine of Britain'. In his *Life of Columba*, Adomnán related that Columba founded monasteries in Pictish territory, east of the Grampians, when he describes the plague that struck Britain and Ireland, during which the people of Scotland were spared. In a rhetorical question, Adomnán asks why Scotland escaped the plague:

> Ireland and Britain were on two occasions totally laid waste by a fearful pestilence, except for two peoples, the Picts and the Irish in Britain, who are separated by the mountains of the Spine of Britain.... To whom else, therefore, can this grace granted them by God be attributed, but to St Columba, whose monasteries founded within the borders of both peoples have been held in great honour by both to the present time?[8]

'The present time' here means the early eighth century.

Monks from Iona in the Highlands

The region around the Tay was then the province of Atholl, a name that may mean 'north pass'; the region served as a gateway to the northern Highlands. By the mid-seventh century, Columban monks had extended their influence northwards as far as Aberdeenshire. Simple cross-marked pillars and slabs are found along routes such as Glen Lyon that link the eastern and western Highlands. They are carved in a style used by early monks on Iona, in which each limb of the cross ends in the shape of a small 'T'. One such cross was found on an eighth-century inscribed cross slab from Dull in Glen Lyon.[9]

Glen Lyon lies to the north-east of Strathfillan and Killin; it follows the River Lyon towards the River Tay, and contains a number of dedications to Adomnán and to Coeti, a bishop of Iona who died in AD 712. At this time, the Pictish King Bridei son of Beli gave his royal support to Iona. We shall trace some of the early monastic settlements in Glen Lyon, starting from Weem, at the eastern end of this natural corridor.

St Cuthbert's Cave, Weem

Weem is 1 mile north-west of Aberfeldy, on the opposite bank of the River Tay. Cuthbert may have visited this area during missionary journeys from the abbey of Melrose in the Scottish Borders. In his *Life and Miracles of St Cuthbert*, Bede described Cuthbert setting out to visit the Picts at Christmas and the problems that arose:

> [Cuthbert] left the monastery for some necessary reason, and went by sea to the land of the Picts.... Two of the brethren accompanied him.... They arrived there the day after Christmas day, hoping, because the weather and sea were both tranquil, that they should soon return; and for this reason, they took no food with them. They were, however, deceived in their expectations; for no sooner were they come to land, than a tempest arose, and prevented them from returning.[10]

They remained snowbound and starving until 6 January, when Cuthbert prayed for food. They found three pieces of dolphin's flesh on the sea shore, which they cooked, and three days later they were able to sail back to Melrose.

We are not told where Cuthbert stayed on this occasion, but according to the Irish *Life of Cuthbert*, he built a chapel and a water cistern at Weem, as a place to rest and pray while evangelising the Picts in the surrounding area. As we have seen, the name of the settlement means 'cave' (or *uaimh* in Gaelic). The cliffs rise steeply above the Tay valley, and Cuthbert's cave is little more than an overhanging rock, where water seeps into a freshwater pool.

St Cuthbert's Pool, Weem, near Aberfeldy, Perth and Kinross.

The well is now called St David's well, after a local fifteenth-century laird, Sir David Menzies, who gave up his comfortable life and came to live as a hermit here. The cave is found by taking the steep track that starts near St Cuthbert's church in the valley below, beside the main road. Do not follow the path to the top of the hill, but turn left, and the cave will soon be signed. The chapel below contains two sturdy early Christian crosses from the nearby Pictish monastery at Dull. The key to the church is held at the nearest house, which is set back behind the church, to the right.

Dull Monastery

The Pictish monastery of Dull was 2 miles west of Weem; it stood on the site of the present church, and was such an important place of learning that it was considered to be the forerunner of St Andrews University. The valley broadens at this point; the name Dull is a Pictish word meaning both 'meadow' and 'valley'. Three sturdy Celtic crosses survive from the monastery, one beside the road leading to the church, in addition to the two preserved in St Cuthbert's church at Weem; a fourth is lost.

Dull became a sanctuary that offered refuge for criminals escaping from the law; its boundaries were marked by the four large sandstone crosses.[11] Several early Christian cross slabs dating from the seventh and eighth centuries have been found in and around

Large cross from Dull monastery, in Weem church, Perth and Kinross.

the graveyard. A Pictish slab, carved with stylised warriors and horsemen, may have formed part of a wall panel or one side of a box shrine built to contain the relics of a saint; it can be seen in the National Museum, Edinburgh.

There is a massive stone font at Dull, dating from early times. The surrounding district is called the Appin of Dull; the name derives from the Old Irish *apdaine* or 'abbey land', and refers to the former monastic estate. Dull was a royal foundation, and was conferred upon the abbot of Dunkeld by King Edgar of Scotland (*c.* 1074–1107); on his death, it reverted to the crown. It may have become a community of Tironensian monks, a reformed order that followed the Benedictine rule. Ruins formerly to be seen in the field below Dull were said to be remains of the late medieval monastery chapel.[12]

Coeti's Church, Fortingall

The ancient settlement of Fortingall is near Dull, and 4 miles west of Aberfeldy, in Glen Lyon. Until 100 years ago, a bonfire was lit here each November on a Bronze Age burial mound, known as *Càrn na Marbh* (or 'cairn of the dead'), to celebrate the pre-Christian Celtic feast of Samhain. This was the forerunner of All Souls' Day, when Christians remember their dead, on 2 November. At Fortingall, the fire was made of furze and sticks; people held hands round the blazing fire, and boys ran into the fields with burning brands.

This was a pre-Christian holy place: half a mile from the church, in a field on the opposite side of the road, are three groups of three standing stones. Beside the churchyard are the remains of Britain's oldest yew tree. It is 17 metres in girth, and has grown by producing saplings around its circumference, despite damage from vandals and Samhain fires in recent centuries. It is at least 3,000 years old and may be the oldest surviving tree in northern Europe. Beside this holy tree, an early church was dedicated to Bishop Coeti of Iona.

There are nine early Christian stones at the church, carved in a style found on Iona in the late seventh century. Another three slabs were carved in about 800 from sandstone brought from elsewhere; their sculptors worked in a style found on the opposite Scottish coast, to the east. Outside the church porch is an early font, carved from a large boulder. It is known as Adomnán's font, after the ninth abbot of Iona, who is said to have worked in Glen Lyon.

Inside the church, protected behind an iron grill, is a monk's hand bell made of iron coated with bronze, dating from the seventh or eighth century. It has no tongue, but would have been struck; it is one of five such bells to survive in Perthshire. They were used as late as the nineteenth century to bless the sick. Hand bells were a characteristic feature of the Irish Church. They were made of both iron and bronze; those made of iron may date from before AD 900, while bronze bells are more likely to date from AD 900 or later.[13]

Above left: 'Adomnán's font', Fortingall church, Glen Lyon, Perth and Kinross.

Above right: Celtic hand bell, Fortingall church, Glen Lyon, Perth and Kinross.

Excavations at Fortingall

Fortingall's Gaelic name is *Fartairchill*, which may mean 'church at the fort'.[14] There is no record of a monastery here, but a crop mark suggested a rectangular monastic enclosure, similar to that of Iona. This was investigated in 2012 by Oliver O'Grady. He found a large enclosure ditch surrounding the church and the yew tree, one section of which appears to enclose the Bronze Age burial cairn.[15]

The enclosure consisted of a wide earthen bank faced with large upright stones dating from the sixth to the eighth centuries: it probably stood 2 metres high. A substantial Pictish road passed through one of the enclosure's main entrances; its surface was built of crushed stones and gravel. Embedded in the road was an opaque yellow glass paste bead, with three red ringlets and a green herringbone motif, dating from the late fifth or early sixth century, of a type found in south-east England in Anglo-Saxon times.[16]

Innerwick: St Adomnán's Bell

Innerwick church was built in 1828 on the east bank of the River Lyon, beside the Bridge of Balgie; it is 13 miles west of Fortingall. There was an ancient chapel and cemetery, *Cladh Bhranno* (or 'Branub's graveyard') near the bridge.[17] Its early font and hand bell are preserved in the nineteenth-century chapel. The bell was lost for 200 years in the churchyard, and then recovered. It is known as the Benrudh Bell, and was said to have belonged to Adomnán.

A mile to the west of Innerwick is Milton Eonan, a name that means 'Mill town of Adomnán'. Two miles to the east of Innerwick is a small hill named Camusvrachan, marked by a standing stone with a cross carved on it, and an ancient ash tree with the largest girth recorded in Scotland. According to tradition, when plague struck, Adomnán prayed here with the people and sent them up to their summer shielings, away from the polluted river; the plague then ceased.

Dunkeld and Iona

Dunkeld is 14 miles north-north-west of Perth. There was an early fort here at a crossing point of the fast-flowing River Tay. The settlement became a frontier town to the Scottish Highlands, with mountains and wilderness to the north. In medieval times, the broad River Tay was too difficult to bridge; it had to be forded. A swimming cow was used to entice herds to swim across in order to be sold at the cattle market in Dunkeld.

There was an early monastery here, which became a daughter house of Iona; a number of carved stones from the monastery are preserved in the cathedral. As Dunkeld was relatively far from the sea, it was safer from Viking attacks than the vulnerable island of

View across the River Tay from Dunkeld Cathedral, Perth and Kinross.

Iona. Columba's relics appear to have been respected by the Norse settlers, but in 849, some of the relics were taken to Kells in Meath for safety, while others were acquired by King Cináed mac Ailpín for an important church, thought to be Dunkeld. As the Irish Scots extended their authority eastwards across Pictish territory, King Cináed mac Ailpín gained authority over both peoples, and he was held in sufficient regard that he was able to acquire these venerated objects.[18]

Cináed mac Ailpín's origins are obscure; he may have been either a Gael or a Pict. He possibly ruled Dál Riata for two years before he also gained control of the land of the Picts. This was not achieved immediately; four Pictish kings are recorded during the early years of his leadership. He was the founder of the first royal Scottish dynasty; his sons succeeded him, and apart from twelve years between 878 and 889, his family line continued to rule until 1034.[19]

Columba's Relics

Columba's relics were contained in a small house-shaped shrine known as the Monymusk reliquary; it used to be thought that this was carried into battle by Scottish kings, but this is now questioned. The magnificent shrine is fashioned from wood, with gilt and silver ornamentation, and is 10.5 cm in width. It dates from about 700 and may have been created by monks on Iona; it is now in the National Museum, Edinburgh.

Dunkeld Cathedral also contained St Columba's crosier, which is now lost. It was venerated by pilgrims in late medieval times, and is depicted on a seal of the Chapter of Dunkeld Cathedral, dating from the early thirteenth century, together with Columba's church-shaped shrine. On either side of these precious relics, a carved angel swings a censer; its incense represents the prayers of the saints rising to heaven.[20]

Dunkeld's Bishops and Abbots

Dunkeld was at the centre of King Cináed mac Ailpín's expanded kingdom, and it may have been at this time that a bishopric was established here. The monastery grew in importance as that of Iona dwindled: at the death of Tuathal, abbot of Dunkeld in 865, he was described as the chief bishop of the kingdom. However, Dunkeld's supremacy was soon eclipsed by St Andrews, where there had been a monastery since at least the eighth century.[21]

By the tenth century, many of the chief monastic offices at Dunkeld were hereditary, including that of the abbot, who was usually a member of the royal family. Dunkeld became the region's mother church, where Columba's shrine was a focus for pilgrimage until the Pictish King Constantine II became abbot of St Andrews in the mid-tenth century, and Columba's relics were removed from Dunkeld to Constantine's church.

At Dunkeld, two abbots were killed in battle in 965 and 1045; these were probably lay officials who had little to do with the spiritual life of the communities they nominally headed. The second of these was Abbot Crinan of Dunkeld, a son of the Lord of the Isles; he married a daughter of Malcolm II. Their son became Duncan I, who was slain by Macbeth in 1040, as portrayed in Shakespeare's *Macbeth*.[22]

Local Pictish Saints

Since most surviving written records of the early Scottish Church derive from Iona, Columba and his followers are portrayed as converting the Picts, but place names in north-east Scotland also indicate the influence of Pictish and British monks. In the seventh and early eighth centuries, a number of local or native saints are named, including Nechtán, Fin(n)an, Drostan, Uoloch, Talorcán, and Garnait.[23]

We know little about these monks, but there are dedications to Finan between the rivers Dee and Don in Aberdeenshire. Talorcán was a common Pictish name, but nothing is known about the monk, who has three dedications in the north; a church and cemetery in a plain above the rocks on the north side of Portree on the Isle of Skye was also named after him.[24]

St Nechtán

Nechtán is described in the Martyrology of Óengus as *Nechtán nár de Albae* ('noble Nechtán of the Scots'); he may be the Nechtán whose death is recorded in the Annals of Ulster in AD 679. Churches were dedicated to him on the islands of Islay and Iona in the west; in the east, he was also known as Nathalan, and has dedications at Tullich, Bethelnie, and Cowie in Aberdeenshire.[25]

The *Aberdeen Breviary* relates that Nechtán was born and buried at Cowie, now part of Stonehaven on the south-east coast of Aberdeenshire. An old couplet from Cowie runs:

Between the kirk and the kirk ford
There lies St Nachlan's hoard.

'Hoard' appears to be a mistranslation of the Scots Gaelic *ulaidh*, which also means 'a stone tomb' or *leacht*. This was an altar, or praying station, built of stones, on which bodies might be placed for burial. Such 'grave verses' are well-known in old Gaelic and Welsh.[26]

St Drostan of Deer

The settlement of Old Deer is beside the River Ugie, 10 miles west of Peterhead in north-eastern Aberdeenshire. The Celtic monastery was probably on the site of the parish church in Deer, and not where the later ruins of Deer Abbey now stand, north-west of the village. From Deer, Celtic monks evangelised the region of Buchan. Nothing remains of the early monastery except a fine manuscript, named the *Book of Deer*; it is now in Cambridge University Library.[27]

In an entry probably written in the early eleventh century, the *Book of Deer* relates that Drostan was a pupil of Columba on Iona; if so, he perhaps died in the early seventh century. He is likely to have been the founding abbot of Deer; there are churches dedicated to him in Aberdeenshire, Buchan, and across the Moray Firth in Caithness. His relics were in the charge of a *dewar*, or hereditary keeper at *Croit Mo-Chrostán* ('my Drostan's croft') in Glen Urquhart, 15 miles south-west of Inverness.[28]

However, Drostan is a common Pictish name, similar to Tristan, and there may have been more than one saint named Drostan. The Annals of Ulster and of Tigernach record the death in AD 719 of a monk with the Pictish name Drestan at the Irish monastery of Ardbraccan in Meath, 19 miles east of Fore. This might be the Drostan who is named on an eighth-century cross slab, the so-called Drostan Stone at St Vigeans in Angus.[29] The slab is a flat rectangular stone with an ornamental cross on one side and Pictish symbols on the other.

This is one of the few Pictish stones with an inscription in Roman letters: at the base of one of the side panels, a ninth-century mason carved 'Drostan, in the time of Ferat and Fergus' (*Drosten, i ré Uoret ett Forcus*). King Ferat reigned from 839 to 842; he is the king mentioned on a stone at Meigle. Fergus, the third person named in the inscription, could be the monk who settled at Glamis, described in Chapter 5. However, the stone may commemorate some cleric or nobleman named Drostan or, indeed, Drostan and Fergus could have been the men who commissioned the stone.[30]

Ornamental cross on the Drostan Stone, St Vigeans, near Arbroath, Angus.

The *Book of Deer*

The *Book of Deer* is a small gospel book produced around AD 900, written in Latin and annotated 200 years later in Scots Gaelic. The pocket gospel book contains John's gospel and portions of those of Matthew, Mark and Luke, with prayers for the sick and the Apostles' Creed. It could have been used by a monk on his travels, who might pray over the sick.

It is written in brown ink on vellum, with eighty-six folios, including full-page illustrations of the four evangelists; while the spelling in the gospel book is poor, its artwork is fascinating. As well as stylised portraits of the evangelists and decorated initials, there are drawings in the margins of men and animals, and simple doodles. The gospel texts could have been sung, and despite our ignorance of Pictish culture and language, the tones used by the monks probably fell within the broad ambit of Gregorian chant.[31]

Gaelic records of grants of land to the monastery were added in the blank spaces and margins from the 1130s to the 1150s. These records were contributed by at least five different hands; they are the earliest continuous examples of written Scots Gaelic. The additions also recount the supposed foundation of the monastery by Columba and Drostan. In 1219, the Cistercian abbey of St Mary of Deer was established, less than a mile upriver, on the opposite bank; the old religious community was probably absorbed into the new foundation. The Cistercian abbey owned some of the land described in the additions to the *Book of Deer*; the abbey survived until the Scottish Reformation of 1560.

Rosemarkie and Curétan

Rosemarkie is a coastal settlement a mile north-east of Fortrose, and 8 miles north-north-east of Inverness, on the shore of the Moray Firth. The parish church of Rosemarkie stands on the site of a Celtic monastery dedicated to Mo Luóc, a monk from north-east Ireland who sailed to Scotland and founded a community on the Isle of Lismore in the sixth century, as we saw at the end of Chapter 2.

Later, Rosemarkie was associated with Curetán (fl. 690–710), who is listed as one of the witnesses to *Cáin Adomnáin* (Adomnán's Law) as *Curetan epscop*. He is also named as bishop and abbot in the Irish martyrologies of Tallaght and of Gorman. His bishopric is thought to have been based at Rosemarkie, where he may have been buried. In the sixteenth-century *Aberdeen Breviary*, he appears to have been confused with St Boniface. There are a number of sites dedicated to Curetán in northern Scotland around Loch Ness and the Firth of Cromarty.

Curetán was a Celtic monk who followed Roman practices and helped Nechtán, King of the Picts, to reform the Pictish Church. As we saw in Chapter 5, Bede relates that in about 715, Nechtán sent messengers to Abbot Ceolfrith of Monkwearmouth in Northumbria, to seek advice on how to introduce Roman traditions and to ask for architects to build churches in the Roman style.

Since Roman practices were already observed in Pictish territory, Nechtán may also have had a political aim. By consolidating relationships with his Northumbrian neighbours at a time of political insecurity, he could thereby strengthen and extend his royal authority. The Northumbrian masons built a church at Rosemarkie, using mortared stone and arches. Curétan carefully named it *Egglespethir*, or 'church of St Peter', the apostle of Rome; this became the chief bishopric of the northern Picts.

A large group of Pictish carved stones was found at Rosemarkie, dating from the eighth and ninth centuries. They include cross slabs, shrine fragments, and architectural pieces that offer a rare glimpse of the interior of a Pictish church. Curetán's reforms appear to have been effective, extending as far as Shetland and Orkney, although these regions were later dominated by the Norse.[32]

St Duthac of Tain

Tain is 23 miles north of Inverness. St Duthac of Tain is usually identified with 'Dubhthach of Alba' (or Scotland), who died in 1065 at Armagh, according to the Annals of Ulster, but the church at Tain became important at an early date, so Duthac may have been a pre-Norse saint. In the west, Loch Duich is named after him; on its shore, Kintail was named *Clachán Dubhthaich*, or 'Dubhthach's stone cell'. There are dedications to him in Forres, Aberdeen, Orkney, St Andrews, Edinburgh and elsewhere. Duthac's 'sanctuary', an area surrounding his shrine at Tain was demarcated by four stone crosses.[33]

Duthac might have lived 130 years earlier than 'Dubhthach of Alba'; he could have been an abbot of Iona recorded in its annals as dying in AD 937. His hand bell and staff were preserved; these early objects suggest that he was a Celtic monk who lived between the eighth and the tenth centuries. At Tain, three churches were dedicated to Duthac. King James IV (1488–1513) made a number of pilgrimages to Tain, and James V (1513–42) commissioned reliquaries to house the bones of St Duthach and St Adrian, which he kept in his possession.[34]

Portmahomack Monastery

Portmahomack is on the north-west side of the Tarbat peninsula, 9 miles east of Tain and 30 miles north-east of Inverness. As we have seen, the name Tarbat means a place of portage, where boats could be hauled across this near-island, between the Firths of Dornoch and Moray. The monastery at Portmahomack was founded in the late sixth century, possibly under Columba's authority, on a site some 30 miles beyond the north-east end of the Great Glen. Monks could have travelled to Portmahomack by boat from Iona, which was situated near the south-western end of the Great Glen.

The site was the focus of excavation and research from 1994 to 2007, under the direction of Martin Carver. No other early Scottish monastery has been excavated so thoroughly and consistently, even Iona. Portmahomack thus offers a unique insight into the lives of Celtic monks in Scotland. I am grateful to Professor Carver for allowing

Above: 1 Iona, viewed from the Sound, Argyll and Bute.

Below: 2 St Blane's monastery, Kingarth, Bute. View from the lower cemetery to the upper (monks') cemetery and the church.

Opposite: 3 St Connán's well, Dalmally, Argyll and Bute.

Above: 4 Site of the Northumbrian church at Whithorn, Dumfries, and Galloway.

Below: 5 Dryburgh Abbey, thirteenth-century north transept, Scottish Borders.

Above: 6 Dumbarton Rock, West Dunbartonshire.

Below: 7 Painted stone fragment, *c.* 1136, from Glasgow's first cathedral.

Opposite: 8 Bandry, where Kessóg is said to have been murdered, Loch Lomond, Argyll and Bute.

Above: 9 View towards Inchtavannach, site of Kessóg's island monastery, Loch Lomond, Argyll and Bute.

Below: 10 View out to sea from hermit's cave, Caiplie, near Anstruther, Fife.

Opposite: 11 Hermit's cave, Caiplie, near Anstruther, Fife.

12 Culdee church of St Mary on the Rock (centre), beyond the wall of St Andrews Cathedral, Fife.

13 East end of St Andrews Cathedral, *c.* 1230, Fife.

Above: 14 Inchailloch, site of Kentigerna's island hermitage, Loch Lomond, Argyll and Bute.

Below: 15 St Fillan's cave, Pittenweem, Fife.

Opposite: 16 St Fillan's pool, Auchtertyre, near Tyndrum, Stirling.

Above: 17 East end of St Macra's church, Kirkibost, Great Bernera, west of Lewis. It stands above Loch Mharcoil, which may be named after her.

Below: 18 St Peter's church, Swainbost, Lewis.

Opposite: 19 St Aula's church, Gress, Lewis.

Opposite: 20 Well of Baptism, Lag ny Keeilley, Isle of Man.

Above: 21 Remains of a medieval chapel on St Cuthbert's Isle, Lindisfarne, Northumberland.

Below: 22 Eighth-century chapel on a headland overlooking Morecombe Bay, Heysham, Lancashire, with a tenth-century doorway.

Above: 23 Crosthwaite church porch, with Mount Skiddaw in the distance, Cumbria.

Below: 24 St Bega's church, Bassenthwaite, at the foot of Mount Skiddaw, Cumbria.

me to summarise at some length his interpretation of the developing monastery at Portmahomack. For a full account of this fascinating story, one must read his book entitled *Portmahomack: Monastery of the Picts* (Edinburgh: Edinburgh University Press, 2nd edition, 2016).

The Monastic Site

At Portmahomack, the monks settled on a sandy ridge where the present church now stands, with dunes and the sea to the north and marsh to the south. They may have built a wooden church, but no evidence for this was found. The monks dug an inner enclosure ditch to collect and canalise water flowing off the hill. By the end of the eighth century, they had built an outer ditch with small wattle fences on both sides, to help retain the water.

A stream flowed through the marsh, which the monks dammed to form a pool. They used both skill and ingenuity with their water supply: channels leading down the hill ended in stone-lined water collectors, which provided a little drinking water. The monks also built a wicker-lined well and dug a shallow pit near the water table that they filled with charcoal to filter the water for drinking.

The land was ploughed with a wooden ard, or foot-plough, in order to grow corn. 'Plough pebbles' were found here, as at Whithorn; the pebbles had one flattened edge and were attached to the ard to give it a longer life. In the sixth and seventh centuries, the gentle slope between the ridge and the marsh was rough pasture, perhaps used for grazing cattle.

Cereal grains were found dating between 540 and 650, and also cattle bones. This suggests that the monks mainly ate bread and beef with its associated products of milk, blood, and marrow, rather than enjoying more exotic imports. Their skeletons indicated that the monks lived into old age. They lived simply, praying and perhaps making trips back to Iona through the Great Glen, or even to Ireland.

The Early Church

Excavation revealed an early church, dating from about AD 700, beneath the wall of the thirteenth-century crypt. The surviving east wall of the crypt is out of alignment with the rest of the church, and its masonry indicates an early date. This is the only known surviving wall of an eighth-century Pictish church. It seems to have been partly subterranean, with its western end built into the hillside. There are similar churches in Northumbria dating from the sixth to the eighth centuries, including the half-buried crypt of St Cedd's church at Lastingham, and the crypts designed to house relics at Hexham and Ripon.

Like Irish examples, the church at Portmahomack perhaps had a window in the south or east wall, so that it could be lit by natural light. It was probably entered through a south door. The surviving wall indicates that it was well-built of good-quality pink and green sandstone. The Tarbat peninsula is famous for its sandstone of various colours, including olive-green, yellow and red. The wall was constructed of rubble, with larger stones at its base. Water flowed westwards off the roof and was collected and conserved in a timber-lined drain. The church could contain about thirty people standing.

Burials

There were twenty-three burials from the sixth and seventh centuries, included three women. These were the monastery's only women, one being among the earliest arrivals, for she died between 535 and 605. Half of these burials were in slab-lined graves; the men were mainly middle-aged or elderly. There were three special graves downhill from the church, one beneath an earth mound covered by a row of stone slabs; perhaps these were graves of founding fathers or early abbots.

There were many burials beneath the nave of the present church. The earliest were slab-lined (or cist) graves and others contained stone head-supports placed on either side of the skull, or on top of it. There were many grave-markers; some were carved with crosses, either simply scratched or in a low relief design, resembling those on Iona and elsewhere along the Scottish west coast.

In the eighth century, some fifty graves were cut into the pink sand, half of them with stone head-supports, one placed at each side of the head. Almost all of the burials were of monks; it is possible that nuns were buried nearby, but a women's cemetery was not discovered. In early Irish monasteries, monks and nuns were interred separately; there was a women's cemetery beside St Rónán's church on Iona.

A Vellum Industry

Sometime after AD 650, the monastery was greatly expanded: the original enclosure ditch was filled in and a larger one was dug, to enclose more land. The valley was dammed to create a pool some 50 metres across; the dam had a sluice to control the flow of water. A paved road was laid on a causeway leading up to a new terrace wall adjoining the dam; the road provided access to running water.

An artisan quarter was developed alongside the road: on the west side, cow hides were processed to produce leather, and on the east side, cattle were probably slaughtered. The leather was used to manufacture vellum for illuminated manuscripts. The cow was first skinned, leaving its feet attached; these were then cut away for use later in the process. The hide was washed and scraped to remove the blood and gore, and then soaked for several days in a tawing tank, which turned the hide white.

A tank, or stone-lined trough was found, its long sides tightly packed with stones and pebbles. Its slabs were stained green: this had been a tawing tank in the vellum factory. Leather was often tanned in oak bark, which darkened it, but since hide for vellum needed to be white, it was tawed in alkali. The tawing tank contained lime made from the burnt shells of winkles, whelks and *spirorbis*, a tiny shellfish that clings to seaweed.

Preparation of the Parchment

The hide was next scraped and thinned with knives on a floor of stone and clay; the skin was then tightly stretched over an oblong frame, using bone pegs made from the cows' feet and small stone toggles. Next, the skin was scraped and shaved with a curved knife, pumice rubbers and smoothing stones. Any gashes were mended with a needle and thread. All the items required for these processes were found at the site. Perhaps heat was required to dry or harden the parchment, since twenty flints for striking a light were found here.

The vellum-makers were sheltered by a large bow-ended building. Each piece of vellum was formed from the skin of a single cow or calf. It was now cut to size and taken to the scriptorium, where the sheets would be planned, prepared, and written by more experienced monks. They were then stitched together and the book fitted with a cover of wooden boards bound with leather and decorated with fine metalwork. The cattle hide workshops flourished for about 100 years, from the late seventh to the late eighth century, when the entire site was destroyed and burnt.

On the opposite side of the road, many cattle bones were found, suggesting that they were slaughtered and skinned here. Much blood and meat would have been produced, and probably prepared for food: blood pudding made from blood and salt, sausages, and dried or smoked meat. Beef might have been preserved in brine from sea water. Most of the monks had dental diseases and worn teeth. This suggests that they had a coarse diet, with tough meat that needed a lot of chewing.

A Smiths' Hall

To the south of the road, church vessels were produced. For this purpose, a beautifully proportioned building, semicircular at one end, was used for metal and glass working. This was a smiths' hall, with a hearth at the semicircular end. Iron fragments were found here and slag, a waste product from forging iron, with fifty fragments of crucibles for melting silver, copper, zinc, and lead.

Glass was also manufactured: 260 pieces of glass moulds were found, with fragments of glass droplets and rods, and lumps of blue and yellow glass. A white glass stud had a geometric metal inlay, and a blue glass stud was inlaid with metal wire and multicoloured glass.

A similar degree of craftsmanship was employed in Ireland to create the magnificent Derrynaflan paten (or Communion dish) and the Ardagh chalice. This suggests that metal workers at Portmahomack were making vessels for use in worship. A considerable number must have been created; perhaps, together with vellum manuscripts, they were 'Mass kits' for other monasteries.

Monumental Cross Slabs

There was evidence that the monks suffered from hernias and back injuries, indicative of heavy lifting. Their injuries suggest that they were dragging enormous stones into place and carving them. By AD 800, the monks had carved four monumental cross slabs, one that stood outside the church and three that marked the monastery's boundaries. A surviving piece of one slab depicts four clerics; when complete, it might have represented the twelve apostles.

A fragment of this slab had been discovered in the nineteenth century—a small section measuring 48 cm by 30 cm, inscribed in Latin in bold, upright letters. They are carved in insular majuscule, resembling that of the Lindisfarne Gospels created on Iona. This suggests that a similar manuscript existed at Portmahomack for the sculptor to copy. The inscription is the longest known from Pictish territory, and has been translated as 'In the name of Jesus Christ, a cross of Christ in memory of Reo[...]lius ... on this day ...'

At this time, three monumental cross slabs were erected elsewhere on the Tarbat peninsula, at Nigg, Shandwick, and Hilton of Cadboll. Together with the cross slabs at Portmahomack, the sophistication of these monumental sculptures indicates that in the late eighth century, the Tarbat peninsula was important and perhaps famous in Britain—perhaps also in Ireland and beyond.

A Viking Raid

This phase of monastic life appears to have been ended abruptly by a catastrophic Viking raid, sometime between 780 and 820. There may have been earlier raids: three monks buried in the cemetery had blade wounds. One had survived an injury from a long sword, but another died from three sharp cuts to his skull. In the final raid, the four monumental cross slabs were destroyed. One great cross shaft at the edge of the enclosure was thrown down and hammered into fragments, with more than 100 pieces of broken sculpture strewn across the site.

A newly carved monument was smashed soon after it was made, and several pieces of it were scorched. The church was burnt or ruined. Heather, wattle, and turf, which had been used to build the monastery, were found still in position, but burnt. Monastic life ended, but the workmen survived. They now served local or Norse landowners, or perhaps both alternately, during struggles for supremacy in the ninth to the eleventh centuries.

The Site is Restored

The artisans reconstructed the road and re-cut the ditches on either side to canalise the water flowing off the hill where the ruined church stood. The fine smiths' hall became a kiln barn for drying corn. Grain could be dried at one end, then malted and stored at the other. The vellum industry was replaced by metal working, first of silver and bronze and later, by the twelfth century, mainly of iron. The workmen now made not church vessels, but simpler objects and ornaments for personal use. There were two bronze dress pins, a bronze strap-end dating from the eighth to the tenth centuries, and an iron snaffle from a horse's bridle. Portmahomack had now become a farmstead with light industrial activity.

Around AD 1000, a hoard was hidden near the north gate of the churchyard. It consisted of silver arm rings used as money by the Norse, and silver coins of English and French kings reigning in the ninth or tenth century. This appears to have been a smith's hoard, buried during time of battle; when peace resumed, he probably intended to create artefacts for the winning warlord. Metalworkers were always valued—warriors did not destroy those who made swords and spears.

For 200 years, the Tarbat peninsula was a battle zone between the Norse invaders and the warlords of Moray. The Annals of Ulster recount that in 839, the heathens (meaning Vikings) won a battle against the men of Fortriu (the northern Picts) and 'almost innumerable' soldiers fell there. The Annals relate that in 865, the chief bishop of Fortriu, Tuathal mac Argusso, died, while in 866, 'Amlaich and Auis went with the foreigners of Ireland and Alba (Britain) to Fortriu, plundered the entire Pictish country and took away hostages from them'. The men of Fortriu defeated the Norse in 906, but Fortriu is not mentioned again—apparently it ceased to exist.

The Site is Abandoned

By the early eleventh century, the region was controlled by the Norse earls of Orkney. The Beauly River at the northern end of Loch Ness appears to have been the frontier between the Norse in Orkney and the Pictish warlords of Moray. Despite many skirmishes, the Norse were unable to open a passage through Loch Ness and the Great Glen in order to reach their territory in the Irish Sea.

The church at Portmahomack was abandoned for 200 years, and there were no more burials until the twelfth century, when men, women, and children were interred once again, sometimes with shroud pins and coffins. These were the families living around a parish church. A pit for casting a bell, dating from the eleventh century, was found inside the present church.

In the twelfth century, a simple rectangular church was built to the west of the buried ruin, with a chancel added soon afterwards. The enclosure ditch was filled in, and the land was ploughed and used by farmers and fishermen. In 1227, Farquhar MacTaggart (a surname meaning 'son of the priest'), first Earl of Ross, founded Fearn Abbey in Tarbat parish, and by 1255, the abbey supplied a priest for Portmahomack. The church was extended several times; in the crypt, the monks created a reliquary chapel dedicated to St Colmán.

Who was St Colmán?

The name Portmahomack means 'Port of my Colmán'. The suffix '*ac*' is a diminutive term of endearment, so the name approximates to 'Harbour of my dear little Columba'. According to the sixteenth-century *Aberdeen Martyrology*, Bishop Colmán was buried on the Tarbat peninsula. His feast day is given as 15 February; this suggests that the saint was not Columba of Iona (whose feast is 9 June), but Colmán of Lindisfarne, who is commemorated on 18 February. He became bishop and abbot of Lindisfarne in about 661.

At the Synod of Whitby in AD 664, when Colmán defended the Celtic method of calculating the date of Easter, the Northumbrian King Oswiu decreed that Northumbria would follow Roman practice instead. Colmán resigned and retired first to Iona and then to Ireland. Perhaps the monks of Fearn acquired a relic of Colmán for Portmahomack church, which might have become a place of pilgrimage once relics were installed in the crypt, since he was revered by the Irish, the Angles, and the Scots. The name Portmahomack was now all that was left to indicate the settlement's monastic roots. We owe a debt of gratitude to Professor Carver and his team for recovering the story of this remarkable monastery.

7

Máelrhuba and the Scottish Islands

In this chapter, we shall focus on the Hebrides and the Northern Isles. The Inner Hebrides is an archipelago off the Scottish west coast, which includes thirty-six inhabited islands and many smaller ones. In the first two chapters, we examined a number of these islands—Iona, Coll and Tiree, Jura, Islay, and Lismore. At the beginning of this chapter, we will survey what is known of the monks and nuns who lived on other islands of the Inner Hebrides, beginning with the Isle of Skye.

The Outer Hebrides (or Western Isles) is an archipelago further to the north-west; it comprises Lewis and Harris, North and South Uist, Benbecula, and Barra, with their surrounding islands. The sculptures and early buildings on these more exposed islands have been ravaged by centuries of Atlantic gales. Here, we shall examine Barra at the southern end of the Outer Hebrides and Lewis in the north; a few early remains can be seen on the other islands in this group. Finally, we will explore the Northern Isles, Orkney, and Shetland.

Our knowledge of early Christianity in the islands to the north and west of Scotland is imprecise: written sources are scanty, and few carved inscriptions survive. The political history of the northern Highlands and islands in early Christian times is also uncertain. When Argyll and the land of the southern Picts became unified, northern Pictish territory may have remained independent.[1]

The extent to which the Vikings conquered Pictish settlements in Orkney, Shetland, and the Outer Hebrides is also unknown. The pagan Vikings were aggressive invaders from Norway and later Denmark. Their first recorded attack on the Hebrides was in 743, when Iona was pillaged and burned. After increasing devastation, they were followed by settlers who colonised the northern and western fringes of Scotland; they also established bases around the Irish Sea. By the later ninth century, there were Norse settlements on Orkney and Shetland.[2]

Máelrubha of Applecross

After Columba, the most well-known Scottish-Irish saint was Máelrubha, who lived in the following century; he was widely revered on the Isle of Skye. He was born in 640 and became abbot of Bangor in north-east Ireland. In 671, he sailed to the Scottish west coast and established a monastery at Applecross on the mainland in 673. He died there in about 722, and his grave is still honoured. Abbots who succeeded Máelrubha are recorded in Irish annals into the ninth century.

There are many dedications to Máelrubha on Skye and throughout northern Scotland. Loch Maree (*Loch Ma-Ruibhe*) in Wester Ross is named after him, while *Aird Ma-Rhuibhe* on the island of Bernera off Lewis means 'High place of Máelrubha'; there is an early cemetery nearby. Another ten sites are named after him in the west, with six more in eastern Scotland. His name means 'lad of the copse', or 'lad of the headland'; it probably refers to an incident concerning his birth or childhood.[3]

In south-west Skye at Borline on Loch Eynort is the early monastic site of Kilmoruy. Its name means 'cell of Máelrubha'; it may have been a daughter house of his monastery at Applecross, on the mainland opposite. The shaft of an elaborately decorated high cross stands in Kilmoruy graveyard, beside a ruined medieval chapel and church. The cross shaft depicts the crucifixion on one side and an abbot on the other; this probably represents Máelrubha, although the cross was carved in later medieval times. The cross and a fifteenth-century font from the site, carved in high relief, are now in the National Museum, Edinburgh.[4]

Applecross

Applecross is on the coast of Wester Ross opposite Skye. Applecross Bay offers a broad, sheltered landing place; it was accessible only by boat until the early twentieth century. A river runs past the monastic site, which is set in a fertile valley. There is an unfinished incised Pictish cross slab, 3 metres high, beside the gate into the modern church. There are also three very fine carved fragments in the church, so this is likely to have been a significant monastery. Isabel Henderson has suggested that some entries in Irish annals, which describe events in Pictish territory, may derive from monastic annals produced at Applecross, since the author uses its Pictish name, *Aporcrosan*, rather than an Old Irish name.[5]

The local Gaelic name for the district is *a' Chomraich*, which means 'the sanctuary'. As at Dull and Tain in the previous chapter, crosses marked its boundaries. The crosses demarcated a sanctuary with a radius of about 6 miles, within which criminals were protected from the law. The stump of one cross survives; it was smashed by a stonemason in the 1870s.[6] The burial ground of Applecross chapel is all that remains of the monastery, which was destroyed by the Vikings within a century of Máelrubha's death.

Máelrubha's Church, Kilmory Knap

On the Scottish mainland, an early church dedicated to Máelrubha can be seen at Kilmory Knap. The hamlet of Kilmory is on the Knapdale peninsula in Argyll, 2 miles

Above left: Early decorated cross slab, St Máelrubha's church, Kilmory Knap, Knapdale, Argyll and Bute.

Above right: MacMillan's Cross, St Máelrubha's church, Kilmory Knap, Knapdale, Argyll and Bute.

north of the Point of Knap, facing the Isle of Jura. Kilmory is reached by a minor road that runs through Knapdale Forest and along the east side of Loch Sween. The present church dates from the early thirteenth century; it contains a number of early Christian decorated cross slabs.

The chapel also contains late medieval grave slabs and standing crosses in West Highland style, dating from the fourteenth to the sixteenth century. These were carved by Irish stone masons after they had finished work on Iona Abbey; the stone was quarried locally from beside the road between Kilmory Knap and Castle Sween.

The finest of these is MacMillan's cross, which was created in the fifteenth century, but executed in twelfth-century Romanesque style. It is an elaborate wheel cross with a figure of the crucified Christ at its centre. On the reverse side, a warrior and his dogs hunt a deer. It is inscribed in Latin: *+hec est crux Alexandri Macmulen* ('this is the cross of Alexander MacMillan'). It is named after the local chieftain who lived in Castle Sween in the fifteenth century.

Kilmuir and Skeabost, Skye

Returning to Skye, near the north-western tip of the peninsula of Trotternish, Kilmuir contains the ruins of a church and graveyard. It was formerly named Kilmaluag, after the sixth-century Irish monk Mo Luóc, who established a monastery on the Isle of Lismore; it was described at the end of Chapter 2. A Celtic hand bell was known at Kilmuir in the 1870s.[7] There is a well-preserved earth-house in Kilmuir; this is an early drystone building, constructed just under the surface of the ground. It consists of a long, narrow tunnel with an oval beehive-shaped cell at the inner end, the roof of which has been destroyed. An earth-house could provide shelter in harsh winters.[8]

Driving south from Kilmuir, one passes *Loch Chaluim Chille*, or Columba's Loch; it is now drained. Fourteen miles south of Kilmuir, in the mouth of the River Snizort, is Skeabost Island, on which are the ruins of two churches. This may have been an early foundation made by monks from Iona; it is also known as St Columba's Isle.

Skeabost Island was probably the headquarters of the Bishopric of the Isles from 1079 until the late fifteenth century. Of the two ruined churches, that to the west, named Columba's chapel, is the earliest: it may have been contemporary with the eleventh-century cathedral, which was founded under the authority of Archbishop Nidoros of Trondheim, Norway.[9] Until the late fourteenth century, this Norse diocese included both the Scottish Islands and the Isle of Man.[10]

Annait, the 'Mother Church'

On Skye's second northern peninsula, Vaternish, 1 mile north-west of Fairy Bridge, is Annait, a Gaelic name meaning 'mother church'; this unusually complete monastery, between Dunvegan and Portree, is one of the oldest Christian settlements on Skye. It is built on a promontory, between two deep gulleys carved by the Bay River and one of its tributaries, a mile south of the sea. The steep scarps rise from 7 metres to 17 metres above the two streams, and they are impossible to climb, so the enclosure is well-protected. A boundary wall 6 metres wide was built across the southern end of the narrow tongue of land, and there are remains of an eastern wall.

There is a single entrance through the wall, and what appear to be four monks' cells with domed roofs are built within the thickness of the wall. Outside the boundary wall are three interlinked cells, with remains of three more scattered inside the enclosure. A rectangular building aligned east-west was probably a church, and there are other rectangular buildings. It was used as a burial ground until the late 1890s, by which time it had become a cemetery for unbaptised children.[11]

The Meaning of *Annaid*

Pronounced 'anyutch', *annaid* is an early monastic word. It may have come from the Desert Mothers and Fathers of the Near East. In Aramaic, *abba* means 'father', hence 'Abba

Antony', 'Abba Macarius', while *amma* means 'mother'; there were a number of Desert Mothers. In Ireland and Scotland, *annaid* is an ecclesiastical word meaning the mother church or monastic community of the earliest Christian settlement in the district.[12]

In Ireland, the term often refers to a church that contains relics of its founder, but in Scotland, the word is used much more frequently in tiny, remote places, where it simply indicates a place connected with an early mother church. At a site named *annaid*, there are normally traces of an ancient chapel or cemetery or both, and often a well or a clear stream, indicating a monastic foundation.[13]

St Donnán's Monastery, Eigg

South of Skye, there is evidence of early Christianity on the three islands of Canna, Rhum, and Eigg. There was a hermitage on Rhum, where a monk named Becchan died around 677, while St Donnán is associated with a monastery on Eigg. This was close to the sixteenth-century chapel at Kildonnan, where there are four early cross slabs.

According to the *Book of Leinster*, Donnán and fifty-four of his brother monks were burnt to death in AD 619; this suggests a large community. The *Martyrology of Óengus* adds an extra detail about the cold weather on Eigg: 'With his followers, a fair assembly, Donnán of chilly Eigg'. It explains that attackers were hired by the Pictish queen of Moidart, angry at losing her grazing rights, but there are other versions of the story.[14]

Donnán is one of Scotland's few recorded martyrs; he and his companions are almost the only saints who lived between AD 400 and 800 that are described as *martires* in Irish chronicles. The Irish references to Donnán appear to derive from the chronicles of Iona, which record other monks being killed, but do not honour them as martyrs. This suggests that Donnán's cult was an early one, and that the monastery on Eigg may have been a daughter house of Iona.[15]

In 2012, John Hunter conducted excavations in the nineteenth-century burial ground near the chapel at Kildonnan. An oval ditch and timber enclosure were found beneath its wall, typical of monastic ramparts around the time of St Donnán. Within the ramparts were mortared foundations of an early building that was probably a chapel, and evidence of cobbled working surfaces, burnt daub, sets of post holes for wooden structures, and coarse pottery. Between the burial ground and the ruined medieval chapel was a Neolithic burial cairn on high ground; this had evidently been a cemetery in ancient times.[16]

Four monks of Eigg are named in early Irish sources, and there are references to monks on the island into the mid-seventh century. Vikings were buried close to the monastic site; a decorated sword hilt and part of a boat have been found here.[17] A song recorded in the Hebrides praises St Donnán:

> *Early gives the sun greeting to Donnán,*
> *Early sings the bird of the greatness of Donnán,*
> *Early grows the grass on the grave of Donnán,*

The warm eye of Christ on the grave,
The stars of the heavens on the grave.
No harm, no harm to Donnán's dust.[18]

A Women's Hermitage on Canna

On Canna there was a medieval church dedicated to St Columba at A' Chill, above the island's chief harbour. A weathered high cross and other sculpture indicate an earlier monastery on the site. About 6 miles away, on the south coast of Canna, are the remains of a hermitage, built on a rocky ledge below steep cliffs; it is difficult to reach by land or water. It is named *Sgòr nam Ban-Naomha*, or 'Cliff of the holy women'.[19]

At the hermitage, a stone wall 2 metres thick enclosed an oval area containing a large circular building and several smaller ones. There is a well-designed drainage system: a stone-lined water channel runs across the enclosure and out through the wall. Built onto the inner face of the wall is a rectangular structure that may have been a bathhouse.[20]

Fragments of three stones with carved crosses were found here. This may have been a hermitage for a group of women who were associated with the early church at Canna harbour. In the nineteenth century, local people believed that the hermitage had a healing spring, and that nuns once lived there. Canna belonged to Iona in 1203, and may have done so from a much earlier date.[21]

The Outer Hebrides

In the Outer Hebrides, agriculture was difficult, so people were mainly hunter gatherers. Deer were a staple food; this was in contrast to the Scottish mainland, where deer hunting was an elite sport rather than a necessity. Animal bones show that later, in Norse times, sheep and cattle were kept. Calves were killed shortly after birth because when cows calve regularly, they yield more milk. Sheep were kept for a year or two in order to provide more meat; at two years old, a fleece could be obtained.[22]

Deep-water fishing was undertaken, probably using limpets as bait for cod, and later, under Norse rule, for herring, as fishing boats were increasingly used. Birds such as gannets and puffins provided meat, eggs, and oil, while their feathers and skins could be used for clothing. Seal meat was eaten; their blubber was used for oil and their skins for leather.[23]

Wild fruit such as raspberries and blackberries, damsons, wild cherries, and crab apples were eaten. Hazelnuts were collected in season, as well as mushrooms, and sorrel for soup. Honey was prized, and was also used for mead. Barley and oats were grown in poor soil, particularly by Norse settlers; sometimes wheat and rye could be cultivated. Flax may have been introduced by Norse farmers: it provided linseed oil, while its stem fibres were used to make linen.[24]

Barra: St Barr's Isle

At the southern tip of the Outer Hebrides, Barra, which is 5 miles wide, was a haven for Viking pirates who launched raids in several directions from the island. They also settled here: most of the early place names on Barra are Norse. Viking sagas describe Norsemen who drove out Barra's Celtic rulers in the mid-ninth century, in order to use the island as a base for plunder, while keeping contact with their relatives in Norway and Iceland. However, the Norwegians appear to have lived here alongside Celtic Christians: the island's name, Barra, is probably an abbreviation of the name of St Finbar (meaning 'white head'), while an islet to the south is named Pabbay, meaning 'priest's isle' in Norse.[25]

Cille Bharra (or 'Barr's cell') is near the northern tip of the island; it might date from the seventh century. There are remains of a ruined twelfth-century church and two chapels, surrounded by an enclosure wall. There are three early grave markers inscribed with Latin crosses in the graveyard.[26] *Cille Bharra* remained a popular place of pilgrimage into medieval times. St Barr was traditionally claimed to be Finbar of Cork, and both their feast days are on or around 25 September, but the *Aberdeen Breviary* relates that Barr was a Scottish monk, born in Caithness. He is the patron of Dornoch in Sutherland, and has dedications elsewhere.[27]

Pagan graves of both men and women dating from the ninth and tenth centuries indicate that the Norwegians brought their wives, but no pagan graves were dug after the tenth century: it appears that the foreigners had accepted Christianity. A grave-slab was discovered at Barr's church dating from the late eleventh or early twelfth century, with an ornamented Celtic cross on one side and an inscription in Norse runes on the other, which reads: 'This cross was raised in memory of Thorgerth, daughter of Steinar'.[28] This suggests the gradual integration of Norse culture with local Christian tradition. The cross is now in the National Museum, Edinburgh.

On the smaller isle of Pabbay, 8 miles south of Barra, there are remains of an early chapel and a cemetery on a mound, containing a stone inscribed with Pictish symbols: a V-rod, a crescent moon, and a flower. A cross was apparently added when it came to be used as a grave marker. There are only five Pictish symbol stones in the Hebrides; this is the only one that remains in its original location. There are three more grave markers inscribed with crosses in Pabbay's graveyard, dating from the sixth to the ninth centuries.[29] This site may have been a cell of a monastery on Barra. There are also remains of chapels on nearby Sandray, Mingulay, and Berneray, with a cemetery on Vatersay.

Lewis

At the northern end of the Outer Hebrides, Lewis is almost 30 miles long. It is barren and mountainous, and subject to fierce gales and short squalls. The early Christian sites are on the coast: monks could land at tiny harbours, and could feed on fish, sea birds, and their eggs. At pre-Norse sites, inhabitants fished from inland waters; Norse settlers favoured deep sea fishing. In Orkney and Shetland, they caught cod and hake; in the Outer Hebrides, herring fishing was common. This was a communal task which involved co-operation between families and investment in boats and nets.[30]

Many of the church sites are found along the north-western shore, where the land shelves more gently down to the sea. We shall follow the coast road in a clockwise direction round Lewis, beginning near its south-western end, on the island of Great Bernera, which is now joined to the mainland by a short road bridge.

St Macra's Church, Great Bernera

St Macra's church is at the village of Kirkibost; its Norse name means 'church farm'. A chapel on the headland east of the village may commemorate a female saint called Macra or Macrel, derived from the Latin name Marcella.[31, 32] The most famous St Marcella was a fourth-century widow, a friend of St Jerome; Macra is likely to have been a later holy woman.

St Macra's church (see colour plate 17) stands above Loch Mharcoil, a lake that may be named after her; the oblong chapel is oriented roughly east-west. Its lower courses are built with huge boulders; the cyclopean masonry is likely to date from Norse times. There is a graveyard nearby, and sunken stone walls of what might be an earth house. There are some early Welsh dedications to a nun named Marcella: she is commemorated, for example, at Whitchurch, the mother church of Denbigh.[33]

Large blocks of cyclopean masonry in the west wall of St Macra's church, Kirkibost, Great Bernera.

St Sgàire's Cell, Bragar

Returning to Lewis, on the coast 8 miles north-east of Kirkibost is a chapel now dedicated to St John (*Teampull Eoin*), close to the village of Bragar. The church was also named Cill Sgàire, meaning the cell or chapel of Sgàire; this is a Norse name still found on Lewis.[34] St John's church is situated on the eastern shore of a small harbour, named Port More, meaning 'large bay', since it is large by Lewis standards. This is a ruined two-chambered church, possible dating from the fifteenth century; there used to be a holy well beside it. The church is situated within a cemetery containing early grave markers; beyond are remains of the former village.

St Peter's Church, Shader

Sixteen miles to the north-east, St Peter's church at Shader is on a windswept clifftop. It may have been dedicated to St Peter after the Synod of Whitby, when the patronage of local saints was replaced by those of the universal church, most often Peter, or one of the other apostles, Andrew, John, and Thomas, or Mary, or the Trinity. In the same way, the church at Lindisfarne, built by Abbot Finan, was later dedicated to St Peter by Archbishop Theodore.[35]

St John's church, Bragar, Lewis, with a flat-headed window in its eastern gable and early grave markers.

The grass-covered foundations of St Peter's church (or *Teampull Pheadair*) survive, only 15 metres from the shore; it was a small two-chambered building with a chancel and a nave. Beside the chapel is 'the rock of the servant of Patrick' (*Creag Gille Phàdraig* in Gaelic); he may have been a monk of the community.[36]

The monastery's land was extensive: an expanse of green pasture, about half a mile north-east of the church is named *Na h'Annaidean*, meaning '[land belonging to] the mother church'. There are two wells on the property, named after St Andrew and St Mary. On the hill above are *Clachan h'Annaid*, or 'stones of the mother church'.[37]

The clifftop is named 'headland of the mother church' (*Rubha na h'Annaid*). On the shore below the church, there was a standing stone named *Clach an t'Sagairt*, meaning 'stone of the priest', but the pillar stone was eroded by the sea in the last hundred years.[38] Thus, although little survives on the ground at this site, the islanders have preserved the names of many small features of this monastery.

Perhaps the earliest are the mother church stones, which may have been pre-Christian holy stones, or they may have marked the early settlement, since *clachan*, meaning 'stones', can denote either a church building or a small settlement. Sailors would have made for the monastery headland, above its tiny harbour, and by Norse times, they could spot the landing place by scanning the horizon for the Priest's pillar stone. The monks had servants, according to the name of the adjacent clifftop, and they farmed the land to the north-east; they drew water from the two wells.

St Andrew's well, Shader, with 'stones of the mother church' on the skyline (top left), Lewis.

St Peter's Church, Swainbost

Swainbost is 4 miles north-east of Shader; its Norse name means 'Sveini's farm'. Here the land slopes gradually down to the sea shore, so this church was more sheltered (see colour plate 18). It stands within a very large medieval graveyard; only the western end of the late medieval church survives, containing a window and two putlog holes in the gable. These were holes for wooden scaffolding, which enabled workmen to construct the upper level.[39]

St Peter's church was still in use in the eighteenth century, but all these north-eastern villages have now moved a few miles inland, where there is more shelter from the gales.[40] Between the church and the sea shore is a hillock named *Cnoc an Annaid* ('hill of the mother church') and, as at Shader, a stretch of land is similarly named *Na h'Annaiden*, meaning '[land belonging to] the mother church'.[41]

The monastery stood on the right bank of the Swainbost River; on the opposite bank is a souterrain, or series of underground chambers, which are a feature of some Irish monastic sites. They were perhaps used to store food, or maybe served to protect people and cattle from the elements. Four examples of such earth-houses, or drystone buildings constructed just below ground level, can be found on Lewis.[42]

No monastic cells survive above ground on Lewis, but beehive shielings continued to be built in the same style for centuries. They were small, circular drystone buildings, roofed with overlapping slabs, arranged to form a false arch; this was protected by an outer covering of turf. One could see them in small clusters in the summer pasture lands; they were normally less than 3 metres in diameter and less than 3 metres high.[43]

St Rónán's Church, Eorpaidh

Eorpaidh is at the northern tip of Lewis. Only a grassy mound survives at the site of St Rónán's church, 500 metres north-east of St Mo Luóc's Cathedral at Eorpaidh. The Irish *Martyrology of Gorman* names twelve Rónáns, but this Rónán appears to have been an abbot of St Catán's monastery on Bute, which was described near the end of Chapter 2. Twenty miles south of Eorpaidh, St Columba's church at Uí is said to have been founded on the site of a cell dedicated to Catán.[44]

According to the Annals of Ulster, Abbot Rónán of Bute died in AD 737, so the church named after him on Lewis may have been an eighth-century foundation. There are a number of dedications to Rónán in the Hebrides. *Teampull Rónaig* on Iona is believed to have been the island's original parish church. He is commemorated on Islay, and an islet off Shetland is called St Rónán's Isle.[45]

A Hermit's Cell on North Rona

St Rónán is believed to have travelled 45 miles north of Lewis to the tiny island of North Rona, where a chapel and cell survive the elements. This is a truly remote 'desert in the sea'. Here, a hermit's drystone beehive cell is one of the most complete in Europe; a chapel was built onto it in about the twelfth century, but its walls have partly collapsed. The cell and chapel are constructed of flat slabs, pinned with smaller stones. They stand within a graveyard, surrounded by a thick drystone wall. The cemetery contains a number of small stone crosses.[46]

West of the church are some simple dwellings: a central oblong enclosure, a low flagged passage, and three beehive huts; five families lived here until about 1680. In his *Description of the Western Islands of Scotland* (1703), the antiquarian Martin Martin wrote a description of life on the stack, drawing on information from Lewis men who had visited it. Families from Lewis again moved out to North Rona, but finally abandoned it in the mid-nineteenth century.[47]

St Rónán's Cross

A carved cross that stood at the centre of the small graveyard on North Rona has been brought to the mainland, where it can now be seen in Niss Historical Museum, (*Comunn Eachdraidh Niss*) south of the Butt of Lewis. It stands 1 metre tall, and may date from the tenth or eleventh century. This is the only Christian carved artefact to survive from early times in the Lewis region.

According to tradition, the cross marked the grave of St Rónán. It is pierced by three holes, and the figure of a naked man is carved in outline on the cross; the holes pass under his armpits and through his throat. This may represent the merging of a pre-Christian belief with the Christian symbol of the cross. Its design is unique, but there was a tradition of carving human figures on crosses along the Scottish west coast from the ninth to the eleventh centuries.[48]

St Mo Luóc's Cathedral, Eorpaidh

Returning to Eorpaidh, Mo Luóc's Cathedral (or *Teampull Mholuaidh*) is at the Butt of Lewis in a field some 250 metres north of the village of Eorpaidh. It is in a dramatic location at the northernmost point of the Outer Hebrides. The single-chambered cathedral was of exceptional importance and was known locally as *Teampull Mòr* (or 'the great church'), although it is only 15 metres by 2.5 metres. The cathedral was restored in 1912, but its foundations and walls are Norse. At its eastern end, a side chapel is entered from the outside, and there is a sacristy on the opposite side. This building plan, with chapels at the eastern end, is typical of twelfth- and thirteenth-century Norse architecture; there are other examples in Norway and Greenland.

This plan is found in the twelfth-century Norse cathedral at Igaliku in the ancient diocese of Garðar in southern Greenland. The arrangement of the side chapels may be a result of Cistercian influence: it resembles the plan of the earliest Cistercian abbey in Norway, Luse Kloster near Bergen, founded in 1146.[49] Another twelfth-century feature of St Mo Luóc's church is the putlog holes in the walls, used for scaffolding during construction.

People came here to pray for healing. In 1630, one Captain Dymes described how those who were unable to visit the church sent a piece of wood similar in shape to their injured

Above left: Cross with three holes and a carving of a naked man, from North Rona, 45 miles north of Lewis.

Above right: St Mo Luóc's Cathedral, Eorpaidh, Lewis.

Early quern stones for grinding corn, Eorpaidh, Lewis.

limb, such as a wooden hand or foot, to be placed on the altar.[50] In the 1890s, Rev. Malcolm MacPhail recorded that those suffering from psychological illness came here to be healed. After arriving at dusk, they walked seven times clockwise round the church and drank water from St Rónán's well before sleeping in St Mo Luóc's church overnight, tied to the altar.[51]

Hallowe'en feasts were also held here before the local people went down to the beach to eat and dance and offer a cup of wine to the local sea god, *Seònaidh* (or Shony). Querns and staddle stones were found outside the church. In Irish tradition, anyone found grinding corn on a Sunday was given the penance of smashing the quern and bringing it to the church.

St Columba's Church, Uí

There are two sites associated with Columba on the more sheltered eastern side of Lewis, where they are protected from the fierce Atlantic breakers on the west coast. St Columba's church at Uí, on the Eye peninsula, is 4 miles east of Stornoway, on the southern shore of a very large bay. The name Uí (or Eye) derives from the Old Norse *Aið*, meaning a narrow neck of land, or isthmus. As we have seen, the church is possibly built on the site of a cell of St Catán of Bute. The present ruined church at Uí dates from the fourteenth century onwards.[52]

This was the principal church of Lewis in medieval times. It had both a north and a south cemetery—that on the north side has been eroded by the sea. The graveyard became the burial place of the MacLeods of Lewis. On the north wall of the church is a memorial slab to Margaret MacKinnon (d. 1503), the mother of John, the last abbot of Iona. There are broken quern stones, used for grinding corn, outside the church porch, like those found at St Mo Luóc's Cathedral. A small stream bisects the graveyard; it could have provided fresh water for the monks.

Viking Chess Sets

In 1831, ninety-three artefacts, including seventy-eight pieces from four chess sets, were discovered in Uí Bay. Most were carved from walrus ivory and a few from whales' teeth. They date from the twelfth century and were perhaps made in Trondheim, Norway. Their lack of wear suggests that they may have been the stock of a trader, perhaps on his way to a wealthy Viking city such as Dublin, or they may have been hidden as a hoard. Eleven pieces are now in the National Museum, Edinburgh, while the others are in the British Museum, London.

They display fascinating details: four of the rooks, depicted as foot soldiers, are depicted biting the rims of their shields. An early thirteenth-century history of the Norwegian kings, entitled *Heimskringla*, describes how the warriors of the god Óðinn entered a state of frenzy and bit their shields as they went into battle.[53] The sixteen Viking bishops, with their mitres and crosiers, stand or sit in various poses; many raise their right hand as they bless their people.

Above: St Columba's church, Uí, Lewis.

Right: Replica of a bishop with a crosier and gospel book, from a twelfth-century Viking chess set found in Uí Bay, Lewis.

A second Columban site is *Eilean Chaluim Chille*, or Columba's Isle, 8 miles south-west of Uí, near Cromore, in the mouth of Loch Erisort. Like Uí, this is a sheltered site, although there is a swift tidal current in this long sea loch. Local people have built up a causeway to the island, which tractors can cross at low tide. On Columba's Isle there are ruins of a rectangular church within a graveyard, and the foundations of a second chapel. According to local tradition, later monks cultivated an orchard on the sheltered south-facing slope on the mainland; the island would have been too exposed for growing fruit.[54] Part of a Viking hogback tomb was found in the neighbourhood; this suggests the presence of Norse Christians.

St Aula's Church, Gress

This is the only church on Lewis dedicated to a Norse saint: St Aula, or Óláfr Haraldsson (995–1030), was King of Norway from 1016 to 1029. After spending time as a soldier and pirate in Normandy and the Baltic, he became a Christian. He seized power in Norway, and converted the country to Christianity both through gentleness and by force.

Óláfr established justice, peace, and security, but after a rebellion encouraged by Cnut, king of England and Denmark, he was exiled, defeated, and killed. His cult was strong in Viking areas of Britain, where over forty churches are dedicated to him in Yorkshire, Lincolnshire, and East Anglia, on the Isle of Man, the Hebrides, Orkney, and Shetland. The Hebridean surname Macaulay, or 'son of Aula' derives from St Óláfr.[55]

Gress is on the east coast of Lewis, 6 miles north of Uí. St Aula's church is on a gently shelving hillside above the shore; its walls and gables survive (see colour plate 19). The doorway is capped by a simple lintel; there are two small windows in the wall, a typical design to keep out the wind and rain. Above the door, the date 1681 is carved; this is likely to mark the date of repairs to the church, since the fabric is older. South of the churchyard, the winding River Gress flows towards the sea. The church is surrounded by a large graveyard, still in use.

Islands West of Lewis and Harris

The names of the smaller islands close to Lewis indicate occupation during several periods. A number of their names end with the Norse suffix '*ey*', meaning island, but the nouns preceding the suffixes tell a different story. Taransay, close to South Harris, off West Loch Tarbert, is named after Taran or Ternan, a saint with a Pictish name. *Tarainus* is the name of a Pictish nobleman in Adomnán's *Life of Columba*.[56] On the island are foundations of a small church named *Teampull Tharáin*, and a burial ground, *Cladh Tharáin*, both of which were solely for the use of women, according to the antiquarian Martin Martin. There was another church and graveyard for men.[57]

St Tarain was a popular saint, with dedications in Aberdeenshire and elsewhere; his skull and hand bell were preserved in Banchory-Ternan on the River Dee in Aberdeenshire until the Reformation.[58] Twelve miles south-west of Taransay is Pabbay, one of four islands with this name in the Outer Hebrides, with a fifth close to the Isle of Skye, 10 miles west of the Kyle of Lochalsh; Pabbay, off Barra, has already been described. The name Pabbay, derived from *abba*, or 'father', may have been given by Norse settlers to islands on which Celtic monks lived; in Iceland, however, the name appears to have been given retrospectively by medieval Norse antiquarians, and the same may apply to those of northern Scotland.

Orkney

In the sixth and seventh centuries, there were already Christians in Orkney and Shetland, as we can tell from the presence of Christian carved stones and other objects bearing Pictish designs. However, most of the early evidence of Christianity in the Northern Isles was obliterated by the arrival of the Vikings. No pre-Viking church has so far been found on Orkney, but the front slab of a carved stone altar was found on the small island of Flotta near the southern end of the Orkneys, while a Pictish cross slab was found at Lady on Sanday at the north-eastern end of the archipelago.[59]

There was a monastery on Papa Westray (or Papay), 20 miles west of Sanday, at the north-western end of the Orkneys, on the safest sea route to Shetland. The twelfth-century church of St Boniface stands above a rocky shore in the north-west corner of the island. There was an extensive early settlement here from Iron Age times into the Pictish period.

A fine carved cross slab was found here, and a second slab brought from the beach, on which a robed standing figure, probably a monk, was carved by pecking. A fragment of a Pictish box-shaped shrine with corner posts, perhaps dating from the eighth century, was discovered; this may have contained the relics of an early abbot. A Viking hogback tomb carved from Old Red Sandstone remains in its original position in the churchyard. This suggests a monastic church that continued into early Norse times.[60]

The Brough of Deerness

There was probably a monastery at the Brough of Deerness on the mainland of Orkney, 10 miles east of Kirkwall, on a projecting headland separated from the mainland by a deep gulley. In earlier times, the site could be reached by a rock bridge. On the sea stack are the remains of a late Viking church and about thirty associated buildings. A strong wall runs along the edge of the settlement that faces the mainland. There was a well and a cemetery that included the graves of at least four children. This was a well-known place of pilgrimage as late as the sixteenth century.[61]

Excavations between 2008 and 2011 led by James Gerrard and James Barrett from Cambridge University demonstrated occupation over a period of a thousand years. An Iron Age copper alloy mount in the shape of an animal was found, dating from Roman times. A fragment of a blue glass vessel with white trails was probably created in the sixth or seventh century. There were Pictish rubbish heaps and a Pictish bone pin. In later levels, there was a tenth- or eleventh-century comb; earlier, an Anglo-Saxon penny of King Eadgar (959–75) had been found. The isolated site is typical of a monastic settlement.

The Brough of Birsay

The Brough of Birsay, an island 20 miles north-west of Kirkwall, was an important Christian centre in Pictish and Viking times; access is by a tidal causeway. The site includes an early monastery, and a later church built by Thorfinn the Mighty, the Norse Earl of Orkney. His grandson, Magnús, was buried here before his relics were transferred to Kirkwall; he was treacherously murdered by his cousin, Haakon, in about 1116, and was venerated as a martyr.

This may have been the site of a sixth-century monastery; Ralegh Radford identified its chapel, graveyard, and enclosure wall.[62] In the ninth century, Viking farmsteads were erected; these had become a larger Norse settlement by the mid-eleventh century. Fragments of a fine Pictish carved stone and a Pictish cross slab were found in the graveyard beneath the Norse enclosure.[63]

The ruins that can be seen today are the lower walls of a church that dates from about 1100. This was probably dedicated to St Peter; it has a square chancel with an eastern apse, a rectangular nave and indications of a western tower or porch. There are stair turrets in the corners of the chancel arch, implying access to a rood screen.[64] It remained a place of pilgrimage until the Reformation.

The earliest known seat of the bishopric of the Norse diocese of Orkney was at Birsay, though it is uncertain whether this was on the tidal island or on the mainland where, again, traces of a twelfth-century building have been found below the present parish church. The bishopric was transferred to Kirkwall in 1137, where St Magnús Cathedral was built to house his relics. The early bishops were subject first to York, and then to Lund, which was then a Danish bishopric within the German archdiocese of Hamburg-Bremen. In 1153, the bishops of Orkney became subject to Trondheim in Norway.[65]

Shetland: Papil Monastery

There were early monks on Shetland, but we do not know their names. The principal monastic site may have been at Papil on West Burra, 6 miles south-west of Lerwick. Situated off the western mainland of Shetland, West Burra is at the northern end of the sea route from Orkney. Burra's limestone soil makes it fertile, and the church is in a sheltered valley; its dedication to St Laurence may date from Norse times or later. As its Norse name, *Papar-byl* ('monks' place') suggests, this was a significant early Christian monastery.[66]

A number of carved cross slabs were found here, and corner posts from slab shrines which may have housed the relics of early abbots. A panel from a richly decorated shrine depicts four monks with hooded cloaks and staffs and a fifth on horseback, perhaps their abbot, moving in procession towards a carved high cross. Each carries a staff and a satchel containing a gospel book. It dates from the late tenth century, and can be seen at the Shetland Museum in Lerwick.[67] Another Pictish sculpture, the Papil Stone, depicts monks below a wheel-headed cross, with various Pictish symbols.

A Hoard on St Ninian's Isle

There was another early Christian foundation on St Ninian's Isle, which is connected to the mainland of Shetland by a gravel bank in summer only. It is off the south-west coast of Shetland, near Bigton. An early church lies beneath a medieval one, surrounded by a graveyard which was in use from pre-Christian times until the nineteenth century. In early Christian times, a group of babies was buried here, aligned east-west, with tiny crosses placed at their heads. Corner posts for stone shrines to enclose the bones of early monks were found, and stones with incised crosses. The dedication to St Ninian is a late one.

Here, a hoard of twenty-eight decorated silver objects and the jawbone of a porpoise, all encased in a larch box, were discovered beneath the east end of the medieval church. The objects were for secular use: eight feasting bowls, parts of swords, eight magnificent penannular brooches that were worn by nobles, and heavy ring chains, thought to have been worn as symbols of power by Pictish chieftains. They were perhaps buried for safekeeping around AD 800 during Viking raids, since the larch box was Scandinavian, although it might have been deposited later by an aristocratic Pictish family who had amassed the treasure over several generations, since the dates of the objects vary.[68]

One of the two elaborate sword chapes, or protective fittings at the end of a scabbard, is an Anglo-Saxon item, probably made in Mercia in the late eighth century. It could have been a gift from a Saxon ruler to his Pictish counterpart. It is inscribed in Old English with a dedication to the Trinity that reads 'In the name of God [the Father]' on one side and 'Property of the Son, of the Holy Spirit' on the other.[69]

More Remote Monasteries

Further north in the Shetland Isles, three sites have been tentatively classified as early Celtic monasteries; each is on a remote rock stack. Their buildings are rectangular in plan, with slightly bowed walls and rounded corners. Kame of Isbister on Unst in the far north is an almost inaccessible rock stack of mica slate with a flat clay-covered top. It is joined to the mainland by a knife-edge ridge. A footpath once crossed the ridge, but it has been eroded by cliff falls. The foundations of nineteen buildings are visible at the monastery.[70]

Another possible early site has been surveyed at Birrier on the island of Yell. This is the second largest island in the Shetlands; it is 20 miles in length and is situated between Shetland and Unst. There are twelve sites of brochs on the island—these are tall stone round houses, dating from the Iron Age. The early monastery at Birrier included fourteen buildings, of which seven form a compact central group. It resembles the monastic settlement at Kame of Isbister, on the opposite side of Yell Sound.[71]

Outer Brough is an exposed rock stack beyond Fetlar, to the east of Yell, where the foundations of sixteen buildings have been traced, and an enclosure wall. There are two groups of buildings: six form an eastern group, with eroded walls, while a western group of about ten buildings is better preserved and contains a larger building subdivided into two compartments.[72] If these are monastic sites, they may have been established by Irish monks who reached the Northern Isles in the seventh and eighth centuries. They favoured inaccessible places such as offshore islands or rocky headlands separated from the mainland by a stout drystone enclosure wall. Now they are best viewed from the air.

8

The Isle of Man: A Vibrant Church

In early Christian times, the Isle of Man was a useful landing place for people travelling between Ireland, Wales, and Scotland. Although it was not the most direct route, it provided safe harbours and fresh water, and successive generations made use of the island as they sailed between the countries surrounding the Irish Sea. From the slopes of Snaefell, the mountain at the centre of the island, one can see Scotland, England, and Wales on a clear day.

Contact with communities overseas brought literacy and new technological ideas. However, Manx life was not greatly affected: Roman civilisation and culture scarcely touched the island. Archaeology has revealed few signs of Roman influence, and nothing to suggest permanent occupation. No local pottery was made after the fifth century BC, and few domestic artefacts have survived. Organic materials such as leather, wood, and stone were used for containers. Wheeled vehicles were not constructed on the island for many centuries.

Celtic Christians

Although the Isle of Man is only 32 miles long and 12 miles wide, it has a rich heritage from early Christian times. In the sixth century, Irish families settled on the Isle of Man, and some of them may have been Christian, though stone carvings suggest that the first Christians might have come from south-west Wales. Burial grounds were consecrated, and most of these were served by a small chapel, or *keeill* in Manx, a name similar to the Gaelic word *cill*.

The first Christian monuments on the island date from the sixth century. One of the earliest is a pillar-shaped tombstone from Ballaqueeney in the parish of Rushen in the south-west; it was discovered in 1874. It is inscribed in ogham, which was mostly used for writing in Old Irish. The inscription, carved up one edge, reads: '[the stone] of Bivaidu, son of the tribe of Cunava[li]'. This refers to Conaille, a small kingdom in eastern Ireland, north of the River Boyne; it confirms the presence of Irish settlers on the Isle of Man.[1]

A sixth-century stone from an early cemetery at Glentraugh in the parish of Santan, in the south-east, indicates that, as well as Irish, Latin was spoken on the island at this time.

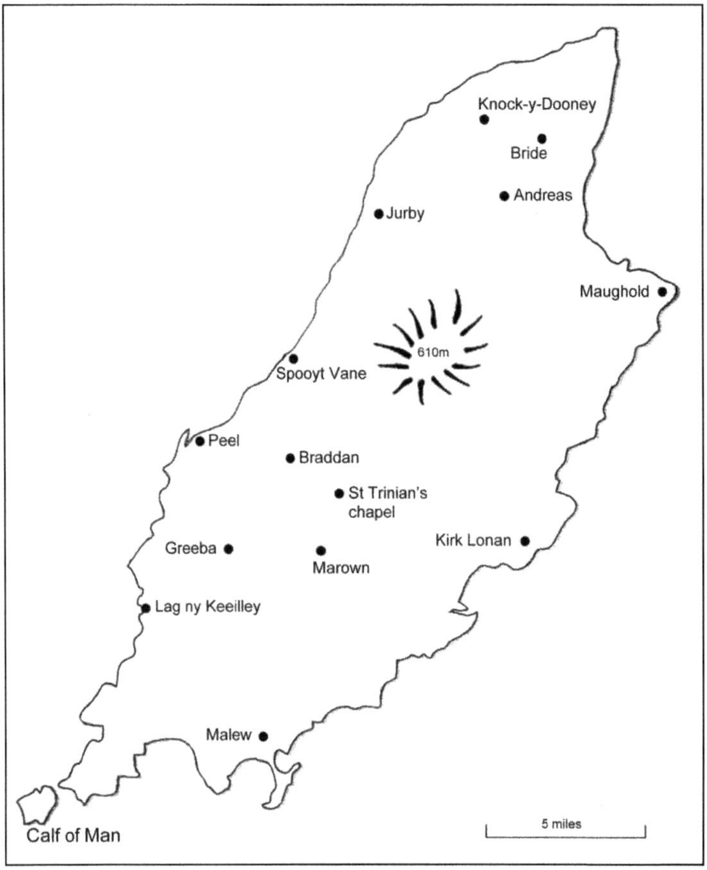

Early Christian sites on the Isle of Man.

The memorial stone is inscribed: 'AVIT MONOMENT', or 'the monument of Avitus'. There are several other Manx cemeteries dating from the sixth or seventh century, including one quite close to Glentraugh, at Speke *keeill*, which will be described in more detail below.

No early liturgical manuscripts survive, but the Manx name for the feast of the Epiphany on 6 January is 'Festival of the Water Well'. The Epiphany is a feast of water and a day for baptism in the Eastern Orthodox Churches, but not in the Roman rite, so the Manx name for the Epiphany may derive from Celtic times, before this tradition died out in the West.[2]

The Vikings

The first Scandinavian raiders arrived on the island in the late eighth century. Most Manx place names derive from Old Norse; this suggests that Vikings took possession of all the useful land. The Celtic language survived, however, and the Norse invaders were converted to Christianity within about 100 years. For the Vikings who lived on the island, it took only a day's sailing or hard rowing to reach Norse trading settlements on the Wirral in north-eastern England, or the new Viking town of Dublin.[3]

The term Viking is an Old Norse word that originally referred to men who adventured overseas to raid and plunder: *vik* means a bay or creek, and describes where they landed. Gaelic peoples called them 'Norsemen', and Anglo-Saxons referred to them as 'the Danes'. However, Vikings rarely spent a lifetime plundering—they normally went on foreign raids in their youth, before settling into adult life.

We do not know whether Scandinavians in the Viking period came to the Isle of Man to attack and pillage or whether they had peaceful intentions and came in search of new land where they could settle. Norse settlements were established on the Isle of Man in the ninth century, and two tenth-century longhouses survive at Braaid in Marown, near the centre of the southern half of the island; smaller Viking farmhouses have also been discovered.[4] At the beginning of the tenth century, the Norse started to bury their dead in existing Christian cemeteries and began to commission stone crosses as memorials for their dead; this suggests that they were now Christian.

In other areas under the control of the kings of Norway, Christianity was adopted after the conversion of King Óláfr Trygvason (*c.* 964–*c.* 1000). The Anglo-Saxon chronicle relates that the Norwegian king, who had already been baptised, was subsequently confirmed in 994 at Andover in Hampshire, with King Æthelred as his sponsor, as part of a Danegeld treaty in which he agreed to no longer raid in England.[5] The Isle of Man remained under Norse control until after the Battle of Largs in 1263, when it came under Scottish rule. It was the Christian culture of the later Norse inhabitants that formed the foundation of the medieval Church on the Isle of Man.

Viking Religion

The inhabitants of Denmark and Norway had various cosmologies, but no single uniform religion. Inhabitants of both countries were converted to Christianity, though many continued to worship their ancestors and to believe in supernatural spirits of the land. A number of Manx crosses bear inscriptions in Norse runes; these would have been commissioned by rich and successful Viking warrior chieftains.

Norse myths may have been adapted by Christians to help explain the new religion. Thor's magic hammer, with which he created thunder and lightning, is depicted as a T-shaped cross on carvings and amulets. This resembles the early Christian tau cross: *tau* is the Greek name for the letter 'T'. About fifty of Thor's amulets have been found across Scandinavia, dating from the ninth to the eleventh centuries, especially in Christian areas. Perhaps a parallel was seen between Thor's hammer and Christ's cross. Some of the hammers are decorated with Christian ornamentation, and a smith's mould from Trend in Jutland includes spaces for fashioning an image of Thor's hammer alongside two Christian crosses.[6]

There are more than 190 carved crosses on the Isle of Man, most of which date from Viking times. Their images and inscriptions provide valuable information about life on the island; occupations such as hunting and fishing are depicted, and stories from Viking sagas. The sculptors adapted and combined Scandinavian patterns as they evolved a distinct regional style.

It is likely that many of the crosses were coloured.[7] They are carved from local stone, normally quarried from the immediate neighbourhood. Most are of clay-slate, while others are of granite, Old Red Sandstone, or limestone. Their carved patterns often resemble those in illuminated manuscripts, and they demonstrate a sophisticated theological awareness, so their sculptors are likely to have been monks.

Keeills

There are records of 174 *keeills* on the Isle of Man; this is a very large number of chapels for such a small island. Thirty-five of them can still be identified. The earliest *keeills* were probably built in the sixth century, but all those that survive date from the ninth century or later. The chapels may have been served by priests from monastic communities like Kirk Maughold, the principal monastery in early times, on the north-east coast. The *keeills* are rectangular, with a stone altar placed against the eastern wall, and often a doorway in the west wall, facing the altar; some have two doors.

The small size of the chapels suggests that people remained outside for most of the services. The great festivals of the church, Christmas and Easter, and the *keeill*'s saint's day were probably celebrated, and weddings, baptisms, and funerals of the local community. Burials were normally in a stone-built box, a lintel grave aligned east-west like the *keeill*, with the head facing east. This was an early Christian tradition: the sun set in the west, which came to symbolise death, and rose in the east, which symbolised resurrection. A slab, sometimes carved with a cross, might be placed flat on top of the grave, or upright at one or both ends, to mark the spot.

Norse *keeills* resembled cottages in small Manx villages today: the roof was thatched with reeds and bound by ropes to pegs fixed in the walls. Altar linen could be washed and hung on bushes to dry. Many of the chapels are built using a primitive drystone technique: their walls are often 1 metre thick, with stone facing on the two surfaces and a filling of earth and small stones. Some, like that of Druidale in the upper valley of the River Sulby, on the shoulder of Snaefell, are built near summer shielings and would not have been used in winter.

We shall begin by exploring what may be the earliest indication of Christianity on the island, a simple preaching station in Marown, and we shall consider a few other inland sites. Then, as with Lewis in the previous chapter, we shall proceed round the Manx coast in a clockwise direction, examining the most interesting sites. In that way, the reader can follow a trail in the course of a week or so, travelling round the island. It would be useful to visit the Manx Museum in Douglas at the start of the journey, to become acquainted with the sites, with their carved crosses and other artefacts that tell us so much about early Christianity on the island.

St Patrick's Chair, Marown

Marown in the southern half of Man is the only Manx parish with no coastline. St Patrick's Chair is thought to be an early Christian preaching station, a site where the

Early preaching station, 'St Patrick's Chair', Marown, Isle of Man.

gospel was proclaimed before *keeills* were built. To find it, take the A1 out of Douglas and turn south on B35; after 1 mile, a farm track leads east to the site. Walk along this path for about ten minutes, and the monument will be visible in the middle of a field, to the left. Its three rectangular slate slabs are set into a small drystone base: they may originally have formed a pre-Christian dolmen.

In an engraving of 1857, two more upright stones are depicted; they have since fallen. At some time between AD 400 and 700, simple crosses were carved on two of the slabs. The field is named *Magher y Chiarn*, or 'Field of the Lord'. There are remains of a holy well in the south-east corner of the field.[8] The site acquired its dedication to Patrick much later: such early saints as Patrick and Brigit became popular in medieval times.

St Trinian's Chapel, Marown

The ruins of St Trinian's chapel can be seen beside the road from Douglas to Peel, south-east of Greeba. Trinian is a Manx and Scots Gaelic form of the name Ninian; there are several churches dedicated to Trinian in northern Scotland.[9] St Ninian's Priory at Whithorn in south-west Scotland was granted land near Greeba in the twelfth century, and the chapel's south door dates from this time; it may have acquired its dedication to Ninian at this point.

There was an earlier *keeill* on the site: a sixth- or seventh-century cross slab survives, while to the right of the altar, paving stones form a plain cross within a circle, and may

St Trinian's chapel, Marown, Isle of Man.

mark the site of the founder's shrine. The Manx word for a burial ground, *rhuillick*, derives from the Latin *reliquae*, meaning 'relics'; the remains of the founding monk might be enshrined in a special grave, or placed beside the altar in the *keeill*, as at St Trinian's.

The old parish church of St Runius in Marown is dedicated to one of the saints called Rónán; the name Marown derives from 'my Rónán'. A *keeill* lies beneath the eastern half of the small church at Marown.

Daniel in the Lions' Den, Braddan

Old Kirk Braddan is off the A1, 2 miles west of Douglas. It is named after St Brendan; this is likely to be a late medieval dedication, when Brendan became a popular saint, especially among seafarers who lived on islands. The church contains twelve well-preserved sculptured crosses, most of which have runic inscriptions. A fragment of a Viking sword was found in the churchyard, and one of the largest hoards, deposited in the 970s, was found in Braddan parish, at Ballaquayle.[10]

A large wheel-headed cross at Braddan is decorated with typical Celtic interlace patterns; it dates from the ninth or tenth century. On the upper limb of the cross, a panel appears to depict the Old Testament prophet Daniel in the lions' den (Daniel 6. 2-25); this story was understood to foreshadow Christ on the cross, taming the ravenous lions of evil and death. The lions on the panel lick Daniel's face.

Daniel licked by two lions, detail from a high cross, Old Kirk Braddan, Isle of Man.

A Cross for Fiacc

Another fine cross at Braddan dates from the late tenth or early eleventh century. It is a tapering pillar over 2 metres tall, with a large, shaped tongue at its base so that it could be inserted into a socket. It is carved from fine blue slate, perhaps from Spanish Head at the south-western tip of the island. It is unique among Manx crosses in that it has a small pierced ring at the cross head; below the ring, the word 'Jesus' is carved in runes.

The body of the cross is decorated on three sides with interlaced dragons. The fourth side is inscribed in runes: 'Thorlief Hnakki erected this cross to the memory of Fiacc, his son, brother's son to Hafr'. Fiacc is a Celtic name, while those of his father and uncle are Norse. This late Norse cross tells us that Fiacc's father probably married a Celtic woman.[11] A high proportion of the names on Manx crosses are Celtic, even though they are mostly inscribed in Scandinavian runes, in the Norse language.

Interlaced dragons and other beasts are a common theme on Manx crosses. We do not know whether their carvers intended to represent the Midgard Serpent, the mighty world-serpent. In Norse mythology, the world-serpent and the god Thor will kill each other at the end of the world. Alternatively, the sculptors may be depicting Satan, the serpent or dragon whose home is in hell; this is a popular early Christian motif found on crosses elsewhere in Britain and Ireland.[12] Both types of imagery depict ever-present supernatural dangers, and perhaps the sculptors had both traditions in mind. These are likely to be reflective statements of belief, created by monastic stonemasons, perhaps from the monastery of Maughold.[13]

Slab to cover a shrine, Greeba, German, Isle of Man.

A Saint's Shrine, Greeba

A stone slab to cover a shrine was found near Greeba, in the parish of German. It dates from the seventh century or later. The cross-shaped hole would have allowed pilgrims to view or touch the remains of the monk who founded the chapel. It was found on top of a slab-lined grave, which suggests that a box-shaped shrine had been erected over the grave. There were other lintel graves at the site, sherds of medieval Manx pottery and some white quartz pebbles.[14]

A Norse plaited gold finger ring was found nearby; it might have been an offering at the shrine. Such shrines could have been created as a result of important conversions to Christianity: they might have been erected at the request of a significant convert, to honour the holy man or woman who converted him. The parish of German may be named after Garmon, a monk from Powys in north Wales, to whom Peel cathedral was also dedicated.

Speke Farm *keeill*

A *keeill* at Speke Farm, Santon, was built on the site of an early Christian cemetery. The site is on a golf course in the grounds of Mount Murray Hotel, 7 miles south-west of Douglas; it was excavated by *Time Team* for Channel 4 in 2006. The site was selected because it was one of the last remaining undisturbed *keeills*, and few of them have been excavated to modern standards. It is quite near the early cemetery at Glentraugh, where the monument to Avitus, described earlier, was discovered. The proximity of these two graveyards suggests a sizeable early Christian population in this area.

The cemetery at Speke Farm was used by Christians in the late sixth century, and was built over a Bronze Age burial mound. There were at least twenty-two burials of a normal domestic population—adults, teenagers, and perhaps a young infant, buried in a very small slab-lined grave. Those investigated by radiocarbon dating spanned two or three generations in the period 530–660. In one grave, a plait of brown hair was found, belonging to a woman aged twenty or thirty. Normally, human hair does not survive, except in dry or waterlogged conditions.[15]

A small slate slab with an ogham inscription in Old Irish was found above a skull fragment of a person aged between fourteen and twenty. The inscription is on a flat surface and uses bound letters: these are letters connected by a stem line, which makes them easier to decipher. It appears to commemorate an unidentified man, '... son of the tribe of Catialli'. The phrase is similar to that on the stone found at Ballaqueeney in 1874, described above. There are another six ogham inscriptions that use the form 'X, son (or grandson) of Y' on the Isle of Man, and two more on which the ogham alphabet is inscribed.[16]

There were large numbers of white pebbles smoothed by the water, in and around Speke *keeill*; they had been brought from a distance, from the nearest river or beach. White pebbles are a typical feature of these early chapels. A large metal bell that could have belonged to an early monastery was found in the area; it has since been lost. In 1981, an early slab incised with a cross was found here; it may have been the lintel of an early grave, later built into the chapel wall, as is typical elsewhere. To the east of the *keeill* was a small, roughly square structure formed of slate and granite slabs; it might have been the founder's grave or reliquary.[17]

Like many Manx *keeills*, this is a typical Scandinavian example built of turf and stone, probably in the tenth or early eleventh century. At its eastern end was an altar, consisting of a rectangular box 1.2 metres long and 1 metre wide, formed from thin slabs of Manx slate. The altar was filled with rubble consisting of granite stones and slate slabs, with blocks and pebbles of white quartz. Unusually, the doorway was not facing the altar but was in the south wall, at its south-west corner.[18]

A Saint's Shrine at Ronaldsway

Ten miles south-west of Douglas, at Ronaldsway in the parish of Malew, there is a *keeill* close to the airport, where the front panel of a stone altar was found, perhaps dating from the eighth century. It was later reused to form the west end of a shrine grave, to mark the burial of a local saint. It is decorated with a compass-arc of crosses; in the lower left corner, three tau crosses suggest a Calvary.

When the site was excavated, it was found that white quartz pebbles weighing several tons covered the hilltop to a depth of 20 cm; they also filled the open-topped shrine and the nearby graves. This suggests that the chapel was an important pilgrimage site for

Front panel of an altar, later used for a shrine grave, Ronaldsway, Malew, Isle of Man.

some centuries, though we do not know the holy man or woman who was buried in the shrine grave.

The medieval parish church, Kirk Christ, Malew, is also likely to be built over an early *keeill*. Malew is named after St Mo Luóc, a sixth-century Irish monk who established a monastery on the Isle of Lismore in the Hebrides, as we saw at the end of Chapter 2.

White Pebbles

Early Christian graves are often marked by numerous white quartz pebbles that symbolised prayers for the dead. This was an ancient and widespread practice: white pebbles decorate the façade of the Neolithic burial chamber at Newgrange in Ireland. On the Isle of Man, white pebbles are found in Neolithic tombs and frequently at Bronze Age burial sites; hundreds of them are found at *keeills*.

In Christian times, white stones were seen as holy. Monks were familiar with the message from St John to the church at Pergamum in the Book of Revelation at the end of the New Testament: 'To those who prove victorious, I will give a white stone, a stone with a new name written on it, known only to the one who receives it' (Revelation 2. 17).

In his *Life of Columba*, Adomnán described how a white stone was used to heal the sick and the dying in the land of the Picts. He relates that Columba sent the stone to Broichan the Druid to save him from death, on condition that he set free an Irish Christian slave girl. Adomnán adds:

> [Columba] said this in the presence of King Brude, and then left the royal house and came to the River Ness. And picking up a white stone from the river, he said to his companions,

> 'See this white stone: through this the Lord will bring about many cures of the sick among this heathen people'.[19]

On the Isle of Man, white pebbles were left at graves, especially against the south wall of a *keeill*, which seems to have been a favoured spot for the burial of significant people.

A Crucifixion from the Calf of Man

The most outstanding early Christian carving on the Isle of Man depicts the Crucifixion. It is carved in low relief and may have formed part of the front panel of an altar. The slab was discovered on the Calf of Man in 1773, when the ruins of a *keeill* were being demolished; it is now in the Manx Museum, Douglas. It is made of local slate, and dates from the late seventh or early eighth century; it would have been a little less than 1 metre in height. Similar crucifixion imagery can be seen on Irish bronze metal plates: an example from Rinnagan, County Roscommon, beside the River Shannon near Athlone, perhaps formed the decoration for the cover of a gospel book.[20]

In the carving on the Calf of Man, Christ is portrayed alive, with open eyes and clothed in royal robes. A large circular ornamented feature at the centre of Christ's body suggests that the sculptor worked from a bronze prototype; it resembles a decorative rivet-head. Beneath Christ's outstretched right arm is a centurion with a spear, about to pierce his side. There would have been another soldier offering Christ vinegar to drink from a stick,

The Crucifixion, perhaps from the front panel of an altar, Calf of Man.

beneath his left arm. The soldiers' actions are described in St John's Gospel (John 19. 29, 34). Similar sculptures indicate that there would have been two angels above the arms of Christ's cross; an angel's foot can be seen above Christ's right shoulder.

Hollow of the Chapel

Lag ny Keeilley, or 'Hollow of the Chapel' is in Patrick parish on the south-west coast of the Isle of Man, 6 miles north of Port St Mary. It is in a beautiful location, where hills fall steeply to the sea and seals bask on the rocks. It can be reached by walking less than a mile along a track from Eary Cushlin car park. In earlier times, this was the packhorse road to the south of the island.

People continued to bring their dead along the track for burial at Lag ny Keeilley until about 1800. An elderly parishioner from Eary Cushlin recalled the last funeral held there; the corpse was wrapped in a winding sheet and strapped to the back of an old mare, supported by a bundle of straw that served as a saddle. The horse was led down the long track to the little burial ground surrounding the chapel.[21]

The solitary monk who founded the *keeill* had levelled the enclosure with considerable effort by digging into the hillside and building up a level platform. Within a retaining embankment, he constructed the chapel and a rectangular stone dwelling for himself. The altar of the *keeill* survives, built of small slabs laid lengthways; a pear-shaped stone that had been brought up the steep track from the beach formed one of its supporting pillars.[22]

Keeill facing the sea, Lag ny Keeilley, Patrick, Isle of Man.

Above the altar was a window with a carved sandstone head. A slab of local slate with a hollow cup in one corner was probably a cresset, containing oil and a wick for a lamp. Some flat stones survive from the original floor, as does the stone socket for a door in the west wall.[23] This is an unusual feature; instead of a door, many are thought to have been closed by a *scraa*, or bundle of willow shoots with a band of heather round the middle. A stick twisted into the band would catch the wall on either side and block the entrance.

Near the *keeill* was a small garden plot for growing vegetables. A piece of a granite quern found near the chapel may indicate that the priest baked bread, or it could have been brought by a penitent: as we have seen, those caught grinding corn in Ireland on a Sunday brought their quern to the church, and smashed it as a penance.[24] The same may have been true on the Isle of Man, since quern fragments are common at *keeill* sites.

The burial ground contains stone-lined lintel graves and three slabs incised with simple crosses. Around 500–600 white quartz pebbles were found in or near the *keeill*, suggesting that it continued as a place of pilgrimage. Near the end of the packhorse road, almost within sight of the chapel, is a spring named *Chibbyr ny Vashtey* in Manx, or 'Well of Baptism' (see colour plate 20); it was visited for healing until the 1900s.[25]

St Patrick's Isle, Peel

St Patrick's Isle at Peel is situated halfway along the west coast of the Isle of Man. Until the eighteenth century it was a tidal islet, accessible on foot at low tide. There is now a causeway leading to the island, which is dominated by the medieval cathedral of St German and a later castle. The islet was inhabited from early times, and a number of large round-houses dating from about 400 BC have been excavated.

There was an extensive early Christian cemetery at the southern end of the islet, near the medieval cathedral; many of the burials date from about 550 onwards. The ruins of a church, a chapel, and a round tower survive, each dating in part from the tenth century. St Patrick's church was constructed of roughly dressed local red sandstone. It had *antae*, or side walls projecting beyond the line of the gables; this style of building was common in Ireland. St Patrick's chapel is smaller, but of similar construction.[26] The front panel of an early stone altar was found when the two buildings were restored in 1873. It is decorated with five small crosses set within a larger, fainter one (see photo overleaf).

The squat round tower is 15 metres high; four windows facing the compass points near the top indicate that this was its original height. It, too, is built of Old Red Sandstone; its battlemented parapet was added in about 1600. Early Christian lintel graves and crosses were found beneath the south transept of the cathedral. The islet became a base for Norse settlers who built a fort of timber or 'pile', which gave Peel its name.[27]

There were at least seven Viking burials within the Christian cemetery beneath Peel castle. The most unusual grave was that of a middle-aged Viking woman who was buried in a slab-lined grave in the tenth century, with her head resting on a feather pillow. She had a magnificent necklace of seventy-three glass, amber, and jet beads, some already

Front panel of a stone altar, decorated with crosses, Peel, German, Isle of Man.

centuries old. She was buried together with unusual objects: two knives, iron shears, and a comb, while on her chest was a pouch containing tiny metal utensils. A small pestle and mortar may have been used to prepare medicines or cosmetics.[28]

At her side was an iron staff 1 metre long, covered with several types of textile and feathers, probably from a goose wing. The iron rod might have been a poker or a roasting spit; alternatively, the woman may have been a shaman, and this could be her staff of office. A carved stone from Kirk Michael depicts a cloaked woman with a similar rod that has split terminals, branching like a plant. There are depictions of a shaman's staff in Denmark and Norway, but the woman's grave at Peel is unique.[29]

Patrick's Chapel at the White Waterfall, Spooyt Vane

Spooyt Vane means 'spout bright' or 'white waterfall'; it is on the west coast 6 miles north-east of Peel, along a signed track off the A1, just south of Kirk Michael. While some *keeills* were in settlements, others such as this were more isolated. Patrick's Chapel (or *Cabbal Pherick* in Manx) at Spooyt Vane is in a wooded glade close to a waterfall, beside a river. The chapel's walls were probably built of slate, with a thatched roof on a timber frame. The altar under the east window was outlined with small stones set on edge, and faced with larger stones.

The priest lived in a hut outside the banked enclosure, with a small well to the west that could have been used for baptisms and for drinking water. There was a burial ground,

Above left: Patrick's chapel, Spooyt Vane, Michael, Isle of Man.

Above right: Waterfall above the chapel, Spooyt Vane, Michael, Isle of Man.

and some slabs carved with simple crosses; they are now in the parish church at Kirk Michael. Only a few white pebbles were found at the site; this suggests that the monk who lived there may have been a hermit, whose retreat was not visited by many pilgrims.

Kirk Michael's Crosses

Kirk Michael church on the north-west coast contains twelve Norse crosses; this forms the largest collection on the island. The head of one cross slab, dedicated to 'Grim the Black', dates from the late tenth or the early eleventh century. Christ is depicted on the cross, wearing a kilt; a semi-circular halo decorated with three small crosses adorns his head. In the upper corners, a cock and a winged angel herald the resurrection—the cock heralds the dawn of a new day for humanity and the angels announce the resurrection to Christ's disciples.

It is unusual for a cross slab to depict the crucifixion: there are fewer than twenty such representations in early medieval British art. As in the carving of the Crucifixion from the Calf of Man and other sculptures from this period, Christ is depicted in glory on the cross.[30] On the reverse side, the corners contain a dragon and the god Óðinn with a raven at his head. Óðinn was the chief god in Norse mythology, the most ancient ruler of their realm, and father of them all.

On another cross slab, the sculptor has carved a ring cross with interlaced panels. On each side of the shaft are animals and figures, including a harper playing a four-stringed harp above another figure who clasps a long drinking horn; two more figures are robed like monks. Harps are rarely depicted on crosses, though there is another on the Dupplin cross, described in Chapter 5. The reverse side of the cross is plain, apart from two inscriptions. One in runes reads: 'Mal Lumkun erected this cross to the memory of Mal-Mura, his foster mother, daughter of Dugald, the wife whom Athisl [or Athish] had'. A comment, or perhaps a proverb, is added in ogham: 'It is better to leave a good foster son than a bad son'.[31]

Gaut the Sculptor

Another cross slab at Kirk Michael was carved by the finest sculptor on the island, named Gaut, perhaps in about 900. The cross stands 2 metres high and bears an inscription in runes along its edge that appears to read: 'Mælbrigde, son of Athakan the smith, raised this cross for his own soul [?to be saved from] sin, but Gaut made this and all in Man'. The long inscription extends up one side of the cross slab and continues round the cross head. The final sentence indicates that Gaut was the chief sculptor in this district.[32]

A runic inscription on a cross from Kirk Andreas reads: 'Gaut made [this], son of Björn from Kolli'. This may mean that Gaut's family came from the island of Coll in the Hebrides, north of Iona.[33] As we saw in Chapter 1, Iona's monks grew grain on Coll to feed their community. Gaut's strong, clear style combines Celtic and Norse elements; it is closer to Scottish than to Irish models. Other crosses on the island are attributed to him; his work was copied and developed by other stonemasons.

Heimdallr's Yelling Horn, Jurby

St Patrick's church at Jurby is 6 miles north of Kirk Michael. It is close to the shore on the exposed north-west coast of the island. On a clear day, one can see down the coast to Peel and across the Irish Sea to Scotland and Ireland. There was a small *keeill*, perhaps dating from the eighth century, about 300 metres south-west of the church. In medieval times, the church belonged to the diocese of Whithorn in Galloway; the dedication to St Patrick is a late one.

One of the cross slabs at Jurby church, dating from the late tenth century, depicts Heimdallr, the watchman of the gods, who sits at the edge of heaven, guarding the rainbow bridge that joins earth to Asgard, the home of the gods. Heimdallr stands above an arm of Christ's cross; he wears a buttoned tunic and a helmet, and is armed with a sword. He blows his giant *Gjallarhorn* (or 'yelling horn') in order to summon the gods to the world's final battle, which is named Ragnarök in Norse mythology. A raven flies ahead of him, bringing news of the battle to the god Óðinn.[34]

Heimdallr blows his horn to summon the gods to the world's final battle. Detail from a cross in St Patrick's church, Jurby, Isle of Man.

Within the circular walled enclosure surrounding the church is a Viking burial site; others have been found in the parish of Jurby, including one at Ballateare, where the mutilated remains of a female slave were found, aged twenty or thirty; she appears to have been buried above her master in order to accompany him into the next life. The back of her skull had been sliced off, probably with a sword. There is evidence of such ritual killings in Scandinavia and elsewhere in Europe. Above her body, the cremated bones of a dog, a horse, an ox, and a sheep were scattered, so they too could accompany their owner after his death.[35]

Knock-y-Dooney, 'Sunday Place'

Knock-y-Dooney is in the parish of Andreas, on the north-west coast of the island, 5 miles north-east of Jurby; it is the site of a Viking ship burial and of a *keeill*. Knock-y-Dooney is one of three Manx place names that incorporate the word *doonee*, meaning 'Sunday' or 'church'. It is an early word deriving from the Latin *dominica*, which was taken into the Irish language as *domnach*. The word was in use only from about 430 to 550, and is not found in Scotland or Wales. It is likely that its usage spread to the Isle of Man from Ireland, and that the Manx *doonee* churches were founded by Irish missionaries or emigrants.[36]

The first reference to Knock-y-Dooney dates from 1627, where its name is translated as 'Sonday hill'; the outline of its *keeill* can still be seen. One of the four early gravestones on the Isle of Man with Latin inscriptions was found at Knock-y-Dooney: it is an early sixth-century pillar stone with an inscription in Irish ogham carved up one side. The text is repeated in Latin in rusticated Roman capitals, on the broad face of the stone. It reads: 'Ammecatus, son of Rocatus, lies here'. These are Irish names, so the chapel may have been attached to the home of a local Irish chieftain. The stone resembles those found in north Wales; it was perhaps carved by a monastic sculptor from the well-established Romano-British church in the Conwy Valley.[37]

Scenes from Norse Myths at Kirk Andreas

Not far from Knock-y-Dooney, Kirk Andreas (or St Andrew's church) is built over a *keeill* dedicated to Columba. One of the finest collections of tenth-century Norse cross slabs can be seen here, including eleven with decorative motifs, runic inscriptions, and carved figures. On one stone, Sigurd the Dragon Slayer roasts the heart of the dragon Fafnir; he holds a skewer over the fire, with portions of its heart simmering like a kebab on a stick. At the same time, he puts his burnt fingers into his mouth and as he tastes the dragon's blood, he gains the ability to understand the language of the birds.[38]

Another tenth-century cross fragment depicts the last great battle, Ragnarök, between the gods and the forces of evil, that takes place at the end of time, when many gods will perish. An inscription in runes down the edge of the cross reads:

Thorwald erected this cross.
Then there shall come One yet mightier,
though him I dare not name.

This is one of a series of crosses unique to the Isle of Man in which scenes from Norse mythology are combined with Christian themes. On one side, Christ treads the ancient serpent, Satan, underfoot, holding aloft his cross and a gospel book. Beneath the cross, a fish is another early symbol for Christ—the letters of the Greek word 'fish' form the initials of the title 'Jesus Christ, Son of God, Saviour'.

The runic inscription offers a rare insight into the beliefs of Viking Christians on the island. Thorwald and his fellow Christian chieftains appear to have valued the mythology of their ancestors, while placing it within the new context of Christianity. Christ is the 'One yet mightier' than Sigurd the Dragon Slayer. Perhaps Viking Christians viewed their mythology as a preparation for Christianity, in the same way that early Jewish Christians saw Christ foreshadowed in the Old Testament.

On the reverse side of Thorwald's cross, the god Óðinn, depicted with a raven on his shoulder, is devoured by a wolf in the final battle of Ragnarök. The wolf has already eaten Óðinn's right foot. Another tenth-century cross slab at Andreas was erected by Sandulf in memory of his wife, who is shown sitting side-saddle on her horse. On one edge of the slab, an inscription in runes reads: 'Sandulf the Black erected this cross in memory of Arinbiörg, his wife'.[39]

Above left: Sixth-century pillar stone, inscribed in Latin, 'Ammecatus, son of Rocatus, lies here', Knock-y-Dooney, Andreas, Isle of Man.

Above right: Christ treads Satan underfoot, from a cross fragment, Kirk Andreas, Isle of Man.

A Window from a *Keeill*, Ballavarkish

The parish of Bride, at the north-eastern end of the island, is named after St Brigit of Kildare: it is a late medieval dedication. Bride church contains a stone with a runic inscription and a small group of carved stones with graffiti in a Roman script; these suggest that their sculptors were monks with a knowledge of church Latin.

Ballavarkish (or St Mark's) *keeill*, in the parish of Bride, is on a farm; a field to the south-west of the farm buildings is known as *Faie Rollag*, or 'enclosure of the cemetery'. A small window frame with two lights, carved from Old Red Sandstone, was found beside the low mound of the former *keeill* (see photo overleaf). Most of the chapel's stones had been removed for later use elsewhere, except from some foundation stones that were boulders collected from the sea shore. A large stone near the middle of the west wall was probably one of its door jambs.[40]

There are several graves to the west of the *keeill*, formed of long lintels and small, flat slabs. Each grave was covered with a layer of white quartz pebbles from the sea shore. At a level lower than the chapel, there was a pathway of carefully fitted water-worn slabs,

Stone window frame with two lights, from Ballavarkish *keeill*, Bride, Isle of Man.

leading to the graves. Inside the *keeill* was the broken upper stone of a granite quern and part of an ornamented cross slab with an inscription in ogham and Latin. A hollowed granite cresset to contain oil for a lamp was also found. There was a holy well named *Chibbyr-y-Varkish* (or St Mark's well) that was visited for sore eyes and other diseases in a field beside the road to the house, 50 metres north-west of the *keeill*.[41]

A Monastery at Kirk Maughold

Kirk Maughold is on the north-east coast of the island, on a hillside above the sea, 8 miles south-east of Kirk Andreas. A monastery may have been established here by the mid-seventh century; some of the earliest Manx crosses were found here. It perhaps contained a library, a scriptorium, and a stone mason's workshop. The present church dates from the twelfth century, but within the graveyard are the remains of three *keeills*, and the sites of three more, including two beneath the medieval church. Each was surrounded by a small cemetery.

Keeill with a later well at its south-east corner, Maughold monastery, Isle of Man.

Maughold was the principal monastery on the Isle of Man. The earliest surviving stone slab, Irneit's cross, suggests that monks may have come from Ireland and even from Gaul, as we shall see. Others perhaps came from north Wales, Northumbria, and Galloway in south-west Scotland. The buildings were probably of timber, like those of Northumbrian monasteries. Some of its monuments appear to have been carved by itinerant Anglian stonemasons. Iron ore was mined at Maughold, which enabled smiths to create metal objects.

By AD 795, the Vikings had begun to rob exposed places on the coast, and Maughold was an easy target. By about 830, colonists arrived and took possession of the arable land. Without land, the monastery could not continue; for a time, no further monuments were constructed here. Norsemen buried their dead in the cemetery, for some graves contain their weapons, including a sword dating from about 900.

The Origin of Maughold's Name

There was a powerful spring on the site, and Norsemen may have named the place *Makt-kelda*, meaning 'forceful spring'.[42] In his *Life of Patrick* (*c.* 1186), the monk Jocelin of Furness described the spring as St Machaldus' well, and offered another meaning of the monastery's name. He linked it with the story of an Irish adventurer told by Muirchú, the seventh-century biographer of St Patrick. Muirchú described a cruel tyrant named Macc Cuill and his dramatic conversion to a holy life. Macc Cuill killed travellers passing through his territory, and when he heard that Patrick was coming, he planned to murder him, but Patrick survived and restored a dead man to life.

According to the story, this miracle converted the tyrant, who then declared his belief in God, confessed his sins, and asked to do penance. Patrick ordered him to abandon everything and set off in a small boat without oars or a rudder. Macc Cuill was set adrift and arrived on the Isle of Man, where two holy bishops trained him. Eventually, he too became a bishop. By telling the story of how a wicked man became a fervent Christian, Muirchú presented a model of holy living. It was based on earlier moral tales: Cassian recounts how one of the desert fathers, Abba Moses, began as a murderer, but was converted and became a wise and holy monk.[43]

Life at the Monastery

It is considered unlikely that there was a Manx saint named Maughold, but we gain glimpses of the monks who lived at the monastery from its fine collection of carved stone slabs. The oldest, as we have seen, is a memorial to Irneit, a seventh-century monastic bishop. His name is inscribed in a circle surrounding a hexafoil cross. This design, resembling a six-petalled flower, is found in post-Roman Britain and Gaul, so the stonemason probably learnt his skill abroad.[44] Below the cross, the monastic sculptor wrote in Latin, using Hiberno-Saxon characters: 'I have made in Christ's name an image of the cross of Christ'.

Bishop Irneit's memorial slab, AD 650–700, Maughold, Isle of Man.

Another slab is inscribed in Latin: 'Branhui led off water to this place.' Branhui was a monk with a Welsh name who provided the monastery with its water supply in about 800. Traces of his stone-lined conduit have been found. Water-powered corn mills with horizontal wheels may have been introduced to the island by monks, probably influenced by Irish monasteries. The corn mills could operate with a small water supply, often led from some distance through wooden troughs. This design remained in use on the island until the nineteenth century.[45]

A ninth-century cross depicts two desert fathers who inspired Celtic monks: St Antony and Paul the Hermit. They sit on solid chairs on either side of a ringed cross, each bearded and dressed in a monk's cowl and hood. Another cross from the same period may have been a memorial to a British king of the Isle of Man named Guriat, whose son came to rule north Wales. It formerly stood at the roadside between Maughold and Ramsey, 3 miles to the north-west.[46]

Runes

Several different types of runes are carved on the cross slabs at Maughold; this suggests that monks who joined the monastery came from various ethnic and cultural backgrounds. The runic alphabet probably originated in first-century Scandinavia; it appears to be derived from the Roman alphabet. So far, runic inscriptions have been discovered on thirty-five Manx crosses; they mainly employ Viking runes.[47]

The runic alphabet is called fuþark (or futhark) after its first six letters. Most Manx crosses use the 'short twig' variant of fuþark, but one cross at Kirk Michael displays the other 'long branch' variant—the names describe the shape of the letters. One inscription at Maughold is carved in a combination of both variants. A cross slab from Kirk Andreas contains cryptic runes that have yet to be deciphered.[48]

The runic inscriptions on two of the carved slabs at Maughold are in Old English instead of Old Norse, so the carver used Anglo-Saxon runes. The two Anglo-Saxon inscriptions both consist of personal names, one of which appears to be the common Old English name Blaecmon (or Blackman). It features on one of a pair of eighth-century stones from the head and foot of a grave. Blaecmon's name is Saxon, but the style of the cross is Celtic; it illustrates how Teutonic settlers spread across northern Britain and adopted Celtic culture.

John, the Priest

John the priest lived at Coroney *keeill*, in an isolated location on the slope of North Barrule, west-south-west of Cornaa farmhouse. It is 3 miles west of Maughold, and is also known as *Keeill Woirrey* (or St Mary's chapel). Like a number of others, it was built at an ancient holy site: remains of a Bronze Age burial were found here. Excavations between the altar and the north wall revealed the paved floor of an earlier chapel beneath the later *keeill*. In the enclosure surrounding the *keeill* were graves with simple markers at their head made of mountain stones set on end; some also had stones at the foot and at each corner.

Three crosses were found, and they are now located at Maughold. On one of the cross slabs, John the priest practised carving the runic alphabet. In English, the inscription reads: 'Ióan, priest, carved these runes'. The alphabet follows, beginning with '[f]uþark'. The runes are as follows: iuan + brist + raisti + þasir + [f]uþarkhniastbmlt.[49] Below the Norse runes, John also carved an alphabet in ogham.

He carved another runic inscription, which reads: 'Christ, Malachi, Patrick and Adomnán. But of all the sheep in Cornadale, John is priest'. His invocation of Malachi dates the stone to the twelfth century, since the Irish monk Malachi, who was an abbot of Bangor and archbishop of Armagh, died in 1148. John may have been the shepherd of both the sheep and the people in the Cornaa valley.

Adomnán's *Keeill* at Old Kirk Lonan

Old Kirk Lonan in Onchan parish is 12 miles south of Maughold. In Ireland and Scotland, Adomnán's name was sometimes shortened to 'Onan', and Lonan is an abbreviation of *Keeill Onan*. The church is built within an early cemetery. An impressive wheel-headed cross in the churchyard still stands, unusually, in its socket stone, which is probably in its original position; it is decorated entirely with interlacing, knots, and plaits. The large cross stands 1.5 metre high and is 1 metre wide; it dates from the ninth or tenth century.

There is a fine collection of crosses at the church. Hundreds of white quartz pebbles were found at Old Kirk Lonan, in two locations: around the slab-lined graves in the churchyard and close to the well at the lower corner of the glebe land that belongs to the church. This suggests that Kirk Lonan may have been a place of pilgrimage.

Although it is tantalising that so little is recorded about the monks, nuns, hermits, and pilgrims who lived on the Isle of Man, at least we catch a glimpse of the monks: John the priest, Gaut the Scottish sculptor, and Branhui the Welsh plumber. There may have been only one significant Manx monastery—that of Maughold—but it is astonishing that there are 170 *keeill* sites and remains of almost 200 carved crosses on an island that is only 32 miles long and 12 miles wide. Furthermore, remains of saints' shrines surrounded by vast quantities of white pebbles suggest a vibrant church in which local people were fully involved.

Wheel-headed cross, standing in its socket stone, Old Kirk Lonan, Isle of Man.

9

Aidan and Northumbria

In early times, English history was entwined with that of Scotland. Northumbrians, Britons, and Anglians made incursions into present-day Scotland, where they occupied territory for considerable periods. In the eighth and ninth centuries, the kingdom of Northumbria extended from the River Humber at the northern boundary of Lincolnshire to the Firths of Forth and Clyde in east and west Scotland.

The Britons and the Anglians tried to expand into Pictish territory. There seem to have been three Pictish kings of British descent between AD 631 and 653, but from then until 685, Anglian puppet kings dominated the land of the Picts. The Anglian king Ecgfrith massacred a Pictish army, which included many of the aristocracy, and seized control of much of Scotland. Bede relates that this was because the Picts had stopped paying tribute to Northumbria.[1]

Meanwhile, Bridei, son of Beli, a Pict who was possibly born of a British father and brought up in the Northumbrian court, attacked forts in Perth and Kinross, and 'the Orkneys were destroyed'. In 685, he routed the Anglians at the Battle of Dunnichen, known as *Nechtansmere* by the Anglians. Dunnichen was formerly thought to be in central Scotland, near Aberlemno in Angus, but the battle is now considered to have taken place in northern Scotland.[2] It is remarkable that the Anglians travelled such a distance in order to fight for territory beyond their own borders.

Christianity in Roman Northumbria

Christianity reached Northumbria in Roman times. A roof tile on which the *chi-rho* symbol for Christ was scratched and a silver finger ring with Christian symbols were found in York. Both date from the third century, before the Emperor Constantine legitimised Christianity in AD 313. Few Christian objects survive from this early date because Christians could expect persecution and therefore kept their faith private.

In 2014, a second silver ring dating from the third century was found at the Roman fort of Binchester in County Durham. It is set with a carnelian gemstone of translucent red quartz, carved with Christian imagery familiar from mainland Europe: a cross-shaped anchor with a fish on either side. Since this valuable ring was found at a fort, it may have belonged to a soldier of high rank.[3]

Research carried out in 2010 on isotopes from the teeth of a young woman from a fourth-century grave in York indicated that she was a wealthy African of black or mixed race, between eighteen and twenty-three years old. Her fine stone sarcophagus had been discovered in Bootham, near the centre of York, in 1901. Her grave contained expensive objects: a glass flagon and necklace, an ivory bangle that might have come from her African homeland, and a bracelet of black jet, probably from Whitby. A bone was found beside her with what appears to be a Christian inscription: 'Hail, sister, may you live in God' (*Sor, ave, vivas in Deo*).[4] Christianity reached North Africa early: St Augustine (354–430) was born at Thagaste in modern Algeria.

Christianity on Hadrian's Wall

At a number of garrisons along Hadrian's Wall, there are rectangular buildings with an apse at the western end; they appear to have been Christian churches. At Vindolanda (or Chesterholm) in Northumberland, 10 miles west of Hexham, the possible church stood in the courtyard of the *praetorium*, or personal residence of the fort's commander; its stone foundations were laid over the flagstones of the yard. It may have been built a little after AD 400, when the courtyard had been abandoned, since the church was 20 cm above the floor of the courtyard.[5]

An earlier apsed building, which may have been a church, was excavated at nearby Housesteads (Northumberland) in 1898; it lies north-west of the Roman fort. Another probable church was found at South Shields (Tyne and Wear), built on the site of the *principia*, or fort's headquarters. It appears to contain a Christian altar, within an eastern apse. The west end of the church may have been attached to a colonnade that surrounded the courtyard, which could have served as a narthex or entrance area for the church. It probably dates to the late fourth or early fifth century.

The churches at Vindolanda and South Shields are both built on the site of military headquarters and are of late date. Their prominent position suggests that they may have replaced earlier pagan regimental shrines. There are similar Roman Christian churches in Germany at forts on the frontier formed by the Danube and the Rhine.[6]

Christian Monuments to the Dead

There is a possible Christian burial inscription, not on a tombstone but on the side of a small child's stone coffin found in York, south-west of the railway station, in an early cemetery. It reads: 'To the spirits of the departed [and] of Simplicia Florentina, a most innocent soul, who lived ten months. Her father, Felicius Simplex, [a soldier] of the Sixth Legion Victrix, made this'. The phrase 'innocent soul' (*anime innocentissime*) suggests a belief in the soul, and the name Simplicia was popular with early Christians.[7]

Three Cumbrian inscriptions giving a person's name and age are simply carved onto rough stone grave slabs, and date from the fifth century. There are two from Maryport on the Cumbrian coast and one from Old Carlisle; they resemble Christian inscriptions on tombstones elsewhere. A possible gravestone fragment from Maryport had the *chi-rho* symbol for Christ carved on it. It was a stone plaque, but is now lost; only a drawing of it survives. There are other fifth- and sixth-century Christian stones in this region.

The names recorded on the gravestones are of men, women, and children. One from Maryport, to Tancorix, and that from Old Carlisle, to Rianorix, employ the native British suffix *-rix*, meaning 'kingly'. The names on tombstones at forts are those of soldiers and civilians, women and children, natives and foreigners. This suggests that churches at forts served the broader community. There seems to have been a baptismal font at Housesteads; this implies an active congregation, with people undergoing instruction and religious formation.[8]

We could think of their priests as army chaplains, with responsibility for military families and perhaps for the population of the *vicus*, or civil settlement that normally served each fort, and for those who lived in the surrounding countryside. For Hadrian's Wall was not a bleak outpost in a barren land; farmers cleared the dense woodland to till the soil, grow food, and pasture their livestock long before the great wall was built. Tim Gates, an aerial archaeologist, has photographed over 200 previously unidentified agricultural sites and six late Iron Age or Romano-British settlements along Hadrian's Wall, with rectangular enclosures, remains of stone buildings, and signs of field systems.[9]

Bede, the Historian

The development of Christianity in Northumbria after the departure of the Romans is described by Bede (672–735), who was considered the most learned man of his time. Bede was an English monk of Monkwearmouth and its companion monastery at nearby Jarrow, in Sunderland. He was an author and scholar who recorded most of what we know about the early history of Northumbria and its surrounding kingdoms in his *Historia ecclesiastica gentis Anglorum*, or the *Ecclesiastical History of the English People*. Bede was also a skilled linguist and translator, who made the Latin and Greek writings of the early Church Fathers accessible to his fellow Anglo-Saxons.

After compiling information for many years, at the age of fifty-nine Bede wrote his *Ecclesiastical History*, in which he also tells us about himself:

> This much of the ecclesiastical history of Britain ... as far as I could learn, either from the writings of the ancients, or the tradition of our ancestors, or of my own knowledge, has, with the help of God, been digested by me, Bede, the servant of God, and priest of the monastery of the blessed apostles Peter and Paul, which is at Wearmouth and Jarrow.
>
> Being born in the territory of that same monastery, I was given, at seven years of age, to be educated by the most reverend abbot Benedict [Biscop], and afterwards by Ceolfrith.

Model of the Saxon monastery at Jarrow, where Bede spent most of his life.

> Spending all the remaining time of my life in that monastery, I wholly applied myself to the study of Scripture … and amidst the daily care of singing in the church, I always took delight in learning, teaching and writing. At the age of nineteen I received deacon's orders; and at thirty, those of priesthood.[10]

As a lad, Bede probably accompanied Abbot Ceolfrith from Monkwearmouth to Jarrow, to continue his education. In 686, the plague struck both monasteries; Ceolfrith and the fourteen-year-old Bede cared for the infected and dying monks. The *Life of Ceolfrith*, written in about 710, recounts that only two survivors were capable of singing the full office—Ceolfrith and a young boy who had been taught by him; this would have been Bede.

Bede's Books

Jarrow had a famous library, which enabled Bede to become acquainted with such authors as Pliny, Virgil, Ovid, and Horace, partly through digests of their work. At the time of his death, he was working on a translation of St John's gospel into English. Earlier, he wrote books designed to teach grammar in the abbey school, where Cuthbert was one of his students. Bede dedicated *De arte metrica*, on the composition of Latin, to Cuthbert, 'his beloved son', and wrote: 'I have laboured to educate you in divine letters and Church laws'.

Bede's *Ecclesiastical History* was completed in about 731. It begins with the advent of the Romans, but his sources become accurate only when they describe facts nearer to Bede's lifetime. He adopted and promoted our continuous dating system. Until this point, various fifteen-year cycles had been used for dating, and also a system of regnal years, counting from the start of the ruler's reign over the kingdom under discussion.

The purpose of the *Ecclesiastical History* was to demonstrate the harmonious growth of the church throughout England, although the book contains more information about Northumbria than about Wessex and Mercia, regions with which Bede was less familiar. Another aim of the work was to present models of holy living: saintly kings and queens, bishops, monks, and nuns, both Celtic and Saxon, to inspire leaders in what Bede considered a somewhat degenerate age.

King Edwin becomes a Christian

Bede relates how Archbishop Paulinus came from Canterbury to Northumbria and baptized King Edwin (586–633) at York on Easter day in 627. Edwin's family and his courtiers were baptised in their turn, and Paulinus spent the next six years, until Edwin's death, evangelising the region. Bede describes how Paulinus used Edwin's royal country seat (*villa regia*) at Yeavering for this purpose.

Yeavering is beside the River Glen, at the edge of the Cheviot Hills, 19 miles south of Berwick-upon-Tweed. There was an Iron Age hill fort at Yeavering, and during Edwin's reign, a series of fine halls were built at the site. The quality of the wood used in their construction, and the height of the walls and roofs suggest that they were perhaps built as sleeping quarters for the royal court. Bede recounts how Edwin's people were instructed:

> So great was then the fervour of the faith … that Paulinus at a certain time coming with the king and queen to the royal country seat, which is called Adgefrin [or Yeavering], stayed there with them thirty-six days, fully occupied in catechising and baptising; during which days, from morning till night, he did nothing else but instruct the people resorting from all villages and places, in Christ's saving word; and when instructed, he washed them with the water of baptism in the river Glen, which is close by.[11]

There had been an earlier pagan temple at the site, inside which was a pit full of the skulls of oxen that had probably been sacrificed. Here, Edwin had ordered the construction of a unique wedge-shaped grandstand. It resembled a wooden amphitheatre, and could seat 150 people; it was later doubled in size. The people would have sat facing a small platform on which a few leaders could stand.[12]

It is possible that this stadium was constructed for Archbishop Paulinus to instruct the new converts. He would have known the Roman theatre in Canterbury, which was the only similar building in Britain. When Bede relates that Paulinus instructed the converts for thirty-six days, he may refer to the customary practice of instructing converts throughout Lent and baptising them at Easter.[13]

Paulinus was able to preach the gospel in Northumbria because King Edwin had married Æthelburg, a Christian princess from Kent. Three artefacts excavated at

Yeavering suggest the presence of Kentish courtiers. First, an iron buckle inlaid with silver, dated between 570 and 640, is of a type made on mainland Europe and otherwise known only in Kent. Secondly, a small filigree ring resembles settings that surround red garnets on many disc brooches made in Kent. Thirdly, a gold-plated imitation coin dating from about 630 was found: these were more frequent in Kent than anywhere else in England.[14]

Oswald, a Warrior Saint

Oswald (*c.* 604–42) was twenty years younger than Edwin; he was the eldest son of the pagan Æthelfrith, King of Bernicia. When Edwin conquered Northumbria, Oswald's family fled to Argyll, where they were converted to Christianity by monks from Iona. Oswald returned at the age of about thirty to his homeland on the River Tweed. Cadwallon, King of Mercia, now occupied Northumbria, but Oswald defeated him in battle at Heavenfield, near Hexham, despite his army being heavily outnumbered.

Although Oswald was Christian, most of his army was probably still pagan. Oswald is said to have set up a cross outside Hexham to mark his victory; this formed a focus for Oswald's later cult, from which the church at Hexham was to benefit considerably.[15] Oswald married the daughter of the king of Wessex, and other Anglo-Saxon kings acknowledged him as their overlord.

Both Adomnán and Bede held Oswald in high regard for his faith, his goodness, and his authority. Adomnán states that he became 'emperor of all Britain' (*imperator totius Brittaniae*).[16] Bede writes that he held authority over all the English and British, except those in Kent. Later, Bede adds: 'he brought under his dominion all the nations and provinces of Britain, which are divided into four languages, *viz.* the Britons, the Picts, the Scots and the English'.[17] Adomnán even relates that before the great battle at Heavenfield, Columba had appeared to Oswald in a vision and promised him victory.[18]

Was Oswald a Model King?

However, Adomnán and Bede wrote about Oswald a century after his death, at a time when he was revered as a soldier saint and a martyr; they honour his cult status, but a closer reading of Bede demonstrates that Oswald was not entirely successful or flawless. Bede was careful to praise his character rather than his conquests, and avoided calling him a martyr. He recounts Oswald's successes, while omitting to mention his struggles with the Saxons. The Irish Annals of Tigernach and of Clonmacnoise record that in about 639, there was 'an alliance of Saxons against Oswald'.[19]

Although Bede relates that Oswald subjugated the Picts and Scots, he undermines this claim by stating that it was Oswald's brother Oswiu, who compelled the Picts and Scots to pay tribute to the king of Northumbria. Bede also states that Northumbria was pagan until Oswald's time, despite the fact that the previous ruler, Cadwallon, was Christian, and that before Cadwallon's time, Bede tells us how Archbishop Paulinus baptised many people at King Edwin's request.[20] Although Bede does not present Oswald as an aggressor, his warfare was mainly offensive. When he died, he was fighting in enemy territory, if Maserfield is indeed close to Oswestry.[21]

Bede also hints that Oswald was unpopular beyond his own native kingdom; when his neice Osryth, queen of Mercia, removed his relics to the double monastery of monks and nuns at Bardney, 9 miles east of Lincoln, Bede relates that its monks at first refused to receive them:

> When the wagon in which [Oswald's] bones were carried arrived towards evening at the aforesaid monastery, they that were in it refused to admit them, because, though they knew him to be a holy man, yet, as he was originally of another province, and had reigned over them as a foreign king, they retained their ancient aversion to him, even after death. Thus it came to pass that the relics were left in the open air all night, with only a large tent spread over them.[22]

It took a miracle to change their minds. It appears that Bede was a little economical with the facts, since he was concerned to present Oswald as the ideal Northumbrian king, and a model for those who would follow him.

Oswald's Personality

When Bede describes Oswald's personality, however, he was able to draw on the knowledge of elderly monks in his own community, and the young king comes to life. Bede tells us that since Oswald wished his people to become Christian, he sent to Iona for a bishop to convert his subjects:

> When King Oswald asked for a Scottish bishop to preach the gospel to himself and his people, first [Colmán] was sent, an austere man who was unsuccessful. The English people ignored him, so he returned home, and reported to the assembled council [on Iona] that he had been unable to do any good among the people to whom he was sent to preach. They were uncivilised, stubborn and barbarous.[23]

The monks on Iona discussed what to do, and an Irishman named Aidan suggested that Colmán might have been too severe. The community therefore decided to consecrate Aidan as bishop, and sent him to Northumbria in place of Colmán.

Aidan comes to Lindisfarne

Aidan (d. 651) arrived in Northumbria with twelve companions in 635. Bede describes Aidan with affection and admiration. He did not approve of the Irish bishop's method of calculating Easter, but he praised his love of prayer and study, his gentleness and humility, and his care for the sick and the poor. It is possible that Bede's unusually lavish words were intended as a reproof for the lax bishops of his own time. Bede relates:

> When [Aidan] arrived, at his request the king [Oswald] gave him the island of Lindisfarne for his bishop's seat. Here the tide ebbs and flows twice a day, so the place is surrounded by the sea and becomes an island. Again twice a day, the shore becomes dry and is joined to the land.... The bishop was not skilled at speaking English, and when he preached the gospel, it was most delightful to see the king himself interpreting God's word to his commanders and ministers, for he had learnt to speak fluent Gaelic during his lengthy exile.[24]

West of the Pennines, both Aidan and Oswald are commemorated in the Eden valley at the village of Kirkoswald, 8 miles north of Penrith. Local tradition relates that here they built a church over a spring, whose water flows under the nave and emerges outside the west wall of the church, where it can be drunk from a well. There are foundations of Saxon pillars in the chancel, and a Saxon ribbed gravestone, with a characteristic herring-bone pattern, outside the church porch; the body of the church is Norman.

St Oswald's well, Kirkoswald, near Penrith, Cumbria.

The Fortress at Bamburgh

King Oswald lived in a fortress on a rocky outcrop at Bamburgh, 15 miles south-east of Berwick-upon-Tweed. There may have been a coastal fort on this site in Roman and pre-Roman times. In AD 547, the Anglian King Ida fought his way northwards to become the first king of Northumbria; he seized the fortress and made it his capital. It is an ideal defensive site, commanding a view of attackers from either land or sea.

From Oswald's fortress, Aidan's island monastery of Lindisfarne was just visible, 6 miles up the coast. Oswald sometimes invited Aidan to join him for dinner. Of Aidan, Bede states:

> When he was invited to eat with the king, which was not often, he went with one or two monks. After eating frugally, he left as soon as possible, in order to read [the scriptures] or write.[25]

On one occasion, after Aidan had celebrated the Easter Vigil with his community, he was invited to join the royal household for a festive meal. Bede relates that when a silver dish of food was put before Aidan and Oswald, the king generously gave it to the poor:

> They were about to say grace, when suddenly the servant entered who was responsible for feeding the poor. He told the king that a large number of beggars had come from everywhere. They were sitting in the streets, begging alms from the king. At once he ordered the food to be taken to the poor, and the dish to be cut up and also given to them.[26]

Oswald's Death

Oswald ruled for only eight years; at the age of thirty-eight, he was killed in battle by the pagan King Penda of Mercia at Maserfield, which was probably near Oswestry, in Shropshire. According to Bede, Penda ordered his soldiers to mutilate Oswald's body: his head, arms, and hands were placed on stakes. Oswestry's name derives from 'Oswald's tree', following a legend that Penda hung him from a tree in mock crucifixion.

The king's holy well can be found near the parish church, in Oswald Place. At one time, there was a stone carving of the king's head here, as it was believed that his head was buried at the well. There was once an oratory above the spring, for in the 1530s the antiquarian John Leland wrote: 'There is a chapel over it of timber, and the fountain environed with a stone wall'.[27] Severed heads are thrown into springs in other early legends, and royal heads were considered particularly potent.

Oswald was soon regarded as a national hero; the Saxons admired his bravery and military skill, his faith and generosity, and his early death in battle. Sixty-two churches were dedicated to him in England, and many more in Europe. Oswald was commemorated in most English calendars, and many places claimed his relics.

St Oswald's well, Oswestry, Shropshire.

Winwick Church

St Oswald's church at Winwick in Lancashire was close to the lowest crossing point of the River Mersey. Oswald's army may have travelled west from Bamburgh and down England's west coast, crossing the Mersey at Winwick Quay as they marched south to fight King Penda at Maserfield. They could also have returned northwards through Winwick after the death of their king.

The present church, in its large, raised churchyard, dates from the fourteenth century. Inside are the arms of an elaborate tenth-century wheel cross. One of its end panels depicts two of Penda's soldiers dismembering Oswald. They look sinister as they trample on the king's head, while severing his legs from his body. The other end panel of the cross appears to depict a priest carrying a bucket of water from Oswald's nearby well. Behind the priest is the parish church and its preaching cross.

The hamlet of Hermitage Green, 1½ miles north of Winwick, is one of several places claimed to be the site of Oswald's death. Bede wrote that the place where Oswald died was the scene of many miracles of healing, and that a depression was made in the ground by people removing soil, in order to heal their sick. Bede wrote: 'as the earth was gradually removed, a pit was left in which a man could stand'.[28] This was said to be the origin of St Oswald's well in Hermitage Green. It is in a field above the hamlet, across the road from Monk House. In the village below, an eighteenth-century inn is named The Hermit. Both names are said to refer to the hermit monk who tended the well.

King Oswin

Oswald was succeeded as king by his cousin, Oswin, who ruled from 644 to 651. Bede thought highly of the new king, and admired his generosity:

> King Oswin was … friendly in speech and courteous in behaviour. He was very generous, to the noble and ignoble alike. Everyone loved him for his physical and mental gifts. From almost every province, people of the highest rank came to serve him. Among his gifts and unusual graces, if I may say so, he was said to be extraordinarily humble.[29]

Bede describes an emotional meal shortly before Oswin's death. Aidan attended the banquet, having recently given away to a beggar a fine horse that he had received from Oswin. The king came into the feast straight from a hunting trip, and chided Aidan for his generosity to the beggar. He went over to the fire with his attendants, to warm himself, and then returned to Aidan to apologise.

In the course of the meal, Aidan felt a premonition of Oswin's approaching death. He wept, and turning to the monk who was with him, he explained in Gaelic the reason for his sadness. The rest of the company did not understand what he said. Soon afterwards, Oswin was treacherously slain by his cousin, Oswiu. Bede adds that Aidan was to die only twelve days later.[30]

Above: St Oswald's martyrdom, reproduced from the arms of a tenth-century high cross, Winwick, Lancashire. His body is dismembered (left) and a priest draws water from his well (right).

Right: St Oswald's well, Hermitage Green, near Winwick, Lancashire.

Aidan's Way of Life

Bede tells us how Bishop Aidan lived: he liked to travel on foot rather than on horseback, and engaged people in conversation. If they were pagan, he taught them about Christianity; if they were believers, he encouraged them. He taught those around him, both monks and lay people, to read the gospels and to learn the psalms. When he received money, he gave it to the poor, or used it to ransom Anglo-Saxon slaves, many of whom he educated and ordained as priests.[31]

He owned a church and a few surrounding fields outside the fortress at Bamburgh, and from here he went on preaching expeditions, staying at Oswald's residences in other parts of his kingdom. This appears to have been quite an itinerant way of life; Bede does not tell us how much time Aidan spent with his community on Lindisfarne.

We learn that Aidan spent each Lent on the Farne Islands, about 2 miles offshore, for an extended period of solitude. He was on Farne when King Penda ravaged Northumbria and reached the royal stronghold at Bamburgh. His soldiers set fire to the fortress, and Aidan, seeing the flames from his cell on Farne, prayed until the wind changed direction and the flames engulfed Penda's troops, who were forced to retreat.[32]

Aidan became ill while in his church at Bamburgh. His followers built a shelter for him beside the church, and Aidan died while resting against a wooden beam for support.

Medieval squint, with a view from the nave to the chancel, St Aidan's church, Bamburgh, Northumberland.

The plank survived when Penda burnt the church; it is still preserved. The impressive church that exists today was built between 1170 and 1230 by a community of Augustinian canons. Its chancel is probably on the site of Aidan's church; a fourteenth-century squint enabled those in the nave to watch the priest at the altar.[33] After Aidan's death, his body was taken back to Lindisfarne for burial. During his sixteen years as bishop, much of Northumbria had become Christian, largely as a result of Aidan's dedicated work.

Hilda of Whitby

Hilda (614–80) was born into the Northumbrian royal family. She was the daughter of a nephew of King Edwin, and she was baptised together with the entire royal court by Archbishop Paulinus at York in 627, at the age of thirteen. She perhaps married and was widowed, since Bede does not refer to her as a virgin. He relates that at the age of thirty-three, Hilda decided to become a nun. She travelled south to her sister and family in East Anglia, intending to join other members of her family in the monastery of Chelles in Gaul.

Before she could do so, Bishop Aidan asked if she would return and found a community in the north. At first, she lived with a few companions on a small plot of land beside the River Wear, given to her by Aidan. She was then invited to become abbess of a double monastery at Hartlepool. At the age of forty-three, she established another double community at Whitby, where she remained until her death; she was chronically ill for the last seven years of her life.[34]

Double Monasteries

In a double monastery, as we have seen, men and women lived separately, but came to church to chant the offices together and celebrate Eucharist. The abbess ruled both communities; she was often a royal widow, and therefore older and more experienced than the other monks and nuns, who could often be teenagers. At this time, women might be married at the age of twelve and men at fourteen, so they had to choose celibate religious life at a young age. Double monasteries were a north European form of religious life, of which Theodore, the Greek archbishop of Canterbury, disapproved. On his arrival in England in 669, he found a number of double communities, most of them established by a woman of the local royal family.[35]

There were such double monasteries in the south at Folkestone (Kent), founded in 630, Minster-in-Sheppey and Minster-in-Thanet (both in Kent), Barking (Essex), and Wimborne (Dorset); 'minster' is a Saxon word meaning 'monastery'. In the west, there were double communities at Much Wenlock (Shropshire) and Gwytherin (Conwy), while they existed in the east at Ely (Cambridgeshire) and Bardney (Lincolnshire). There were also a number in the north, at Repton (Derbyshire), Hartlepool (Cleveland), Carlisle (Cumbria), and Coldingham (Berwickshire), as well as at Whitby and Hackness in Scarborough—both founded by Hilda.

Many of the royal abbesses were widows whose husbands had been killed in battle. When a queen was past the age of child-bearing, she lost much of her value as a political or dynastic tool, and monastic life was considered an appropriate form of retirement in both England and Gaul. Her position as abbess would pass to her daughter, sister, or niece.[36] Although he disapproved of double monasteries, Theodore of Canterbury tolerated them. He wrote: 'It is not permitted for men religious to have women [among them], nor for women, men: nonetheless we shall not overthrow that which is the custom of this province.'[37]

Hilda's Community at Whitby

For a time, it was thought that Hilda's double monastery was not at Whitby, but in the village of Strensall, 5 miles north of York, since Bede relates that Hilda's community was at *Streaneshalch*. Due to its proximity to York, which was the royal capital of Deira, Strensall would have been more accessible to participants in the so-called Synod of Whitby. On its clifftop, Whitby would have been more remote. However, monasteries were often located on a cliff top above a navigable harbour, and although the present ruins at Whitby date only from the thirteenth century, extensive excavation has revealed a large early monastery that is likely to be that of Hilda.

Her monastery at Whitby seems to have included forty or fifty stone cells, each probably intended for the use of one or two nuns, with a number of wooden buildings and a cluster of workshops for the production of sculpture, fine metalwork, ceramics, and also books, since styli, or writing instruments, were found.

There were many commemorative stone crosses dating from the seventh century, each with a simple border and sometimes an inscribed name. Some are very small, no more than 19 cm high; they were sometimes buried under the head of the dead person. These resemble 'pillow stones' found on Iona. It is possible that among the dead commemorated at the monastery was Acha, the mother of King Oswald—a cross-head inscribed +AHHAE is likely to be hers.[38]

In her monastery, Hilda gave importance to education, and to copying, reading, and studying the scriptures and Latin literature. Under Hilda, a lay brother named Caedmon, whom Bede describes as having care of the animals at the monastery, was given the gift of translating the scriptures into vernacular poetry, which Hilda encouraged him to do.[39] However, little of the poetry once attributed to Caedmon is considered likely to have been composed by him.

The Synod of Whitby

At least five bishops were clerics in Hilda's monastery, which was chosen as the venue for the Synod of Whitby in 664.[40] This was a royal council convened by King Oswiu, rather than a church synod. It is described by Bede, who appears to have edited and added to an account of the gathering in a *Life of Wilfrid* by Eddius Stephanus, written soon after 710, some twenty years before Bede wrote his *Ecclesiastical History*.

According to Bede, the chief purpose of the council was to settle the correct date for the celebration of Easter, and so bring Northumbrian Christians into line with the rest of Western Europe. Bede's *Ecclesiastical History* is presented, somewhat artificially, as a triptych with the Synod of Whitby as its central panel. His reported 'conversations' of the participants appear to be Bede's own views, put into the mouths of both parties.

King Oswiu of Northumbria celebrated Easter according to the Irish dating system, which he had learned when in exile on Iona, while his queen, Eanflæd, followed the continental practice with which she had been brought up in Kent. However, the royal couple had already been married for twenty years, and the gathering may have been less significant than Bede suggests.[41] Other practices were also discussed, including the form of monastic tonsure, or haircut.

The method of calculating the date of Easter and the style of tonsure represented deeper traditions and allegiances. The Celtic tonsure, with the head shaved at the front and the hair long at the back was also practised by the druids.[42] Again, the spring equinox, from which Easter was calculated by Celtic peoples, had been celebrated from prehistoric times onwards by Britons, Saxons, and the Irish, as their stone circles indicate. For Celts, stone circles still marked the seasons and the movement of the heavenly bodies.[43] It was only natural that Celtic peoples would prefer their ancestral calculations of the springtime festival.

At the synod, the main debate took place between Wilfrid and Colmán, the abbot of Lindisfarne. Wilfrid was an ambitious monk who had trained at Lindisfarne and later studied in Rome. The Celtic monk Colmán was no match for Wilfrid, with his European training. The king favoured the Irish position, but was compelled by Wilfrid's arguments. After the debate was concluded, Colmán resigned as abbot of Lindisfarne. He returned to Iona, taking with him most of the Celtic monks and thirty Anglo-Saxons.

Although Bede presents the council as a church synod, the decision was political: King Oswiu decided that Northumbria would follow Roman customs. As a result of the synod, the chief bishopric of Northumbria was transferred from Lindisfarne to York. Wilfrid later became bishop of York, and King Oswiu replaced the monks of Lindisfarne with Irish monks from monasteries that already observed the Roman date of Easter, which by now was followed by most of the Irish communities.

Cuthbert and Wilfrid at Ripon

In about 655, ten years before the Synod of Whitby, King Oswiu appointed his son Alchfrith as sub-king of Deira, the southern portion of Northumbria. Five years later, King Alchfrith gave the abbot of Melrose in the Scottish Borders a tract of land at Ripon in north Yorkshire, 120 miles south of Melrose, on which to build a monastery.

Wilfrid's crypt in Ripon Cathedral, North Yorkshire, with a doorway and a cavity for an oil lamp.

The abbot of Melrose, named Eata, selected a group of monks to travel south with him to Ripon, and chose Cuthbert (*c.* 634–87), now aged twenty-five, to accompany him to Ripon as guest master. However, the community spent only two years in Ripon before being ousted by Wilfrid, who enjoyed royal patronage, and was appointed by the king as abbot in place of Eata.

Wilfrid introduced the Benedictine rule, and built a new stone church with an impressive crypt that perhaps housed the relics of saints. These would have been relics that Wilfrid brought back from Rome, intending to install them in the new churches that he planned to build. There are cavities for oil lamps in the walls of the crypt. Wilfrid built a similar crypt at Hexham, near Hadrian's Wall; it too survives intact.

Wilfrid's church at Ripon was dedicated in 672; later, when monks from Lindisfarne were fleeing from the Vikings, bearing Cuthbert's body, they stopped for a while at Ripon, before eventually settling at Durham. Vikings also destroyed Wilfrid's church at Ripon, apart from its crypt; it was later rebuilt by the Normans.

Cuthbert becomes Prior of Lindisfarne

Eata, Cuthbert, and the other Celtic monks returned to Melrose. Not long afterwards, in 664, Eata was appointed abbot of Lindisfarne and brought Cuthbert with him as prior. Eata came to a troubled community: the Synod of Whitby had recently taken place, and abbot Colmán had returned to Iona with many of Lindisfarne's monks. It was left to Eata and his young prior to rebuild the community, to restore its shattered morale, and implement Roman customs peacefully. Cuthbert was an experienced monk, with patience and discretion. Bede describes his skill at mediation:

> In discussion with the brothers, when he was weary of the bitter taunts of those who opposed him, he would quietly rise from his seat and dismiss the meeting until the following day. Then he would use the same exhortations as before, as if he had not been attacked, until he brought them round to his own views. He showed remarkable patience.[44]

Bede approved of Lindisfarne because, as he said, even though the island was small, the monastery was well-organised, with the abbot, priests and deacons, singers and readers leading an ordered monastic life. As the first bishop of Lindisfarne, Aidan had set a model of living simply as one of the monks, and this tradition continued in Cuthbert's day.

Bede describes Cuthbert busy praying, making something with his hands, or walking around the island to inspect his property. He noted that Cuthbert used to celebrate Eucharist not in a loud voice, but quietly, often shedding tears. While he did not dress in a slovenly way, he preferred simple materials, and the monks wore unbleached vestments of natural wool.[45]

The Early Monastery

Little survives on Lindisfarne from Cuthbert's day; the monastery was destroyed by Vikings in 793 and the monks left the island a generation later, dismantling their wooden church and taking its timbers with them.[46] The surviving priory ruins date from the twelfth century. The nearby parish church of St Mary may stand on the site of an Anglo-Saxon one. The extent to which Lindisfarne was occupied by monks after the Viking raids in the ninth, tenth, and eleventh centuries is not yet known.

A geophysical survey carried out in 2012 provided evidence of at least three buildings dating from after the Viking raids. Excavations in the summer of 2016 directed by David Petts focussed on the search for evidence of these, and of earlier monastic buildings.[47] They discovered the upper end of an Anglo-Saxon grave marker dating from the mid-seventh century, close to the time when the monastery was built. The name on the stone is half visible, and ends in '*frith*', a common Anglo-Saxon name element. This is the earliest evidence of a monastery on Lindisfarne.

South-west of the priory is a rocky islet which Cuthbert used as a retreat (see colour plate 21). At low tide, it is ten minutes' walk from the priory, but at high tide, it is cut off from the mainland. Visible in the photograph are the remains of a medieval chapel on the island, its ruined walls covered with pink thrift, and yellow bird's-foot trefoil. At its east end, a tall wooden cross marks the site of the altar. More fragmentary stones may be the remains of Cuthbert's hermitage.

Twelfth-century priory, Lindisfarne, Northumberland. View from the nave, facing east.

Cuthbert on Inner Farne

After ten years as prior of Lindisfarne, Cuthbert went to live as a hermit on Inner Farne, following Aidan's example. However, while his predecessor spent only short periods on the island, Cuthbert remained on Farne for ten years, constructing buildings to suit his needs. Bede describes these in some detail. He built a circular hut, taller than himself, with walls made of rough stones and turf dug from the floor. Its roof was constructed of poles thatched with straw. A second chamber formed Cuthbert's chapel.

Further away, beside the landing stage, he built a large guest-house for visiting monks. He thatched its roof, although crows caused problems by pulling out straw in order to build their nests. Visitors could drink water from a nearby well. By digging, Cuthbert also discovered a spring in his own compound. He asked the monks from Lindisfarne to bring him farm tools and wheat seed, which he planted in the springtime. When it failed to germinate, he tried barley, and this grew well.[48]

At first, when monks came to visit him, Cuthbert would leave his hermitage in order to make them welcome. He washed their feet in warm water, and Bede records that the monks would persuade Cuthbert to have his feet washed also, for he became so used to seclusion that he often forgot to take off his leather gaiters for months, and sometimes removed his shoes only on Maundy Thursday in Holy Week, when feet are ceremonially washed during the Lord's Supper. Over the years, however, Cuthbert stopped visiting his guests, and remained in his cell to pray.[49]

Sometimes his visitors found themselves put on the spot. Bede describes how Cuthbert left his cell to give advice to some guests; he also told them to cook and eat a goose that was hanging on the wall, rather than sail away hungry. Presumably the goose had been brought by a previous visitor. The guests had sufficient provisions, and decided to leave the bird for Cuthbert. A storm forced them to return to Farne, however, and Cuthbert made them boil the kettle and cook the goose.[50]

Cuthbert Returns to a Bishop's Life

After ten years, King Ecgfrith and Theodore, Archbishop of Canterbury, prevailed on Cuthbert to become bishop of Hexham. Parts of the Saxon abbey church at Hexham still survive. Cuthbert would have been familiar with its crypt and its bishop's throne, probably commissioned by Wilfrid; it was also used as a sanctuary seat for criminals fleeing from the law (see photo overleaf).

Cuthbert, aged fifty, agreed to become bishop of Hexham, but soon exchanged his diocese with that of Eata, and became responsible for Lindisfarne instead. He once more began to preach, teach, and travel throughout his diocese. He gave out food and clothing, and consecrated churches. Cuthbert journeyed back and forth along Hadrian's Wall to Carlisle. Here there was a double monastery, whose abbess was the sister of Queen Iurminburg. Bede describes the queen waiting apprehensively in her sister's monastery,

Saxon bishop's throne, also used as a sanctuary seat for criminals, Hexham Abbey, Northumberland.

while her husband Ecgfrith fought his last fatal battle against the Picts in Scotland. Cuthbert prepared the queen to hear the news she dreaded.[51]

Cuthbert and Herbert

In 686, Cuthbert again visited Carlisle to ordain priests and to visit Queen Iurminburg. A hermit named Herbert also travelled to Carlisle to spend time with Cuthbert. Herbert lived on an island in Cumbria, on Derwentwater, a mile south of Keswick. Derwentwater was then a marshy lake; remains of a circular stone building on St Herbert's Isle may be his hermitage.

On the lake-shore opposite is Friar's Crag, from which point monks set out to visit Herbert on his island. Bede recounts how, each year, Herbert used to travel 100 miles to Lindisfarne in order to visit Cuthbert. Since Carlisle was only 20 miles north of Derwentwater, Herbert took advantage of Cuthbert's visit for what proved to be their final encounter, since the two men were both to die on 20 March the following year.

Cuthbert's Death

After only two years as bishop of Lindisfarne, Cuthbert returned to Inner Farne to die. Monks from Lindisfarne visited him regularly, but in the last week of his life, storms prevented them from reaching Cuthbert for five days. Herefrid, abbot of Lindisfarne, was Cuthbert's attendant, and told Bede the story of Cuthbert's death in considerable detail. On his arrival after the storm, he found that Cuthbert had collapsed in the guest-house by the landing stage.

Herefrid warmed some water to wash Cuthbert's feet, for he had an ulcer on his leg. He also warmed some wine that he had brought because, since his collapse, Cuthbert had managed to eat only a piece of raw onion. The abbot returned home, leaving two monks to care for Cuthbert. Herefrid returned frequently and, as Cuthbert weakened, the sick man asked to be carried to his chapel to die. Herefrid described Cuthbert's final hours: 'I went in to him at about the ninth hour and found him lying in the corner of his chapel, before the altar. I sat beside him but he spoke very little, for the burden of his suffering prevented him from speaking much'.[52]

The abbot asked Cuthbert for some final words of advice to the community and Cuthbert spoke, little by little, as he found the strength to do so. Herefrid gave him the Eucharist, and Cuthbert stretched out his hands in prayer and then died. Herefrid went out to tell the waiting monks, one of whom lit two torches and climbed to a high point on the island to signal to the brothers waiting on Lindisfarne that Cuthbert was dead.[53]

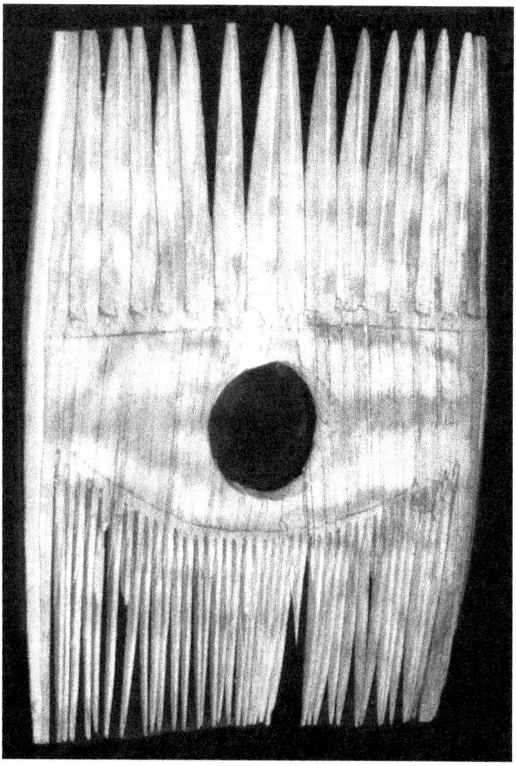

St Cuthbert's comb made from a walrus tusk, Durham Cathedral.

A monk was standing at a similar high spot on Lindisfarne and, seeing the signal, he ran to the monastery to tell the community. Cuthbert's body was taken back to Lindisfarne for burial. Some of Cuthbert's belongings were preserved by the monks and were buried with him, including an ivory comb made from a walrus tusk, with a row of thick teeth along one edge and thin teeth along the other (see photo on p. 201).

Eleven years later, the monks dug up Cuthbert's remains in order to enshrine them. His body had not decayed; it was placed in a carved oak casket. When Lindisfarne was devastated by Norsemen, the monks fled, taking Cuthbert's relics with them. After many years of wandering around northern Britain with their precious coffin, the brothers selected Durham for its resting place. Fragments of the finely carved shrine can still be seen in Durham Cathedral.

St Patrick's Chapel, Heysham

There are some early Christian sites in Northumbria that were not associated with Lindisfarne. In the eighth century, a small chapel was built on a headland at Heysham, which overlooks Morecambe Bay (see colour plate 22). It was decorated with yellow, red, white, and green-brown wall plaster; traces of both paintings and lettering were found. In the chapel was a ceremonial stone chair, or throne, for the president at the Eucharist. One of its arms was discovered, shaped like a bird's head, with prominent eyes and a hooked beak; it is now in Lancaster museum.

The stone blocks that form the chapel walls are held together by mortar made with burnt sea shells for lime, poured between the stones while it was still hot. This was a style used by the Romans. The tall, narrow building was extended by the Saxons in the tenth century; its new doorway was decorated with a ribbed arch.

No evidence of a monastery has been found on the headland, but carved into the rock outside each end of the chapel are repositories for bones, six in a row on one side, with others lower down the slope. The cavities are too small for graves. Each has a rim to take a lid, and a socket at its head, into which a cross was inserted. The cemetery was also extended: the graves of ninety Vikings and later Christians have been found in and around the chapel, near the shrines of the monks.

An ancient stone passage leads downhill from St Patrick's chapel and its graveyard to a flat, sheltered spot where the parish church of St Peter now stands. If there was a monastery, it may have been here. The lower portion of an elaborate Anglian cross can be seen in the churchyard; it dates from the ninth century and is carved from local Old Red Sandstone. Carved on its north face is a gabled building with windows and a doorway, in which a human figure stands, apparently swathed in grave clothes. The panel may depict Christ raising Lazarus from the dead (John 11. 43-4).

The church was rebuilt in the mid-tenth century as a barn-like building with small stone doorways, two of which survive. A fine Viking hogback tombstone also dates from this time. It is shaped like a feasting hall, with an animal's head at each end of its gabled roof. Along each side is a procession of creatures and people

Above: Early monks' shrine beside St Patrick's chapel, Heysham, Lancashire.

Right: Anglian cross shaft, perhaps depicting the raising of Lazarus, St Peter's church, Heysham, Lancashire.

Cumbrian Dedications to Kentigern

In the later medieval period, there was a resurgence of interest in early British saints. At this time, a number of churches in Cumbria were dedicated to the seventh-century saint, Kentigern of Glasgow. The British princes of Strathclyde re-occupied Cumbria from 900 to 1092, and held their territory against both the English and the Norse. They appear to have named churches after their Glasgow patron.

In the twelfth century, the diocese of York attempted, unsuccessfully, to establish its authority in southern Scotland, and Jocelin of Furness in Cumbria wrote a *Life of Kentigern*, as we saw in Chapter 4. He wove his story around the churches dedicated to Kentigern, and depicts him travelling southwards to Cumbria.

Crosthwaite

Jocelin portrays Kentigern arriving in Carlisle and proceeding to Crosthwaite:

> When he came to Carlisle, he heard how many people in the mountain district were idolatrous and ignorant of God's law. So he turned aside, and converted many from strange beliefs to Christianity, and corrected the errors of believers. He stayed for a while in a wooded area, to encourage and confirm in their faith the people who lived there. He planted a cross there as a symbol of faith, and so it is called Crosthwaite in English.[54]

Crosthwaite church (see colour plate 23) is on the northern outskirts of Keswick; it looks towards Skiddaw's peak, 2 miles distant. 'Thwaite' is Norse for a forest clearing; it well describes the 'wooded area' mentioned by Jocelin. The earliest remains in Crosthwaite church are from the twelfth century. The church has a unique set of twelve crosses around its inside walls, with another twelve on its external walls. These were carved when the church was rededicated in 1523, according to the English rite of consecration.

Mungrisdale and Castle Sowerby

Of the eight medieval churches named after Kentigern in Cumbria, that of Mungrisdale uses his pet name, Mungo, or 'My dear one', the name by which he is honoured at Glasgow cathedral. The hamlet is situated to the east of Skiddaw's peak, between Keswick and Penrith. The name Mungrisdale may mean 'Valley of Mungo's pigs'; these were a staple food in Celtic times. The tiny church was rebuilt in 1756, and the porch retains its floor of cobblestones.

There is another church dedicated to Kentigern at Castle Sowerby. This is a small country house with a church and a holy well in the churchyard wall, beside the track that leads to the church and the house; the well is now dry. The church is in a beautiful,

Right: Cobbled porch, St Mungo's church, Mungrisdale, near Keswick, Cumbria.

Below: St Kentigern's church, Castle Sowerby, near Sebergham, Cumbria.

though isolated, location, surrounded by farmland and bleak moors. The small twelfth-century church was enlarged in the sixteenth century and repaired in the eighteenth; its whitewashed walls gleam in the sunlight.

To find Castle Sowerby, leave the M6 at junction 41. Take the B5305 as if for Sebergham. After 6 miles, turn left for Lamonby; then turn right for Castle Sowerby. Other Cumbrian churches dedicated to Kentigern can be found at Kirkcambeck and Irthington, both north of Carlisle, and at Caldbeck, near Castle Sowerby, where a fine holy well can be seen beside the river. There are three more churches names after Kentigern at Grinsdale, where the River Eden flows into the Solway Firth, and at Bromfield and Aspatria, near the Cumbrian coast.

St Kentigern's Church, Aspatria

Aspatria is the earliest Christian site among the Cumbrian churches dedicated to Kentigern. It is 3 miles from the coast, on the A596, 18 miles south-west of Carlisle. Its name derives from 'Patrick's ash'; it was perhaps a pre-Christian holy site beside a sacred ash tree. Aspatria's first name element, *askr*, is Old Norse, but the order of the two elements (the name was *ascpatric* in about 1230) is Celtic, suggesting both Gaelic and Norse influence.[55] An incised tomb slab carved with a swastika was found here, dating from around 430. This indicates the presence of early British Christians in the area.

In the church, there are also two shafts of crosses with spiral decorations carved from white sandstone, and remains of a Saxon wheel-headed cross of Old Red Sandstone, with the socket in which it stood. These fine monuments suggest that there might have been a monastic community here. St Kentigern's well in the churchyard is now dry, but it was formerly fed from an underground spring and used for baptisms. Aspatria suffered from Norse-Irish coastal raids, and part of a Viking hogback tombstone marks a wealthy Norseman's burial.

St Martin's Church, Brampton

Another early church is that of St Martin near Brampton, 9 miles north-east of Carlisle. The tiny church is 1½ miles out of the town, at the end of a road to the right of William Howard School, signed 'Old Church Cemetery'. The church lies within a Roman camp, one of a series of forts along the Stanegate, constructed before Hadrian's Wall was built. It is situated beside the River Irthing, and was used by a Roman auxiliary unit for a brief period of twenty-five years; it was abandoned in about AD 150. Amphorae and other artefacts were discovered at the site. The church was built some time after the Romans withdrew from Britain in the first decade of the fifth century; it hugs the Roman rampart and is not aligned with the camp, but made use of the Roman earthworks for shelter.[56]

St Martin's church, built inside a Roman fort at Brampton, near Carlisle, Cumbria.

There used to be a holy tree here, named St Martin's oak. At the foot of the esker on which the fort was built is a well that may have been a shrine to the local water spirit, since there are signs of a Roman concrete surround. It was later known as 'Ninewells', which was taken to mean 'Ninian's well', but may derive from the Celtic word *nyen*, or 'holy'. The first graveyard here was oval, following Celtic tradition. The church was rebuilt in Norman times, using some stone from the abandoned fort; only its chancel remains. This is possibly one of the earliest Christian sites in Cumbria.[57]

St Bega's Priory and Cave

The Norman priory of St Bees on the Cumbrian coast was founded by monks from the Benedictine abbey of St Mary's, York. Norsemen arrived here in the eleventh century and called the settlement *Kirkeby Begoc*, or 'the village near Bega's church'. The fine west door of St Bees priory is decorated with chevrons and beak-heads of grotesque birds or beasts; it was built around 1220. There is an early Christian cross in the cemetery, opposite the great west door, and inside is the stump of a fine carved cross dating from the tenth or eleventh century.

According to her legend, Bega was an Irish chieftain's daughter who vowed chastity. She escaped before an arranged marriage and fled across the sea, landing at St Bees,

St Bega's cave, Fleswick Bay, St Bees, Cumbria.

where she founded a convent. Her cult may have arisen from a bracelet kept at her shrine in St Bees, which was said to have healing properties. Its Old English name, *beag*, may have suggested the saint's name; the bracelet disappeared in the twelfth century. An hour's walk westwards from the priory leads along the cliffs to St Bees Head, where one can climb down to Smuggler's Cave in Fleswick Bay. On reaching the Cumbrian coast, Bega was said to have taken shelter in the cave.

Who was Bega?

Bega might be the nun Begu who spent thirty years at the double monastery of Hackness in Scarborough, North Yorkshire, and died in about 660. According to Bede, Begu saw the death of Hilda, her abbess and friend, in a vision; the communities of both Hackness and Whitby were founded by Hilda.[58] The legend of Bega's life is related in a Latin hymn in a fifteenth-century *Book of Hours* in the Bodleian Library, Oxford. A copy of the hymn, translated by W. F. Ewbank in 1980, can be seen in St Bega's church beside Lake Bassenthwaite, at the foot of Mount Skiddaw, north of Keswick (see colour plate 24).

St Bega's church is 3 miles south of Bassenthwaite village; it was part of Crosthwaite parish until the late sixteenth century. The small church is beside an ancient track leading from Little Crosthwaite to Bowness. Random courses of large stones in the north and east outer walls may be pre-Norman; inside, there is a Norman chancel arch. The church was given to the Augustinian priory at Jedburgh in the Scottish Borders in the eleventh century; it was heavily restored in the nineteenth century.

Kilbucho in the Upper Tweed valley, 12 miles south-west of Peebles may be named after Bega. It appears as *Kylbeuhoc* in about 1200, meaning 'church of my dear Begu'; the suffix *-oc* is an affectionate diminutive. The name *Killebeccocestun*, recorded in about 1200 at Eddleston, 4 miles north of Peebles, means '*tun* , or settlement, of Begu's ghillie, or attendant'. At Dunbar on the Scottish coast, 28 miles east of Edinburgh, Bega may be commemorated by a holy well named 'St Bais wall' in 1603.[59]

Bega's legend is the subject of the novel *Credo* by Melvyn Bragg; the book conveys a vivid impression of early Christian Northumbria, its monks and nuns, and the people whom they served.[60] Bega might be considered a typical Celtic saint: a highborn Irish lady who left her homeland and became a holy woman in a foreign country. However, like so many other Celtic saints, she must be considered as a figure in a landscape—the figures are medieval, yet the landscape remains.

Endnotes

Chapter 1

1. Quotations from Adomnán's *Life of Columba* are transl. by J. Gregory, in J. Marsden, *The Illustrated Columcille* (London: Macmillan, 1991). Here, bk. 3, ch. 2, p. 153.
2. Adomnán, second preface, Marsden, p. 56.
3. Adomnán, bk 1. ch. 1, Marsden, p. 57; bk. 2. ch. 1, Marsden, p. 104; bk. 3, ch. 4, Marsden, p. 154.
4. P. Ó Riain, 'St Finbarr: A Study in a Cult', *Journal of the Cork Historical and Archaeological Society*, vol. 82 (1977), pp. 72-5.
5. T. O. Clancy, 'The Real St. Ninian', *Innes Review*, vol. 52 (2001), pp. 13-14.
6. Adomnán, bk. 3, ch. 3, Marsden, p. 154.
7. Bede, *Ecclesiastical History of the English People*, transl. L. Sherley-Price, revised R. E. Latham (London: Penguin Classics, 1990), bk. 1, ch. 1.
8. E. Campbell, *Saints and Sea-kings: The First Kingdom of the Scots* (Edinburgh: Canongate, 1999) pp. 11-15.
9. *Ibid.*, pp. 53, 56.
10. *Ibid.*, pp. 58-9.
11. A. Ritchie, *Iona* (London: Batsford, 1997), p. 51.
12. E. Campbell, *Saints and Sea-kings*, pp. 49, 50.
13. S. Foster, *Picts, Gaels and Scots* (Edinburgh: Birlinn, 2014), pp. 49-50.
14. E. Campbell, *Saints and Sea-kings*, pp. 23-5.
15. A. Ritchie, *Iona*, p. 52.
16. S. Foster, *Picts, Gaels and Scots*, p. 132.
17. E. Campbell, *Saints and Sea-kings*, p. 58.
18. In Old Irish, '*Sliab óir iarthair domuin*', from the *Martyrology of Óengus*.
19. W. J. Watson, *The History of the Celtic Place-names of Scotland* (Edinburgh: Birlinn, 1926, revised ed. 1993), p. 291.
20. A. Ritchie, *Iona*, p. 90.
21. Adomnán, bk. 1, ch. 17, Marsden, p. 73.
22. *Ibid.*, ch. 18, Marsden, p. 73.
23. Adomnán, bk. 2, ch. 8, Marsden, pp. 107-8.
24. *Ibid.*, ch. 9, Marsden, p. 108.
25. Adomnán, bk. 3, ch. 24, Marsden, p. 171.
26. E. Campbell, *Saints and Sea-kings*, pp. 33, 36.
27. Adomnán, bk. 1, ch. 19, Marsden, p. 73.
28. *Ibid.*, ch. 33, Marsden, p. 82.
29. Information from Elizabeth MacLennan, Barrhead, Renfrewshire, aged eighty-six, 06.01.2015. She lived for many years in the Highlands at Ardelve, Kyle of Lochalsh, near Skye.
30. S. Foster, *Picts, Gaels and Scots*, pp. 63, 65.
31. Adomnán, bk. 2, ch. 26, Marsden, p. 120.
32. *Ibid.*, bk. 3, ch. 4, Marsden, p. 155.
33. A. Ritchie, *Iona*, p. 47.
34. Adomnán, bk. 3, ch. 24, Marsden, pp. 172-4.
35. S. Foster, *Picts, Gaels and Scots*, p. 108.
36. A. Ritchie, *Iona*, p. 98.
37. J. Dunbar and I. Fisher, *Iona: A Guide to the Monuments* (Edinburgh: Her Majesty's Stationery Office, 1995), p. 27.

38. A. Ritchie, *Iona*, pp. 15, 21.
39. Adomnán, bk. 2, ch. 46, Marsden, p. 140.
40. *Ibid.*, bk. 3, ch. 24, Marsden, p. 172.
41. A. Ritchie, *Iona*, pp. 43, 35.
42. Adomnán, bk. 2, ch. 3, Marsden, p. 105.
43. J. Dunbar and I. Fisher, *Iona*, p. 15.
44. Adomnán, bk. 1, ch. 35; bk. 3, ch. 24, Marsden, pp. 85, 170.
45. A. Ritchie, *Iona*, pp. 68, 19.
46. E. Campbell, *Saints and Sea-kings*, pp. 40-41.
47. *Ibid.*, pp. 41, 47.
48. A. Ritchie, *Iona*, pp. 75, 78.
49. Adomnán, bk. 3, ch. 24, Marsden, pp. 172-3.
50. J. Dunbar and I. Fisher, *Iona*, p. 13.
51. B. Lacy, 'The Discovery Project, *Slí Chomcille* (St. Columba Trail), Dublin, 2015.
52. Adomnán, Second Preface, Marsden, p. 56.
53. W. J. Watson, *Celtic Place-names of Scotland*, p. 284.

Chapter 2

1. E. Campbell, *Saints and Sea-kings* (Edinburgh: Canongate, 1999), p. 34.
2. Bede, *Ecclesiastical History of the English People*, transl. L. Sherley-Price, revised R. E. Latham (London: Penguin Classics, 1990), bk. 5, chs. 15-17.
3. *Ibid.*, bk. 5, ch. 15.
4. Adomnán, *Life of Columba*, transl. J. Gregory, in J. Marsden, *The Illustrated Columcille* (London: Macmillan, 1991), bk. 3, ch. 6, p. 155.
5. S. Foster, *Picts, Gaels and Scots* (Edinburgh: Birlinn, 2014), p. 44.
6. *Ibid.*, pp. 44-5.
7. E. Campbell, *Saints and Sea-kings*, p. 34.
8. Bede, *Ecclesiastical History*, bk. 3, ch. 25.
9. *Cáin Adomnáin*. For a more detailed account of the Synod of Birr, see G. Márkus, *Adomnán's Law of the Innocents: Cáin Adomnáin* (Glasgow: Blackfriars Books, 1997).
10. *Book of Raphoe*, Treatise, 3, quoted in M. Ní Dhonnchadha, 'The *Lex Innocentium*: Adomnán's Law for Women, Clerics and Youths, 697 AD', from M. O'Dowd and S. Wichert, eds., *Chattel, Servant or Citizen: Women's Status in Church, State and Society* (Belfast: Historical Studies, vol. 19, 1995), p. 64.
11. *Book of Raphoe*, Treatise, 7, M. Ní Dhonnchadha, pp. 65-6.
12. *Ibid.*, Treatise, 33, M. Ní Dhonnchadha, p. 66.
13. Adomnán, bk. 2, ch. 26; Marsden, p. 119.
14. H. J. Macdonald, MA diss., Guelph, *Cáin Adomnáin: The* Familia Columbae *and the politics of piety*, 2001, pp. 89-121.
15. J. E. Fraser, *From Caledonia to Pictland: Scotland to 795* (Edinburgh: Edinburgh Press, 2014), pp. 367, 369.
16. W. J. Watson, *The History of the Celtic Place-names of Scotland* (Edinburgh: Birlinn, 1926, revised ed. 1993), p. 282.
17. A. Ritchie, *Iona* (London: Batsford, 1997), p. 78.
18. E. Campbell, *Saints and Sea-kings*, p. 34.
19. J. Stevenson, *Altus Prosator*, 'Celtic Studies', School of Celtic Studies, DIAS, 1999, pp. 345-7.
20. Transl. T. O'Loughlin, in *Celtic Spirituality*, The Classics of Western Spirituality series, ed. O. Davies, (Mahwah, New Jersey: Paulist Press, 1999), pp. 405-10. It appears in ninth-century manuscripts on mainland Europe and in two eleventh-century copies of the Irish *Liber Hymnorum*, all of which were preserved in monastic libraries. I am grateful to Professor Thomas O'Loughlin for permission to reproduce extracts from his translation of *Altus Prosator*.
21. Isidore of Seville, *Etymologiae* 13, 1-3; see J. Stevenson, *Altus Prosator*, p. 333. The *Etymologiae* was an encyclopaedia in which Isidore assembled extracts of many books from classical antiquity that would otherwise have been lost.
22. J. Stevenson, *Altus Prosator*, p. 356.
23. *Ibid.*, *Altus Prosator*, p. 351.
24. A. Woolf, *From Pictland to Alba* (Edinburgh: Edinburgh University Press, 2014), pp. 2-3.
25. J. E. Fraser, *From Caledonia to Pictland*, p. 368.
26. R. Fawcett, *Scottish Cathedrals* (London: Batsford, 1997), p. 15.
27. A. Ritchie, *Iona*, pp. 91, 93.
28. *Ibid.*, p. 98.
29. *Ibid.*, p. 92.
30. *Ibid.*, p. 97.
31. S. Foster, *Picts, Gaels and Scots*, p. 155.

32. *Ibid.*, p. 156.
33. C. Plummer ed., *Latin Lives of the Irish Saints, Vitae Sanctorum Hiberniae* (Oxford: Oxford University Press, 1910), vol. 1, p. 143.
34. Adomnán, bk. 3, ch. 17; Marsden, p. 165.
35. Report by I. Fisher: CANMORE, 'Garvellachs, Eileach an Naoimh enclosure grave', ID 22364, 2001.
36. Bede, *Ecclesiastical History*, bk. 3, ch. 3.
37. R. Fawcett, *Scottish Abbeys and Priories* (London: Batsford, 1994), p. 14.
38. '*Bláán buadach Bretan*', from the *Félire* of Gorman, quoted in Watson, *Celtic Place-names of Scotland*, pp. 164-5.
39. R. Fawcett, *Scottish Cathedrals*, p. 115.
40. C. Lowe, *Inchmarnock. An Early Historic Island Monastery and its Archaeological Landscape* (Edinburgh: Society of Antiquaries of Scotland, 2008), p. xxiii.
41. *Ibid.*
42. RCAHMS, Bute, 'St Ninian's Chapel', CANMORE, ID 40437, Site no. NS065W 4, Archaeology Notes, 2009.
43. *Ibid.*
44. W. J. Watson, *Celtic Place-names of Scotland*, pp. 78, 256-7.
45. P. Dransart, 'Saints, stones and shrines: the cults of Sts Moluag and Gerardine in Pictland' in *Celtic Hagiography and saints' cults*, ed. J. Cartwright (Cardiff: University of Wales Press, 2003), p. 234.
46. A. Ritchie, *Iona*, p. 81.
47. I. Carmichael, *Lismore in Alba* (Perth: D. Leslie, ?1948), p. 35.
48. P. Dransart, 'Saints, stones and shrines', p. 238.
49. *Ibid.*, p. 235.

Chapter 3

1. G. and A. Ritchie, *Scotland: Archaeology and Early History* (Edinburgh: Edinburgh University Press, 1991), p. 142.
2. *Ibid.*, p. 143.
3. J. Fraser, *From Caledonia to Pictland: Scotland to 795* (Edinburgh: Edinburgh University Press, 2009), pp. 88-9.
4. G. and A. Ritchie, *Scotland: Archaeology*, pp. 143-4, 147-8.
5. S. Foster, *Picts, Gaels and Scots* (Edinburgh: Birlinn, 2014), p. 102.
6. P. Yeoman, *Pilgrimage in Medieval Scotland* (London: Batsford, 1999), p. 35.
7. A. Cox, S. Gall, P. Yeoman, *Whithorn Priory and St Ninian's Chapel and Cave* (Edinburgh: Historic Scotland, 2015), p. 38.
8. *Ibid.*, p. 38.
9. *Ibid.*, p. 37.
10. Bede, *Ecclesiastical History of the English People*, transl. L. Sherley-Price, revised R. E. Latham (London: Penguin Classics, 1990), bk. 3, ch. 4.
11. P. Yeoman, *Pilgrimage in Medieval Scotland*, p. 33.
12. A. Cox, *Whithorn Priory*, pp. 20-21.
13. P. Hill, *Whithorn and St Ninian: The Excavation of a Monastic Town 1984-91* (Stroud: Sutton Publishing, 1997), pp. 69, 300-301.
14. Information from Elizabeth MacLennan, Barrhead, Renfrewshire, aged eighty-six, 6. 1. 2015. She lived for many years in the Highlands at Ardelve, Kyle of Lochalsh, near Skye.
15. P. Hill, *Whithorn and St Ninian*, p. 124.
16. *Ibid.*, p. 128.
17. *Ibid.*, pp. 37-8, 52.
18. *Aut ipse beatus Martinus, verus Dei cultor, in Christiano imperio minus venerari fas est, quam Scolapius falsator in paganorum potestate habuit?* Alcuin, *Epistolae*, 245.
19. P. Yeoman, *Pilgrimage in Medieval Scotland*, p. 36.
20. P. Yeoman, *Medieval Scotland* (London: Batsford, 1995), p. 16.
21. I. MacDonald, ed. *Saint Ninian, by Ailred, Abbot of Rievaulx* (Edinburgh: Floris, 1993), p. 39.
22. J. and W. MacQueen, *St Nynia. With a translation of the* Miracula Nynie episcope *and the* Vita Niniani (Edinburgh: Birlinn, 2005), *Miracula*, ch. 4.
23. P. Hill, *Whithorn and St Ninian*, p. 19.
24. Ibid., p. 19.
25. *Ibid.*, pp. 20, 47.
26. P. Yeoman, *Pilgrimage in Medieval Scotland*, pp. 41-2.
27. P. Connor, 'The Ruthwell Monument Runic Poem in a Tenth-Century Context', *Review of English Studies*, no. 59 (238), March 2007, pp. 1-27.
28. Translation from T. O. Clancy and G. Markús, ed. and transl., *The Triumph Tree: Scotland's Earliest Poetry, 550-1350* (Edinburgh: John Wiley, 2008).
29. Clancy and Markús, *The Triumph Tree.*

30. É. Ó Carragaáin, 'Christian Inculturation in Eighth-Century Northumbria: The Bewcastle and Ruthwell Crosses', *Colloquium*, vol. 4, autumn 2007 (Yale Institute of Sacred Music).
31. C. Lowe, *Excavations at Hoddom, Dunfriesshire* (Edinburgh: Society of Antiquaries of Scotland, 2006), pp. 102-13, 150-55.
32. *Ibid.*, pp. 134-44.
33. *Ibid.*, pp. 123-30.
34. '*abbaten Hodda Helmi*', see M. Parker, 'An Eighth-century Reference to the Monastery at Hoddom', *The Journal of Scottish Name Studies*, vol. 6, 2012, pp. 51-80.
35. RCAHMS, ID 731596, 1997, 'Hoddom'.
36. T. Ward, 'Excavation of three Early Christian graves at Lyne, near Peebles', Biggar Archaeology Group, 2005.
37. R. Fawcett, *Scottish Abbeys and Priories* (London: Batsford, 1994), p. 16.
38. P. Yeoman, *Pilgrimage in Medieval Scotland*, p. 45.
39. 'The Life and Miracles of St Cuthbert', ch. 6, in Bede, *Ecclesiastical History of the English People.*
40. *Ibid.*, ch. 6.
41. *Ibid.*, ch. 8.
42. P. Yeoman, *Medieval Scotland*, pp. 15-16.
43. W. J. Watson, *The History of the Celtic Place-names of Scotland* (Edinburgh: Birlinn, 1926, revised ed. 1993), p. 288.
44. E. G. Bowen, *The Settlements of the Celtic Saints in Wales* (Cardiff: University of Wales Press, 1954), pp. 74-8.
45. J. Randall and C. Seymour, *Stobo Kirk* (Selkirk: Stobo Kirk, 1997), pp. 8-9.
46. W. J. Watson, *The Celtic Place-names of Scotland*, p. 257.
47. W. J. Watson, *The Celtic Place-names of Scotland*, p. 257, n. 2.
48. Bede, *Ecclesiastical History*, bk. 4, ch. 19.
49. P. Rumsey, *Women of the Church: the religious experience of monastic women* (Dublin: Columba Press, 2011), pp. 138-41.
50. Bede, *Ecclesiastical History*, bk. 4, ch. 25.
51. P. Rumsey, *Women of the Church*, p. 147.

Chapter 4

1. S. Foster, *Picts, Gaels and Scots* (Edinburgh: Birlinn, 2014), p. 5.
2. S. Hothershall, *Archaeology around Glasgow* (Glasgow: Glasgow Archaeological Society, 2007), p. 61.
3. *Ibid.*
4. Adomnán's *Life of Columba*, transl. J. Gregory, in J. Marsden, *The Illustrated Columcille* (London: Macmillan, 1991), bk. 1, ch. 8, p. 68.
5. Bede, *Ecclesiastical History of the English People*, transl. L. Sherley-Price, revised R. E. Latham (London: Penguin Classics, 1990), bk. 1, end of ch. 1.
6. T. Thompson, ed., *A Collection of Inventories* (Edinburgh, 1815), pp. 299-302.
7. Patrick's *Acknowledgement*, 1, in T. O'Loughlin, *Saint Patrick: The Man and his Works* (London: SPCK, 1999), p. 52.
8. W. J. Watson, *The History of the Celtic Place-names of Scotland* (Edinburgh: Birlinn, 1926, revised ed. 1993), p. 194.
9. S. Hothershall, *Archaeology around Glasgow*, p. 134.
10. P. Yeoman, *Pilgrimage in Medieval Scotland* (London: Batsford, 1999), p. 32.
11. CANMORE, 'Loch Lomond, Inchmurrin, St Mirren's Chapel', ID 42465, 1995.
12. M. Carver, *Portmahomack: Monastery of the Picts* (Edinburgh: Edinburgh University Press, 2008), p. 107.
13. S. Hothershall, *Archaeology around Glasgow*, pp. 36-7.
14. P. Yeoman, *Pilgrimage in Medieval Scotland*, p. 29.
15. *Ibid.*, pp. 28-9.
16. S. Hothershall, *Archaeology around Glasgow*, p. 37.
17. *Ibid.*, pp. 118-9, 132-3.
18. P. Yeoman, *Pilgrimage in Medieval Scotland*, p. 18.
19. 'Life of Kentigern by Jocelin of Furness', ed. and transl. A. W. Wade-Evans, *Vitae Sanctorum Britanniae et Genealogiae* (Cardiff, University of Wales Press Board, 1944).
20. P. Yeoman, *Pilgrimage in Medieval Scotland*, p. 46.
21. K. Jankulak, 'Alba Longa in the Celtic regions? Swine, saints and Celtic hagiography' in *Celtic Hagiography and Saints' Cults*, ed. J. Cartwright (Cardiff, University of Wales Press, 2003), pp. 272, 274.
22. I. MacDonald, *Saint Mungo, Also Known as Kentigern, by Jocelinus, a Monk of Furness* (Edinburgh: Floris, 1993), p. 32.
23. *Ibid.*
24. E. Rees, *Celtic Saints of Wales* (Stroud: Fonthill, 2015), pp. 146-8.

25. 'Life of Kentigern by Jocelin of Furness', ch. 25, 210.
26. *Ibid.*, ch. 25, 213.
27. I. MacDonald, *Saint Mungo*, p. 46.
28. *Ibid.*, pp. 50-51.
29. *Ibid.*, pp. 40-41.
30. P. Yeoman, *Pilgrimage in Medieval Scotland*, pp. 18-19.
31. I. Macdonald, *Saint Ninian, by Aelred, Abbot of Rievaulx* (Edinburgh: Floris, 1993), pp. 56-7.
32. I. MacDonald, *Saint Mungo*, p. 63.
33. D. McRoberts, 'The death of St Kentigern of Glasgow', *Innes Review*, vol. 24, 1973, pp. 43-50.
34. 'Life of Kentigern by Jocelin of Furness', ch. 44, 343-6.
35. I. MacDonald, *Saint Mungo*, p. 62.
36. S. Hothershall, *Archaeology around Glasgow*, p. 25.
37. P. Yeoman, *Medieval Scotland* (London: Batsford, 1995), pp. 51-2.
38. S. Hothershall, *Archaeology around Glasgow*, p. 24.
39. P. Yeoman, *Medieval Scotland*, p. 52.
40. Adomnán's *Life of Columba*, bk. 3, ch. 16, p. 165.
41. V. Glenn, 'Court and Patronage in Scotland 1240-1340', in *Medieval Art and Architecture in the Diocese of Glasgow*, ed. R. Fawcett, British Archaeological Association Conference Transactions 23 (Leeds, 1998), pp. 112-21, at pp. 112-4.
42. A. P. Forbes, *Kalendars of Scottish Saints* (Edinburgh: Edmondston and Douglas, 1872), pp. 284-7.
43. W. J. Watson, *The Celtic Place-names of Scotland*, pp. 189, 274.
44. *Ibid.*, pp. 305-6.
45. CANMORE, 'Holy Island, St Molaise's Cave', ID 40079, 2001.
46. CANMORE, 'Loch Lomond, Inchtavannach', ID 129719, 1995.
47. Adomnán's *Life of Columba*, bk. 1, ch. 27, p. 78.
48. J. Sinclair, *St Mackessog's Church, Luss, Loch Lomond* (Luss Church Promotions, n. d.), p. 1.
49. W. Fraser, *The chiefs of Colquhoun and their country* (Edinburgh, 1869), vol. 2, pp. 46, 56, 58.
50. W. J. Watson, *The Celtic Place-names of Scotland*, p. 278.
51. Adomnán's *Life of Columba*, Second Preface, p. 56.
52. W. J. Watson, *The Celtic Place-names of Scotland*, p. 272.
53. CANMORE, 'Cardross, Kilmahew, St Mahew's Chapel', ID 42385, 2001.
54. Information at the chapel, 2015.

Chapter 5

1. More than sixty kings are listed, of whom about thirty are known from other sources. Both groups of copies may have a common source dating from the ninth century, with an initial version written by the 660s. See S. Foster, *Picts, Gaels and Scots* (Edinburgh: Birlinn, 2014), p. 14.
2. S. Foster, *Picts, Gaels and Scots*, pp. 149-50.
3. Patrick, *Address to the soldiers of Coroticus*, 2, in T. O'Loughlin, *St. Patrick: the Man and his Works* (London: SPCK, 1999), p. 94.
4. T. O'Loughlin, *St. Patrick: the Man and his Works*, pp. 90-91.
5. S. Foster, *Picts, Gaels and Scots*, p. 14.
6. W. J. Watson, *The History of the Celtic Place-names of Scotland* (Edinburgh: Birlinn, 1926, revised ed. 1993), p. 332.
7. J. E. Fraser, *From Caledonia to Pictland: Scotland to 795* (Edinburgh: Edinburgh University Press, 2009), pp. 255-6.
8. The manuscript is in Marsh's Library, Dublin. See A. Macquarrie, '*Vita Sancti Servani*: The Life of St Serf', *The Innes Review*, vol. 44, no. 2, autumn 1993, pp. 122-52.
9. J. E. Fraser, *From Caledonia to Pictland*, p. 256.
10. I. MacDonald, ed., *Saint Mungo, Also Known as Kentigern, by Jocelinus, a Monk of Furness* (Edinburgh: Floris, 1993), pp. 12-18.
11. See N. Aitchison, *Forteviot: A Pictish and Scottish Royal Centre* (Stroud: History Press, 2001).
12. S. Foster, *Picts, Gaels and Scots*, p. 133.
13. W. J. Watson, *The Celtic Place-names of Scotland*, p. 510.
14. D. Keys, 'Ancient royal tomb found in Scotland', *The Independent*, 14. 8. 2009.
15. O. O'Grady, *Iona Workshop: Culdee Archaeology Project*, unpublished paper, 2012.
16. *Ibid.*
17. S. Toulson, *Celtic Journeys in Scotland and the North of England* (London, Fount, 1995), p. 137.
18. W. Follett, *Céli Dé in Ireland: Monastic Writing and Identity in the Early Middle Ages*, in *Studies in Celtic History* Series (Woodbridge: Boydell & Brewer, 2006), p. 3.
19. T. O. Clancy, 'Iona, Scotland and the Céli Dé' in B. E. Crawford, ed., *Scotland in Dark Age Britain* (St. Andrews: St. John's House Papers, no. 6, 1996), pp. 111-30.

20. W. Follett, *Céli Dé in Ireland*, p. 3.
21. J. Harris, *Dysart Carmelite Monastery (Ancient & Modern)* (Carnock, Fife: John Harris, n.d. [*c.* 2000]), pp. 4-5.
22. P. Yeoman, *Pilgrimage in Medieval Scotland* (London: Batsford, 1999), p. 63.
23. H. James, P. Yeoman et al., *Excavations at St Ethernan's Monastery, Isle of May, Fife, 1992-7* (Perth: Tayside and Fife Archaeological Committee, 2008), Monograph 6.
24. *Ibid.*
25. 'Early Christian Church Found on the Isle of May' in *British Archaeology* no. 18, October 1996. News, p. 4.
26. P. Yeoman, *Medieval Scotland* (London: Batsford, 1995), p. 13.
27. *Ibid.*, p. 26.
28. *Ibid.*, p. 25.
29. P. Yeoman, *Pilgrimage in Medieval Scotland*, p. 64.
30. SCAPE: Scotland's Coastal Heritage at Risk, NMRS no. NO50NE6: Caiplie Caves, 'The Coves'. Coastal Assessment Survey for Historic Scotland Fife – Kincardine to Fifeness, 1996.
31. S. Foster, *Picts, Gaels and Scots*, pp. 120-21.
32. W. J. Watson, *The Celtic Place-names of Scotland*, p. 275.
33. A. Woolf, *From Pictland to Alba 789-1070* (Edinburgh: Edinburgh University Press, 2007), p. 319.
34. R. Fawcett, *Scottish Abbeys and Priories* (London: Batsford, 1994), p. 132.
35. See R. Samson, 'The reinterpretation of the Pictish symbols', *Journal of the British Archaeological Association*, vol. 145, 1992, pp. 29-62; K. Forsyth, 'Some thoughts on Pictish symbols as a formal writing system' in D. Henry (ed.), *The Worm, the Germ and the Thorn. Pictish and Related Studies presented to Isabel Henderson* (Balgavies: Pinkfoot Press, 1997), pp. 85-98.
36. R. Lee, 'The use of information theory to determine the language character type of Pictish symbols', *Scottish Archaeological Journal*, vol. 32, no. 2, 2010, pp. 137-76.
37. S. Foster, *Picts, Gaels and Scots*, pp. 97-100.
38. M. Carver, *Portmahomack*, p. 96.
39. R. Fawcett, *St Andrews Cathedral* (Edinburgh: Historic Scotland, 1993), p. 4.
40. S. Foster, *Picts, Gaels and Scots*, p. 45.
41. R. Fawcett, *St Andrews Cathedral*, pp. 4-5.
42. R. Fawcett, *Scottish Cathedrals* (London: Batsford, 1997), pp. 17, 19.
43. R. Fawcett, *St Andrews Cathedral*, p. 6.
44. R. Fawcett, *Scottish Cathedrals*, pp. 20-21.
45. W. J. Watson, *The Celtic Place-names of Scotland*, pp. 286-7.
46. I. Fisher, 'Medieval parish church of St Fyndoca', CANMORE, ID 922082, 2001.
47. W. J. Watson, *The Celtic Place-names of Scotland*, pp. 188, 276-7.
48. GUARD Archaeology Project 4063, 'Abbots, Kings and lost Harbours: Looking for Cambuskenneth Watergate', 9. 11. 2015.
49. J. E. Fraser, *From Caledonia to Pictland*, p. 336.
50. A. Ritchie, *Meigle Museum: Pictish Carved Stones* (Edinburgh: Historic Scotland, 1997), p. 6.
51. *Ibid.*, p. 15.
52. *Ibid.*, p. 16.
53. S. Foster, *Picts, Gaels and Scots*, p. xx.
54. N. Atkinson, *Aberlemno to Glamis* (Balgavies, Angus: The Pinkfoot Press, 1997). pp. 4-5.
55. Bede, *Ecclesiastical History of the English People*, transl. L. Sherley-Price, revised R. E. Latham (London: Penguin Classics, 1990), bk. 5, ch. 21.
56. N. Atkinson, *Aberlemno to Glamis*, pp. 8-9.
57. R. Fawcett, *Scottish Cathedrals*, p. 17.
58. *Ibid.*, p. 112.
59. S. Foster, *Picts, Gaels and Scots*, p. 16.

Chapter 6

1. W. J. Watson, *The History of the Celtic Place-names of Scotland* (Edinburgh: Birlinn, 1926, revised ed. 1993), pp. 228-9.
2. The *Leabhar Breac*, or 'Speckled Book' dates from the early fifteenth century. The note is on p. 90.
3. W. J. Watson, *The Celtic Place-names of Scotland*, p. 285.
4. *Ibid.*, pp. 164, 284.
5. CANMORE, 'Loch Lomond, Inchcailloch, Church of St Kentigerna and Burial Ground', ID 70202, 1995.
6. G. and A. Ritchie, *Scotland: Archaeology and Early History* (Edinburgh, Edinburgh University Press, 1991), p. 160.
7. P. L. Henry, ed., transl., *Amra Choluim Chille: Dallán's elegy for Columba* (Belfast: Colmcille; Ultach Trust, 2006).
8. Adomnán, *Life of Columba*, transl. J. Gregory, in J. Marsden, *The Illustrated Columcille* (London: Macmillan, 1991), bk. 2, ch. 47, p. 141.

9. S. Foster, *Picts, Gaels and Scots* (Edinburgh: Birlinn, 2014), p. 121.
10. 'The Life and Miracles of St Cuthbert', ch. 11, in Bede, *Ecclesiastical History of the English People*, transl. L. Sherley-Price, revised R. E. Latham (London: Penguin Classics, 1990).
11. CANMORE, 'Dull, Cross', ID 25618, 2016.
12. J. F. S. Gordon, *Monasticon*, vol. 1 (Glasgow: John Tweed, 1868), p. 487.
13. S. Foster, *Picts, Gaels and Scots*, p. 122.
14. W. J. Watson, *The Celtic Place-names of Scotland*, p. 69.
15. O. O'Grady, *Iona Workshop: Culdee Archaeology Project*, unpublished paper, 2012.
16. *Ibid.*
17. W. J. Watson, *The Celtic Place-names of Scotland*, p. 312.
18. R. Fawcett, *Scottish Cathedrals* (London: Batsford, 1997), p. 15.
19. S. Foster, *Picts, Gaels and Scots*, pp. 150-52.
20. P. Yeoman, *Pilgrimage in Medieval Scotland* (London: Batsford, 1999), pp. 86-7.
21. R. Fawcett, *Scottish Cathedrals*, pp. 15-16, 113.
22. *Ibid.*, p. 18.
23. T. O. Clancy, 'Deer and the early Church in north-eastern Scotland' in K. Forsyth, ed., *'This Splendid Little Book': Studies on the Book of Deer* (Dublin: Four Courts Press, 2008).
24. W. J. Watson, *The Celtic Place-names of Scotland*, p. 298.
25. *Ibid.*, p. 308.
26. *Ibid.*, pp. 329-30.
27. Cambridge University Library, Ms. li .6. 32.
28. W. J. Watson, *The Celtic Place-names of Scotland*, pp. 317-8.
29. J. E. Fraser, *From Caledonia to Pictland: Scotland to 795* (Edinburgh: Edinburgh University Press, 2009), pp. 336-7.

Chapter 7

1. S. Foster, *Picts, Gaels and Scots* (Edinburgh: Birlinn, 2014), p. 154.
2. *Ibid.*, pp. 5-6.
3. W. J. Watson, *The History of the Celtic Place-names of Scotland* (Edinburgh: Birlinn, 1926, revised ed. 1993), pp. 288-9.
4. CANMORE, 'Skye, Eynort: St Maelrubha's Churches', ID 11030, 2008.
5. A. Ritchie, *Iona* (Edinburgh: Batsford, 1997), p. 82.
6. W. J. Watson, *The Celtic Place-names of Scotland*, p. 125.
7. J. Anderson, *Scotland in early Christian times: the Rhind lectures in archaeology, 1879, no. 1* (Edinburgh: David Douglas, 1881), p. 208.
8. H. Maxwell, ed., *Royal Commission on Ancient and Historical Monuments of Scotland: Ninth Report with Inventory of Monuments and Constructions in the Outer Hebrides, Skye and the Small Isles* (Edinburgh: His Majesty's Stationary Office, 1928), p. xli.
9. CANMORE, 'Skye, Skeabost Island: Cemetery, Chapel, Church, Monastic Settlement (possible)', ID 11282, 2007.
10. R. Fawcett, *Scottish Cathedrals* (London: Batsford, 1997), p. 117.
11. H. Maxwell, *Royal Commission on Ancient and Historical Monuments of Scotland*, no. 499, pp. 149-50.
12. *Ibid.*, p. xlv.
13. W. J. Watson, *The Celtic Place-names of Scotland*, pp. 250-54.
14. A. Ritchie, *Iona*, p. 82.
15. J. E. Fraser, *From Caledonia to Pictland: Scotland to 795* (Edinburgh: Edinburgh University Press, 2009), pp. 343-4.
16. The Highland Council Historic Environment Record (HER), MHG 5687, 2012.
17. A. Ritchie, *Iona*, p. 82.
18. K. Mcleod, ed., *Songs of the Hebrides, and other Celtic songs from the Highlands of Scotland* (London: Boosey & Co., 1909), vol. 2.
19. A. Ritchie, *Iona*, p. 84.
20. *Ibid.*, p. 84.
21. RCAHMS (SC), Broadsheet 5, 'Canna, The Archaeology of a Hebridean Landscape'. Site no. NG20SW 2, 2007.
22. D. Etheridge, M. Hart, E. Heans-Glogowska, P. Kupiec, ed. B. Schorn and J. Quinn, *Languages, Myths and Finds, vol. 2: The Vikings. Centre for the Study of the Viking Age, Nottingham University* (Rzeszów, Poland: Mitel Publishing, 2014), p. 19.
23. S. Foster, *Picts, Gaels and Scots*, pp. 66-7.
24. *Ibid.*, pp. 67-8.
25. A. Macquarrie, *Cille Bharra* (Droitwich: Grant Books, 1989), pp. 8, 10-11.
26. CANMORE, 'Barra, Eoligarry, Cille-bharra: Burial Ground, Chapel(s), Church', ID 9767, 2002.
27. W. J. Watson, *The Celtic Place-names of Scotland*, pp. 272-3.

28. D. Etheridge, *Languages, Myths and Finds*, p. 35.
29. CANMORE, 'Pabbay: Chapel, Cross Slab(s), Midden, Pictish Symbol Stone', ID 21381, 2001.
30. D. Etheridge, *Languages, Myths and Finds*, p. 14.
31. *Origines parociales Scotiae: the antiquities ecclesiastical and territorial of the parishes of Scotland*, vol. 2, part 1 (Edinburgh: W. H. Lizars, 1854), p. 386.
32. M. Martin, *Description of the Western Islands of Scotland* (London: Andrew Bell, 1703), p. 106 (new ed. Birlinn: Edinburgh, 2014).
33. E. Rees, *Celtic Saints of Wales* (Stroud: Fonthill, 2015), pp. 149-50.
34. F. MacLeod, *The Chapels in the Western Isles* (Stornoway: Acair, 1997), p. 19.
35. Bede, *Ecclesiastical History of the English People*, transl. L. Sherley-Price, revised R. E. Latham (London: Penguin Classics, 1990), bk. 3, ch. 25.
36. F. MacLeod, *The Chapels in the Western Isles*, p. 17; M. Robson, *A Desert Place in the Sea: the early churches of northern Lewis* (Ness: Comunn Eachdraidh Nis, 1997), p. 80.
37. *Ibid.*, p. 17.
38. *Ibid.*, p. 17.
39. H. Maxwell, ed., *Royal Commission on Ancient and Historical Monuments*, no. 6, p. 2.
40. M. Robson, *A Desert Place in the Sea*, p. 72.
41. F. MacLeod, *The Chapels in the Western Isles*, p. 15.
42. H. Maxwell, *Royal Commission on Ancient and Historical Monuments*, p. xli.
43. *Ibid.*
44. W. C. Makenzie, *The Book of the Lews* (Paisley: Alexander Gardner, 1919), pp. 137-9.
45. W. J. Watson, *The Celtic Place-names of Scotland*, p. 309.
46. M. Robson, *A Desert Place in the Sea*, pp. 30-41.
47. *Ibid.*, pp. 36-7.
48. Information at Comunn Eachdraidh Niss, 2016.
49. W. D. Simpson, *Portrait of Skye and the Outer Hebrides* (London: Robert Hale, 1967), p. 121.
50. M. Robson, *A Desert Place in the Sea*, pp. 58-9.
51. *Ibid.*, pp. 64-5.
52. CANMORE, 'Lewis, Aignish: St Columba's Church', ID 4308, 2013.
53. D. Etheridge, *Languages, Myths and Finds*, p. 6.
54. Information from a local inhabitant, August 2005.
55. D. H. Farmer, *The Oxford Dictionary of Saints* (Oxford: Oxford University Press, 2nd ed. 1987), p. 325.
56. Adomnán, *Life of Columba*, transl. J. Gregory, in J. Marsden, *The Illustrated Columcille* (London: Macmillan, 1991), bk. 2, ch. 24, p. 118.
57. M. Martin, *Description of the Western Islands of Scotland*, p. 49; A. Carmichael, *Carmina Gaedelica* (Edinburgh: Floris, 1994), notes to vol. 2, no. 164, pp. 610-11.
58. W. J. Watson, *The Celtic Place-names of Scotland*, pp. 300, 515.
59. S. Foster, *Picts, Gaels and Scots*, p. 125.
60. CANMORE, 'Papa Westray, St Boniface's Church: Burial Ground (Twelfth Century), Church (Twelfth Century)', ID 2856, 1998; P. Yeoman, *Pilgrimage in Medieval Scotland* (London: Batsford, 1999), p. 99.
61. CANMORE, 'Brough of Deerness: Chapel, Monastic Settlement (possible)', ID 2927, 2011.
62. C. A. Ralegh Radford, 'Birsay and the spread of Christianity to the north', *Orkney Heritage*, vol. 2, 1983, pp. 13-35.
63. CANMORE, 'Brough of Birsay: Chapel, Settlement', ID 1796, 1997.
64. R. Fawcett, *Scottish Cathedrals*, p. 115.
65. *Ibid.*, pp. 112, 115.
66. The Papar Project. Shetland: S9. Papil, Burra, 2015.
67. The Papar Project.
68. S. Foster, *Picts, Gaels and Scots*, pp. 84-5, 91.
69. *Ibid.*, p. 144.
70. CANMORE, 'Kame of Isbister: Monastic Settlement', ID 883, 1970.
71. CANMORE, 'Yell, Birrier of West Sandwick, Monastic Settlement', ID 1262, 2001.
72. CANMORE, 'Fetlar, Outer Brough: Building(s), Monastery', ID 1421, 2001.

Chapter 8

1. A. M. Cubbon, *The Art of Manx Crosses* (Douglas: Manx Museum and National Trust, 1977), p. 5.
2. D. S. Dugdale, *Manx Church Origins* (Lampeter: Llanerch, 1998), p. 190.
3. L. Gardela and C. Larrington, eds., *Viking Myths and Rituals on the Isle of Man*, Centre for the Study of the Viking Age, University of Nottingham (Rzeszów, Poland: Mitel Publishing, 2014), Introduction, p. 3.
4. L. Gardela and C. Larrington, *Viking Myths and Rituals on the Isle of Man*, ch. 2, 'The Vikings: Myths and Misconceptions', by B. McMahon, pp. 12-14; ch. 5, 'Viking Death Rituals on the Isle of Man', by L. Gardela, p. 30.
5. R. Lavelle and S. Roffey, eds., *Danes in Wessex: The Scandinavian impact on Southern England, c. 800–c. 1100* (Oxford: Oxbow Books, 2016), p. 126.

6. 'The Vikings: Myths and Misconceptions', by B. McMahon, p. 13.
7. R. N. Bailey, *Viking Age Sculpture in Northern England* (London: Collins, 1980), p. 254.
8. A. M. Cubbon, *Ancient And Historic Monuments of the Isle of Man* (Douglas: The Manx Museum and the National Trust, 4th edition, 1973): St Patrick's Chair, Marown.
9. W. J. Watson, *The History of the Celtic Place-names of Scotland* (Edinburgh: Birlinn, 1926, revised ed. 1993), p. 294.
10. L. Gardela and C. Larrington, *Viking Myths and Rituals on the Isle of Man*, Introduction, p. 6.
11. M. Costain Richards, *The Manx Crosses Illuminated* (Port St Mary, Isle of Man: Croshag Publications, 1988), p. 14.
12. L. Gardela and C. Larrington, *Viking Myths and Rituals on the Isle of Man*, ch. 3, 'Viking-Age Stones and Crosses', by H. Stoner, p. 19.
13. R. N. Bailey, *Scandinavian Myth on Viking-period Stone Sculpture in England*, 2015, sydney.edu.au/arts/medieval/saga/pdf015-bailey.pdf.
14. Isle of Man Natural History and Antiquarian Society, Proceedings, vol. 10, part 3, p. 289; vol. 11, part 2, p. 249.
15. 'Speke Keeill, Mount Murray Hotel, Isle of Man, Archaeological Evaluation and Assessment of Results' (Ref. 62511.01), July 2007, pub. Wessex Archaeology, pp. 12, 15, 20.
16. A. West, babelstone.blogspot.com/2008, 15. 5. 08.
17. 'Speke Keeill, Mount Murray Hotel', pp. 3, 4, 9, 22.
18. *Ibid.*, p. 21.
19. Adomnán's *Life of Columba*, transl. J. Gregory, in J. Marsden, *The Illustrated Columcille* (London: Macmillan, 1991), bk. 2, ch. 34, pp. 125-6.
20. S. Young, *Works of Angels, Masterpieces of Celtic Metalwork, 6th – 9th centuries AD* (London: British Museum Press, 1989), catalogue no. 133.
21. W. C. Corlett, W. K. Kermode, P. Cadman et al., *Annual Report of the Manx Archaeological Society* (1909), p. 19.
22. *Ibid.*, pp. 20-21.
23. *Ibid.*, pp. 20, 23.
24. *Ibid.*, p. 25.
25. *Ibid.*, pp. 23-5.
26. R. A. Curphey, *Peel Castle* (Douglas: Manx National Heritage, n.d.), pp. 3-4.
27. *Ibid.*, p. 4.
28. 'Viking Death Rituals on the Isle of Man', by L. Gardela, p. 33.
29. *Ibid.*, p. 36.
30. 'Viking-Age Stones and Crosses', by H. Stoner, pp. 19-20.
31. M. Costain Richards, *The Manx Crosses Illuminated*, p. 31.
32. 'Viking-Age Stones and Crosses', by H. Stoner, p. 18.
33. A. M. Cubbon, *The Art of Manx Crosses*, p. 18.
34. *Ibid.*, p. 31.
35. 'Viking Death Rituals on the Isle of Man', by L. Gardela, p. 31.
36. D. S. Dugdale, *Manx Church Origins*, pp. 20-23.
37. *Ibid.*, pp. 24-5.
38. A. M. Cubbon, *The Art of Manx Crosses*, p. 29.
39. *Ibid.*, pp. 32-3; 23
40. Manx Archaeological Survey, 3rd Report, 1911, Parish of Kirk Bride: Ballavarkish.
41. *Ibid.*
42. D. S. Dugdale, *Manx Church Origins*, pp. 62, 113-5.
43. T. O'Loughlin, *Journeys on the Edges: the Celtic Tradition* (London: Darton, Longman & Todd, 2000), pp. 90-91.
44. A. M. Cubbon, *The Art of Manx Crosses*, p. 7.
45. Information at the Manx Museum, Douglas, Isle of Man, 2016.
46. A. M. Cubbon, *The Art of Manx Crosses*, pp. 11, 12.
47. 'Viking-Age Stones and Crosses', by H. Stoner, p. 18.
48. *Ibid.*, p. 18.
49. *Ibid.*, pp. 19, 21.

Chapter 9

1. S. Foster, *Picts, Gaels and Scots* (Edinburgh: Birlinn, 2014), pp. 40-41.
2. *Ibid.*, p. 40.
3. P. Wilkinson, 'Finds shed light on early faith', *Church Times*, 1. 8. 2014.
4. H. Eckardt, 'A Lady of York; migration, ethnicity and identity in Roman Britain', *Antiquity*, vol. 84, March 2010, pp. 131-45.
5. D. Petts, *Christianity in Roman Britain* (Stroud: Tempus, 2003), pp. 75-6.
6. *Ibid.*, pp. 77-8, 167.
7. *Ibid.*, pp. 151-2.
8. *Ibid.*, pp. 152-4, 167.

9. T. Gates, 'Hadrian's Wall Amid Fields of Corn', in *Archaeology*, no. 49, November 1999, p. 6 ff.
10. Bede, *Ecclesiastical History of the English People*, transl. L. Sherley-Price, revised R. E. Latham (London: Penguin Classics, 1990), bk. 5, ch. 24.
11. *Ibid.*, bk. 2, ch. 14.
12. H. Leyser, 'Yeavering: Northumberland', in *Beda: A Journey to the Seven Kingdoms in the Time of Bede* (London: Harper/Collins, 2015).
13. *Ibid.*
14. D. Hinton, 'Great Sites: Yeavering', in *British Archaeology Magazine,* no. 58, Council for British Archaeology, April 2001.
15. J. E. Fraser, *From Caledonia to Pictland: Scotland to 795* (Edinburgh: Edinburgh University Press, 2009), p. 168.
16. Adomnán's *Life of Columba*, transl. J. Gregory, in J. Marsden, *The Illustrated Columcille* (London: Macmillan, 1991), bk. 1, ch. 1, p. 58.
17. Bede, *Ecclesiastical History*, bk. 2, ch. 5; bk. 3, ch. 6.
18. Adomnán's *Life of Columba*, bk. 1, ch. 1, pp. 57-8.
19. J. E. Fraser, *From Caledonia to Pictland*, pp. 168-9.
20. Bede, *Ecclesiastical History*, bk. 2, ch. 5; bk. 2, ch. 4.
21. C. Stancliffe, 'Where was Oswald Killed?', in C. Stancliffe and E. Cambridge, eds., *Oswald: Northumbrian King to European Saint* (Stamford: Paul Watkins, 1995).
22. Bede, *Ecclesiastical History*, bk. 3, ch. 11.
23. *Ibid.*, bk. 3, ch. 5.
24. *Ibid.*, bk. 3, ch. 3.
25. *Ibid.*, bk. 3, ch. 5.
26. *Ibid.*, bk. 3, ch. 6.
27. J. and C. Bord, *Sacred Waters: Holy Wells and Water Lore in Britain and Ireland* (London: Paladin, 1986), pp. 20, 122, 205–6.
28. Bede, *Ecclesiastical History*, bk. 3, ch. 9.
29. *Ibid.*, bk. 3, ch. 14.
30. *Ibid.*
31. *Ibid.*, bk. 3, ch. 5.
32. *Ibid.*, bk. 3, ch. 16.
33. J. Bird, *St Aidan's Church, Bamburgh, and its Story through 1400 Years* (Bamburgh: John Bird, 1985), pp. 5-8.
34. Bede, *Ecclesiastical History*, bk. 4, ch. 23.
35. P. Rumsey, *Women of the Church*, (Dublin: Columba Press, 2011), pp. 143, 145.
36. *Ibid.*, pp. 145-6.
37. Penitential of Theodore, 6. 8, in J. T. McNeill and H. M Gamer, *Medieval Handbooks of Penance: A Translation of the Principle* Libri Poenitentiales (New York: Columbia University Press, 1938, revised ed. 1990), p. 204.
38. H. Leyser, 'Yeavering: Northumberland'.
39. Bede, *Ecclesiastical History*, bk. 4, ch. 24.
40. *Ibid.*, bk. 4, ch. 23.
41. P. Rumsey, *Women of the Church*, pp. 142-3.
42. N. Venclova, 'The Venerable Bede, druidic tonsure and archaeology', *Antiquity*, vol. 76, 2002, pp. 488-71.
43. M. Carver, *Portmahomack: monastery of the Picts* (Edinburgh: Edinburgh University Press, 2008), pp. 10, 195.
44. 'The Life and Miracles of St Cuthbert', ch. 16, in Bede, *Ecclesiastical History of the English People.*
45. 'The Life and Miracles of St Cuthbert', ch. 16.
46. E. Cambridge, *Lindisfarne Priory and Holy Island* (London: English Heritage, 1995), p. 15.
47. D. Keys, 'Lindisfarne dig to be crowd-funded', in *Church Times*, 11. 3. 2016.
48. 'The Life and Miracles of St Cuthbert', chs. 17-20.
49. *Ibid.*, ch. 18.
50. *Ibid.*, ch. 12.
51. *Ibid.*, ch. 27.
52. *Ibid.*, ch. 39.
53. *Ibid.*, chs. 39, 40.
54. I. MacDonald (ed), *Saint Mungo, Also Known as Kentigern, by Jocelinus, a Monk of Furness* (Edinburgh: Floris, 1993), pp. 29-30.
55. E. Ekwall, *The Concise Dictionary of English Place Names* (Oxford: Clarendon Press, 5th ed. 1964), entry: Aspatria.
56. 'Saint Martin's Church, Brampton', in *Transactions of the Cumberland and Westmoreland Antiquarian Society*, vol. 82, 1982.
57. *Ibid.*
58. Bede, *Ecclesiastical History*, bk. 4, ch. 23.
59. W. J. Watson, *The History of the Celtic Place-names of Scotland* (Edinburgh: Birlinn, 1926, revised ed. 1993), p. 151.
60. M. Bragg, *Credo* (London: Sceptre, 1996).

Index